POLITICAL SCIENCE AND HISTORY

A HISTORY OF THE UNITED STATES

POLITICAL SCIENCE AND HISTORY

Additional books in this series can be found on Nova's website under the Series tab.

Additional e-books in this series can be found on Nova's website under the eBooks tab.

POLITICAL SCIENCE AND HISTORY

A HISTORY OF THE UNITED STATES

CECIL CHESTERTON

Copyright © 2018 by Nova Science Publishers, Inc.

All rights reserved. No part of this book may be reproduced, stored in a retrieval system or transmitted in any form or by any means: electronic, electrostatic, magnetic, tape, mechanical photocopying, recording or otherwise without the written permission of the Publisher.

We have partnered with Copyright Clearance Center to make it easy for you to obtain permissions to reuse content from this publication. Simply navigate to this publication's page on Nova's website and locate the "Get Permission" button below the title description. This button is linked directly to the title's permission page on copyright.com. Alternatively, you can visit copyright.com and search by title, ISBN, or ISSN.

For further questions about using the service on copyright.com, please contact:
Copyright Clearance Center
Phone: +1-(978) 750-8400   Fax: +1-(978) 750-4470   E-mail: info@copyright.com.

NOTICE TO THE READER

The Publisher has taken reasonable care in the preparation of this book, but makes no expressed or implied warranty of any kind and assumes no responsibility for any errors or omissions. No liability is assumed for incidental or consequential damages in connection with or arising out of information contained in this book. The Publisher shall not be liable for any special, consequential, or exemplary damages resulting, in whole or in part, from the readers' use of, or reliance upon, this material. Any parts of this book based on government reports are so indicated and copyright is claimed for those parts to the extent applicable to compilations of such works.

Independent verification should be sought for any data, advice or recommendations contained in this book. In addition, no responsibility is assumed by the publisher for any injury and/or damage to persons or property arising from any methods, products, instructions, ideas or otherwise contained in this publication.

This publication is designed to provide accurate and authoritative information with regard to the subject matter covered herein. It is sold with the clear understanding that the Publisher is not engaged in rendering legal or any other professional services. If legal or any other expert assistance is required, the services of a competent person should be sought. FROM A DECLARATION OF PARTICIPANTS JOINTLY ADOPTED BY A COMMITTEE OF THE AMERICAN BAR ASSOCIATION AND A COMMITTEE OF PUBLISHERS.

Additional color graphics may be available in the e-book version of this book.

Library of Congress Cataloging-in-Publication Data

ISBN: 978-1-53613-600-5

Published by Nova Science Publishers, Inc. † New York

*Dedicated to
My Comrade and Hospital Mate, Lance-Corporal Wood, of the King's
Own Liverpools, Citizen of Massachusetts, Who Joined the British Army in
August, 1914*

CONTENTS

Preface		ix
Introduction		xi
Author's Preface		xix
Chapter 1	The English Colonies	1
Chapter 2	Arms and the Rights of Man	15
Chapter 3	"We, the People"	37
Chapter 4	The Mantle of Washington	51
Chapter 5	The Virginian Dynasty	65
Chapter 6	The Jacksonian Revolution	89
Chapter 7	The Spoils of Mexico	109
Chapter 8	The Slavery Question	129
Chapter 9	Secession and Civil War	155
Chapter 10	"The Black Terror"	201
Chapter 11	The New Problems	225
Index		239

PREFACE[*]

This book, originally published in 1919, is a telling of U.S. history from colonial times to Reconstruction. Written by a British soldier mostly from the battlefields of World War One, it provides a British perspective of U.S. history that was reflective of the author's time. Modern scholars take issue with this telling and have proven many inaccuracies in its pages, but the text still stands as a reflection of the sometimes rich and inspiring and sometimes base and unfortunate attitudes and perspectives of America's birth and rise.

---

[*] This is an edited, reformatted and augmented version of "A History of the United States" by Cecil Chesterton was previously published by Chatto & Windus, London, England in 1919.

INTRODUCTION

"... O more than my brother, how shall I thank thee for all? Each of the heroes around us has fought for his house and his line, But thou hast fought for a stranger in hate of a wrong not thine. Happy are all free peoples too strong to be dispossessed, But happiest those among nations that dare to be strong for the rest."
— Elizabeth Barrett Browning.

The author of this book, my brother, died in a French military hospital of the effects of exposure in the last fierce fighting that broke the Prussian power over Christendom; fighting for which he had volunteered after being invalided home. Any notes I can jot down about him must necessarily seem jerky and incongruous; for in such a relation memory is a medley of generalisation and detail, not to be uttered in words. One thing at least may fitly be said here. Before he died he did at least two things that he desired. One may seem much greater than the other; but he would not have shrunk from naming them together. He saw the end of an empire that was the nightmare of the nations; but I believe it pleased him almost as much that he had been able, often in the intervals of bitter warfare and by the aid of a brilliant memory, to put together these pages on the history, so necessary and so strangely neglected, of the great democracy which he never patronised, which he not only loved but honoured.

Cecil Edward Chesterton was born on November 12, 1879; and there is a special if a secondary sense in which we may use the phrase that he was born a fighter. It may seem in some sad fashion a flippancy to say that he argued from his very cradle. It is certainly, in the same sad fashion, a comfort, to remember one truth about our relations: that we perpetually argued and that we never quarrelled. In a sense it was the psychological truth, I fancy, that we never quarrelled because we always argued. His lucidity and love of truth kept things so much on the level of logic, that the rest of our relations remained, thank God, in solid sympathy; long before that later time when, in substance, our argument had become an agreement. Nor, I think, was the process valueless; for at least we learnt how to argue in defence of our agreement. But the retrospect is only worth a thought now, because it illustrates a duality which seemed to him, and is, very simple; but to many is baffling in its very simplicity. When I say his weapon was logic, it will be currently confused with formality or even frigidity: a silly superstition always pictures the logician as a pale-faced prig. He was a living proof, a very living proof, that the precise contrary is the case. In fact it is generally the warmer and more sanguine sort of man who has an appetite for abstract definitions and even abstract distinctions. He had all the debating dexterity of a genial and generous man like Charles Fox. He could command that more than legal clarity and closeness which really marked the legal arguments of a genial and generous man like Danton. In his wonderfully courageous public speaking, he rather preferred being a debator to being an orator; in a sense he maintained that no man had a right to be an orator without first being a debater. Eloquence, he said, had its proper place when reason had proved a thing to be right, and it was necessary to give men the courage to do what was right. I think he never needed any man's eloquence to give him that. But the substitution of sentiment for reason, in the proper place for reason, affected him "as musicians are affected by a false note." It was the combination of this intellectual integrity with extraordinary warmth and simplicity in the affections that made the point of his personality. The snobs and servile apologists of the régime he resisted seem to think they can atone for being hard-hearted by being soft-headed. He reversed, if ever a man did, that

Introduction

relation in the organs. The opposite condition really covers all that can be said of him in this brief study; it is the clue not only to his character but to his career.

If rationalism meant being rational (which it hardly ever does) he might at every stage of his life be called a red-hot rationalist. Thus, for instance, he very early became a Socialist and joined the Fabian Society, on the executive of which he played a prominent part for some years. But he afterwards gave the explanation, very characteristic for those who could understand it, that what he liked about the Fabian sort of Socialism was its hardness. He meant intellectual hardness; the fact that the society avoided sentimentalism, and dealt in affirmations and not mere associations. He meant that upon the Fabian basis a Socialist was bound to believe in Socialism, but not in sandals, free love, bookbinding, and immediate disarmament. But he also added that, while he liked their hardness, he disliked their moderation. In other words, when he discovered, or believed that he discovered, that their intellectual hardness was combined with moral hardness, or rather moral deadness, he felt all the intellectual ice melted by a moral flame. He had, so to speak, a reaction of emotional realism, in which he saw, as suddenly as simple men can see simple truths, the potterers of Social Reform as the plotters of the Servile State. He was himself, above all things, a democrat as well as a Socialist; and in that intellectual sect he began to feel as if he were the only Socialist who was also a democrat. His dogmatic, democratic conviction would alone illustrate the falsity of the contrast between logic and life. The idea of human equality existed with extraordinary clarity in his brain, precisely because it existed with extraordinary simplicity in his character. His popular sympathies, unlike so many popular sentiments, could really survive any intimacy with the populace; they followed the poor not only at public meetings but to public houses. He was literally the only man I ever knew who was not only never a snob, but apparently never tempted to be a snob. The fact is almost more important than his wonderful lack of fear; for such good causes, when they cannot be lost by fear, are often lost by favour.

Thus he came to suspect that Socialism was merely social reform, and that social reform was merely slavery. But the point still is that though his attitude to it was now one of revolt, it was anything but a mere revulsion of feeling. He did, indeed, fall back on fundamental things, on a fury at the oppression of the poor, on a pity for slaves, and especially for contented slaves. But it is the mark of his type of mind that he did not abandon Socialism without a rational case against it, and a rational system to oppose to it. The theory he substituted for Socialism is that which may for convenience be called Distributivism; the theory that private property is proper to every private citizen. This is no place for its exposition; but it will be evident that such a conversion brings the convert into touch with much older traditions of human freedom, as expressed in the family or the guild. And it was about the same time that, having for some time held an Anglo-Catholic position, he joined the Roman Catholic Church. It is notable, in connection with the general argument, that while the deeper reasons for such a change do not concern such a sketch as this, he was again characteristically amused and annoyed with the sentimentalists, sympathetic or hostile, who supposed he was attracted by ritual, music, and emotional mysticism. He told such people, somewhat to their bewilderment, that he had been converted because Rome alone could satisfy the reason. In his case, of course, as in Newman's and numberless others, well-meaning people conceived a thousand crooked or complicated explanations, rather than suppose that an obviously honest man believed a thing because he thought it was true. He was soon to give a more dramatic manifestation of his strange taste for the truth.

The attack on political corruption, the next and perhaps the most important passage in his life, still illustrates the same point, touching reason and enthusiasm. Precisely because he did know what Socialism is and what it is not, precisely because he had at least learned that from the intellectual hardness of the Fabians, he saw the spot where Fabian Socialism is not hard but soft. Socialism means the assumption by the State of all the means of production, distribution, and exchange. To quote (as he often quoted with a rational relish) the words of Mr. Balfour, that is Socialism and nothing else is Socialism. To such clear thinking, it is at

Introduction xv

once apparent that trusting a thing to the State must always mean trusting it to the statesmen. He could defend Socialism because he could define Socialism; and he was not helped or hindered by the hazy associations of the sort of Socialists who perpetually defended what they never defined. Such men might have a vague vision of red flags and red ties waving in an everlasting riot above the fall of top-hats and Union Jacks; but he knew that Socialism established meant Socialism official, and conducted by some sort of officials. All the primary forms of private property were to be given to the government; and it occurred to him, as a natural precaution, to give a glance at the government. He gave some attention to the actual types and methods of that governing and official class, into whose power trams and trades and shops and houses were already passing, amid loud Fabian cheers for the progress of Socialism. He looked at modern parliamentary government; he looked at it rationally and steadily and not without reflection. And the consequence was that he was put in the dock, and very nearly put in the lock-up, for calling it what it is.

In collaboration with Mr. Belloc he had written "The Party System," in which the plutocratic and corrupt nature of our present polity is set forth. And when Mr. Belloc founded the Eye-Witness, as a bold and independent organ of the same sort of criticism, he served as the energetic second in command. He subsequently became editor of the Eye-Witness, which was renamed as the New Witness. It was during the latter period that the great test case of political corruption occurred; pretty well known in England, and unfortunately much better known in Europe, as the Marconi scandal. To narrate its alternate secrecies and sensations would be impossible here; but one fashionable fallacy about it may be exploded with advantage. An extraordinary notion still exists that the New Witness denounced Ministers for gambling on the Stock Exchange. It might be improper for Ministers to gamble; but gambling was certainly not a misdemeanor that would have hardened with any special horror so hearty an Anti-Puritan as the man of whom I write. The Marconi case did not raise the difficult ethics of gambling, but the perfectly plain ethics of secret commissions. The charge against the Ministers was that, while a government contract was being considered, they tried to make money out of a secret tip, given them by the very government contractor with whom their government was supposed to be bargaining. This was what their accuser asserted; but this was not what they attempted to answer by a prosecution. He was prosecuted, not for what he had said of the government, but for some secondary things he had said of the government contractor. The latter, Mr. Godfrey Isaacs, gained a verdict for criminal libel; and the judge inflicted a fine of £100. Readers may have chanced to note the subsequent incidents in the life of Mr. Isaacs, but I am here only concerned with incidents in the life of a more interesting person.

In any suggestion of his personality, indeed, the point does not lie in what was done to him, but rather in what was not done. He was positively assured, upon the very strongest and most converging legal authority, that unless he offered certain excuses he would certainly go to prison for several years. He did not offer those excuses; and I believe it never occurred to him to do so. His freedom from fear of all kinds had about it a sort of solid unconsciousness and even innocence. This homogeneous quality in it has been admirably seized and summed up by Mr. Belloc in a tribute of great truth and power. "His courage was heroic, native, positive and equal: always at the highest potentiality of courage. He never in his life checked an action or a word from a consideration of personal caution, and that is more than can be said of any other man of his time." After the more or less nominal fine, however, his moral victory was proved in the one way in which a military victory can ever be proved. It is the successful general who continues his own plan of campaign. Whether a battle be ticketed in the history books as lost or won, the test is which side can continue to strike. He continued to strike, and to strike harder than ever, up to the very moment of that yet greater experience which changed all such military symbols into military facts. A man with instincts unspoiled and in that sense almost untouched, he would have always answered quite naturally to the autochthonous appeal of patriotism; but it is again characteristic of him that he desired, in his own phrase, to "rationalize patriotism," which he did upon the principles of Rousseau, that contractual theory which, in these pages, he connects with the great name of Jefferson. But things even deeper than patriotism impelled him against Prussianism. His enemy was the barbarian when he enslaves, as something more hellish even than the barbarian when he slays. His was the spiritual instinct by which Prussian order was worse than Prussian anarchy; and nothing was so inhuman as an inhuman humanitarianism. If you had asked him for what he fought and died amid the wasted fields of France and Flanders, he might very probably have answered that it was to save the world from German social reforms.

This note, necessarily so broken and bemused, must reach its useless end. I have said nothing of numberless things that should be remembered at the mention of his name; of his books, which were great pamphlets and may yet be permanent pamphlets; of his journalistic exposures of other evils besides the Marconi, exposures that have made a new political atmosphere in the very election that is stirring around us; of his visit to America, which initiated him into an international friendship which is the foundation of this book. Least of all can I write of him apart from his work; of that loss nothing can be said by those who do not suffer it, and less still by those who do. And his experiences in life and death were so much greater even than my experiences of him, that a double incapacity makes me dumb. A portrait is impossible; as a friend he is too near me, and as a hero too far away.

G. K. Chesterton

AUTHOR'S PREFACE

I have taken advantage of a very brief respite from other, and in my judgment more valuable, employment, to produce this short sketch of the story of a great people, now our Ally. My motive has been mainly that I do not think that any such sketch, concentrated enough to be readable by the average layman who has other things to do (especially in these days) than to study more elaborate and authoritative histories, at present exists, and I have thought that in writing it I might perhaps be discharging some little part of the heavy debt of gratitude which I owe to America for the hospitality I received from her when I visited her shores during the early months of the War. This book is in another sense the product of that visit. What I then saw and heard of contemporary America so fascinated me that—believing as I do that the key to every people is in its past—I could not rest until I had mastered all that I could of the history of my delightful hosts. This I sought as much as possible from the original sources, reading voraciously, and at the time merely for my pleasure, such records as I could get of old debates and of the speech and correspondence of the dead. The two existing histories, which I also read, and upon which I have drawn most freely, are that of the present President of the United States and that of Professor Rhodes, dealing with the period from 1850 to 1876. With the conclusions of the latter authority it will be obvious that I am in many respects by no means at one; but I think it the more necessary to say that without a careful study of his book I could neither have formed my own conclusions nor ventured to challenge his. The reading that I did at the time of which I speak is the foundation of what I have now written. It will be well understood that a Private in the British Army, even when invalided home for a season, has not very great opportunities for research. I think it very likely that errors of detail may be discovered in these pages; I am quite sure that I could have made the book a better one if I had been able to give more time to revising my studies. Yet I believe that the story told here is substantially true; and I am very sure that it is worth the telling.

If I am asked why I think it desirable at this moment to attempt, however inadequately, a history of our latest Ally, I answer that at this moment the whole future of our civilization may depend upon a thoroughly good understanding between those nations which are now joined in battle for its defence, and that ignorance of each other's history is perhaps the greatest menace to such an understanding. To take one instance at random—how many English writers have censured, sometimes in terms of friendly sorrow, sometimes in a manner somewhat pharisaical, the treatment of Negroes in Southern States in all its phases, varying from the provision of separate waiting-rooms to sporadic outbreaks of lynching! How few ever mention, or seem to have even heard the word "Reconstruction"—a word which, in its historical connotation, explains all!

I should, perhaps, add a word to those Americans who may chance to read this book. To them, of course, I must offer a somewhat different apology. I believe that, with all my limitations, I can tell my fellow-countrymen things about the history of America which they do not know. It would be absurd effrontery to pretend that I can tell Americans what they do not know. For them, whatever interest this book may possess must depend upon the value of a foreigner's interpretation of the facts. I know that I should be extraordinarily interested in an American's view of the story of England since the Separation; and I can only hope that some degree of such interest may attach to these pages in American eyes.

It will be obvious to Americans that in some respects my view of their history is individual. For instance, I give Andrew Jackson both a greater place in the development of American democracy and a higher meed of personal praise than do most modern American historians and writers whom I have read. I give my judgment for what it is worth. In my view, the victory of Jackson over the Whigs was the turning-point of American history and finally decided that the United States should be a democracy and not a parliamentary oligarchy. And I am further of opinion that, both as soldier and ruler, "Old Hickory" was a hero of whom any nation might well be proud.

I am afraid that some offence may be given by my portrait of Charles Sumner. I cannot help it. I do not think that between his admirers and myself there is any real difference as to the kind of man he was. It is a kind that some people revere. It is a kind that I detest—absolutely leprous scoundrels excepted—more than I can bring myself to detest any other of God's creatures.

Cecil Chesterton
Somewhere in France,
May 1st, 1918.

Chapter I

THE ENGLISH COLONIES

In the year of Our Lord 1492, thirty-nine years after the taking of Constantinople by the Turks and eighteen years after the establishment of Caxton's printing press, one Christopher Columbus, an Italian sailor, set sail from Spain with the laudable object of converting the Khan of Tartary to the Christian Faith, and on his way discovered the continent of America. The islands on which Columbus first landed and the adjacent stretch of mainland from Mexico to Patagonia which the Spaniards who followed him colonized lay outside the territory which is now known as the United States. Nevertheless the instinct of the American democracy has always looked back to him as a sort of ancestor, and popular American tradition conceives of him as in some shadowy fashion a founder. And that instinct and tradition, like most such national instincts and traditions, is sound.

In the epoch which most of us can remember pretty vividly—for it came to an abrupt end less than five years ago—when people were anxious to prove that everything important in human history had been done by "Teutons," there was a great effort to show that Columbus was not really the first European discoverer of America; that that honour belonged properly to certain Scandinavian sea-captains who at some time in the tenth or eleventh centuries paid a presumably piratical visit to the coast of Greenland. It may be so, but the incident is quite irrelevant. That one set of barbarians from the fjords of Norway came in their wanderings in contact with another set of barbarians living in the frozen lands north of Labrador is a fact, if it be a fact, of little or no historical import. The Vikings had no more to teach the Esquimaux than had the Esquimaux to teach the Vikings. Both were at that time outside the real civilization of Europe.

Columbus, on the other hand, came from the very centre of European civilization and that at a time when that civilization was approaching the summit of one of its constantly recurrent periods of youth and renewal. In the North, indeed, what strikes the eye in the fifteenth century is rather the ugliness of a decaying order—the tortures, the panic of persecution, the morbid obsession of the danse macabre—things which many think of as Mediæval, but which belong really only to the Middle Ages when old and near to death. But all the South was already full of the new youth of the Renaissance. Boccaccio had lived, Leonardo was at the height of his glory. In the fields of Touraine was already playing with his fellows the boy that was to be Rabelais.

Such adventures as that of Columbus, despite his pious intentions with regard to the Khan of Tartary, were a living part of the Renaissance and were full of its spirit, and it is from the Renaissance that American civilization dates. It is an important point to remember about America, and especially about the English colonies which were to become the United States, that they have had no memory of the Middle Ages. They had and have, on the other hand, a real, formative memory of Pagan antiquity, for the age in which the oldest of them were born was full of enthusiasm for that memory, while it thought, as most Americans still think, of the Middle Ages as a mere feudal barbarism.

Youth and adventurousness were not the only notes of the Renaissance, nor the only ones which we shall see affecting the history of America. Another note was pride, and with that pride in its reaction against the old Christian civilization went a certain un-Christian scorn of poverty and still more of the ugliness and ignorance which go with poverty; and there reappeared—to an extent at least, and naturally most of all where the old religion had been completely lost—that naked Pagan repugnance which almost refused to recognize a human soul in the barbarian. It is notable that in these new lands which the Renaissance had thrown open to

European men there at once reappears that institution which had once been fundamental to Europe and which the Faith had slowly and with difficulty undermined and dissolved—Slavery.

The English colonies in America owe their first origin partly to the English instinct for wandering and especially for wandering on the sea, which naturally seized on the adventurous element in the Renaissance as that most congenial to the national temper, and partly to the secular antagonism between England and Spain. Spain, whose sovereign then ruled Portugal and therefore the Portuguese as well as Spanish colonies, claimed the whole of the New World as part of her dominions, and her practical authority extended unchallenged from Florida to Cape Horn. It would have been hopeless for England to have attempted seriously to challenge that authority where it existed in view of the relative strength at that time of the two kingdoms; and in general the English seamen confined themselves to hampering and annoying the Spanish commerce by acts of privateering which the Spaniards naturally designated as piracy. But to the bold and inventive mind of the great Raleigh there occurred another conception. Spain, though she claimed the whole American continent, had not in fact made herself mistress of all its habitable parts. North of the rich lands which supplied gold and silver to the Spanish exchequer, but still well within the temperate zone of climate, lay great tracts bordering the Atlantic where no Spanish soldier or ruler had ever set his foot. To found an English colony in the region would not be an impossible task like the attempt to seize any part of the Spanish empire, yet it would be a practical challenge to the Spanish claim. Raleigh accordingly projected, and others, entering into his plans, successfully planted, an English settlement on the Atlantic seaboard to the south of Chesapeake Bay which, in honour of the Queen, was named "Virginia."

In the subsequent history of the English colonies which became American States we often find a curious and recurrent reflection of their origin. Virginia was the first of those colonies to come into existence, and we shall see her both as a colony and as a State long retaining a sort of primacy amongst them. She also retained, in the incidents of her history and in the characters of many of her great men, a colour which seems partly Elizabethan. Her Jefferson, with his omnivorous culture, his love of music and the arts, his proficiency at the same time in sports and bodily exercises, suggests something of the graceful versatility of men like Essex and Raleigh, and we shall see her in her last agony produce a soldier about whose high chivalry and heroic and adventurous failure there clings a light of romance that does not seem to belong to the modern world.

If the external quarrels of England were the immediate cause of the foundation of Virginia, the two colonies which next make their appearance owe their origin to her internal divisions. James I. and his son Charles I., though by conviction much more genuine Protestants than Elizabeth, were politically more disposed to treat the Catholics with leniency. The paradox is not, perhaps, difficult to explain. Being more genuinely Protestant they were more interested in the internecine quarrels of Protestants, and their enemies in those internecine quarrels, the Puritans, now become a formidable party, were naturally the fiercest enemies of the old religion. This fact probably led the two first Stuarts to look upon that religion with more indulgence. They dared not openly tolerate the Catholics, but they were not unwilling to show them such favour as they could afford to give.

Therefore when a Catholic noble, Lord Baltimore, proposed to found a new plantation in America where his co-religionists could practise their faith in peace and security, the Stuart kings were willing enough to grant his request. James approved the project, his son confirmed it, and, under a Royal Charter from King Charles I., Lord Baltimore established his Catholic colony, which he called "Maryland." The early history of this colony is interesting because it affords probably the first example of full religious liberty. It would doubtless have been suicidal for the Catholics, situated as they were, to attempt anything like persecution, but Baltimore and the Catholics of Maryland for many generations deserve none the less honour for the consistency with which they pursued their tolerant policy. So long as the Catholics remained in control all sects were not only tolerated but placed on a footing of complete equality before the law, and as a fact both the Nonconformist persecuted in Virginia and the Episcopalian persecuted in New England frequently found refuge and peace in Catholic Maryland. The English Revolution of 1689 produced a change. The new English Government was pledged against the toleration of a Catholicism anywhere. The representative of the Baltimore family was deposed from the Governorship and the control transferred to the Protestants, who at once repealed the edicts of toleration and forbade the practice of the Catholic religion. They did not, however, succeed in extirpating it, and to this day many of the old Maryland families are Catholic, as are also a considerable proportion of the Negroes. It may further be noted that, though the experiment in religious equality was suppressed by violence, the idea seems never to have been effaced, and Maryland was one of the first colonies to accompany its demand for freedom with a declaration in favour of universal toleration. At about the same time that the persecuted Catholics found a refuge in Maryland, a similar refuge was sought by the persecuted Puritans. A number of these, who had found a temporary home in Holland, sailed thence for America in the celebrated Mayflower and colonized New England on the Atlantic coast far to the north of the plantations of Raleigh and Baltimore. From this root sprang the colonies of Massachusetts, Connecticut, Vermont and Rhode Island, and later the States of New Hampshire and Maine. It would be putting it with ironical mildness to say that the Pilgrim Fathers did not imitate the tolerant example of the Catholic refugees. Religious persecution had indeed been practised by all parties in the quarrels of the sixteenth and seventeenth centuries; but for much of the early legislation of the Puritan colonies one can find no parallel in the history of European men. Calvinism, that strange fierce creed which Wesley so correctly described as one that gave God the exact functions and attributes of the devil, produced even in Europe a sufficiency of madness and horror; but here was Calvinism cut off from its European roots and from the reaction and influence of Christian civilization. Its records read like those of a madhouse where religious maniacs have broken loose and locked up their keepers. We hear of men stoned to death for kissing their wives on the Sabbath, of lovers pilloried or flogged at the cart's tail for kissing each other at all without licence from the deacons, the whole culminating in a mad panic of wholesale demonism and witch burning so vividly described in one of the most brilliant of Mrs. Gaskell's stories, "Lois the Witch." Of course, in time the fanaticism of the first New England settlers cooled into something like sanity. But a strong Puritan tradition remained and played a great part in American history. Indeed, if Lee, the Virginian, has about him something of the Cavalier, it is still more curious to note that nineteenth-century New England, with its atmosphere of quiet scholars and cultured tea parties, suddenly flung forth in John Brown a figure whose combination of soldierly skill with maniac fanaticism, of a martyr's fortitude with a murderer's cruelty, seems to have walked straight out of the seventeenth century and finds its nearest parallel in some of the warriors of the Covenant.

The colonies so far enumerated owe their foundation solely to English enterprise and energy; but in the latter half of the seventeenth century foreign war brought to England a batch of colonies ready made. At the mouth of the Hudson River, between Maryland and the New England colonies, lay the Dutch settlement of New Amsterdam. The first colonists who had established themselves there had been Swedes, but from Sweden its sovereignty had passed to Holland, and the issue of the Dutch wars gave it to the English, by whom it was re-christened New York in honour of the King's brother, afterwards James II. It would perhaps be straining the suggestion already made of the persistent influences of origins to see in the varied racial and national beginnings of New York a presage of that cosmopolitan quality which still marks the greatest of American cities, making much of it a patchwork of races and languages, and giving to the electric stir of Broadway an air which suggests a Continental rather than an English city, but it is more plausible to note that New York had no original link with the Puritanism of New England and of the North generally, and that in fact we shall find the premier city continually isolated from the North, following a tradition and a policy of its own.

With New Amsterdam was also ceded the small Dutch plantation of Delaware, which lay between Maryland and the Atlantic, while England at the same time established her claim to the disputed territory between the two which became the colony of New Jersey.

Shortly after the cession of New Amsterdam William Penn obtained from Charles II. a charter for the establishment of a colony to the north of

Maryland, between that settlement and the newly acquired territories of New Jersey and New York. This plantation was designed especially as a refuge for the religious sect to which Penn belonged, the Quakers, who had been persecuted by all religious parties and especially savagely by the Puritan colonists of New England. Penn, the most remarkable man that ever professed the strange doctrines of that sect, was a favourite with the King, who had a keen eye for character, and as the son of a distinguished admiral he had a sort of hereditary claim upon the gratitude of the Crown. He easily carried his point with Charles, and himself supervised the foundations of the new commonwealth of Pennsylvania. Two surveyors were sent out by royal authority to fix the boundary between Penn's concession and the existing colony of Maryland—Mr. Mason and Mr. Dixon by name. However elated these two gentlemen may have been by their appointment to so responsible an office, they probably little thought that their names would be immortalized. Yet so it was to be. For the line they drew became the famous "Mason-Dixon" line, and was to be in after years the frontier between the Slave States and the Free.

In all that he did in the New World Penn showed himself not only a great but a most just and wise man. He imitated, with happier issue, the liberality of Baltimore in the matter of religious freedom, and to this day the Catholics of Philadelphia boast of possessing the only Church in the United States in which Mass has been said continuously since the seventeenth century. But it is in his dealings with the natives that Penn's humanity and honour stand out most conspicuously. None of the other founders of English colonies had ever treated the Indians except as vermin to be exterminated as quickly as possible. Penn treated them as free contracting parties with full human rights. He bought of them fairly the land he needed, and strictly observed every article of the pact that he made with them. Anyone visiting to-day the city which he founded will find in its centre a little strip of green, still unbuilt upon, where, in theory, any passing Indians are at liberty to pitch their camp—a monument and one of the clauses of Penn's celebrated treaty.

In the same reign the settlement of the lands lying to the south of Virginia had begun, under the charter granted by Charles II. to the Hyde family, and the new plantations were called after the sovereign "Carolina." But their importance dates from the next century, when they received the main stream of a new tide of immigration due to political and economic causes. England, having planted a Protestant Anglo-Scottish colony in North-East Ireland, proceeded to ruin its own creation by a long series of commercial laws directed to the protection of English manufacturers against the competition of the colonists. Under the pressure of this tyranny a great number of these colonists, largely Scotch by original nationality and Presbyterian by religion, left Ulster for America. They poured into the Carolinas, North and South, as well as into Pennsylvania and Virginia, and overflowed into a new colony which was established further west and named Georgia. It is important to note this element in the colonization of the Southern States, because it is too often loosely suggested that the later division of North and South corresponded to the division of Cavalier and Puritan. It is not so. Virginia and Maryland may be called Cavalier in their origin, but in the Carolinas and Georgia there appears a Puritan tradition, not indeed as fanatical as that of New England, but almost as persistent. Moreover this Scotch-Irish stock, whose fathers, it may be supposed, left Ireland in no very good temper with the rulers of Great Britain, afterwards supplied the most military and the most determined element in Washington's armies, and gave to the Republic some of its most striking historical personalities: Patrick Henry and John Caldwell Calhoun, Jackson, the great President, and his namesake the brilliant soldier of the Confederacy. The English colonies now formed a solid block extending from the coasts of Maine—into which northernmost region the New England colonies had overflown—to the borders of Florida. Florida was still a Spanish possession, but Spain had ceased to be formidable as a rival or enemy of England. By the persistence of a century in arms and diplomacy, the French had worn down the Spanish power, and France was now easily the strongest nation in Europe. France also had a foothold, or rather two footholds, in North America. One of her colonies, Louisiana, lay beyond Florida at the mouth of the Mississippi; the other, Canada, to the north of the Maine, at the mouth of the St. Lawrence. It was the aim of French colonial ambition to extend both colonies inland into the unmapped heart of the American continent until they should meet. This would necessarily have had the effect of hemming in the English settlements on the Atlantic seaboard and preventing their Western expansion. Throughout the first half of the eighteenth century, therefore, the rivalry grew more and more acute, and even when France and England were at peace the French and English in America were almost constantly at war. Their conflict was largely carried on under cover of alliances with the warring Indian tribes, whose feuds kept the region of the Great Lakes in a continual turmoil. The outbreak of the Seven Years' War and the intervention of England as an ally of Prussia put an end to the necessity for such pretexts, and a regular military campaign opened upon which was staked the destiny of North America.

It is not necessary for the purposes of this book to follow that campaign in detail. The issue was necessarily fought out in Canada, for Louisiana lay remote from the English colonies and was separated from them by the neutral territory of the Spanish Empire. England had throughout the war the advantage of superiority at sea, which enabled her to supply and reinforce her armies, while the French forces were practically cut off from Europe. The French, on the other hand, had at the beginning the advantage of superior numbers, at least so far as regular troops were concerned, while for defensive purposes they possessed an excellent chain of very strong fortresses carefully prepared before the war. After the earlier operations, which cleared the French invaders out of the English colonies, the gradual reduction of these strongholds practically forms the essence of the campaign undertaken by a succession of English generals under the political direction of the elder Pitt. That campaign was virtually brought to a close by the brilliant exploit of James Wolfe in 1759—the taking of Quebec. By the Treaty of Paris in 1763 Canada was ceded to England. Meanwhile Louisiana had been transferred to Spain in 1762 as part of the price of a Spanish alliance, and France ceased to be a rival to England on the American continent.

During the French war the excellent professional army which England was able to maintain in the field was supported by levies raised from the English colonies, which did good service in many engagements. Among the officers commanding these levies one especially had attracted, by his courage and skill, and notably by the part he bore in the clearing of Pennsylvania, the notice of his superiors—George Washington of Virginia.

England was now in a position to develop in peace the empire which her sword had defended with such splendid success and glory. Before we consider the causes which so suddenly shattered that empire, it is necessary to take a brief survey of its geography and of its economic conditions. The colonies, as we have seen, were spread along the Atlantic seaboard to an extent of well over a thousand miles, covering nearly twenty degrees of latitude. The variations of climate were naturally great, and involved marked differentiations in the character and products of labour. The prosperity of the Southern colonies depended mainly upon two great staple industries. Raleigh, in the course of his voyages, had learned from the Indians the use of the tobacco plant and had introduced that admirable discovery into Europe. As Europe learned (in spite of the protests of James I.) to prize the glorious indulgence now offered to it, the demand for tobacco grew, and its supply became the principal business of the colonies of Virginia and Maryland. Further to the south a yet more important and profitable industry was established. The climate of the Carolinas and of Georgia and of the undeveloped country west of these colonies, a climate at once warm and humid, was found to be exactly suited to the cultivation of the cotton plant. This proved the more important when the discoveries of Watt and Arkwright gave Lancashire the start of all the world in the manipulation of the cotton fabric. From that moment begins the triumphant progress of "King Cotton," which was long to outlast the political connection between the Carolinas and Lancashire, and was to give in the political balance of America peculiar importance to the "Cotton States."

But at the time now under consideration these cotton-growing territories were still under the British Crown, and were subject to the Navigation Laws upon which England then mainly relied for the purpose of making her colonies a source of profit to her. The main effect of these was to forbid the colonies to trade with any neighbour save the mother country. This condition, to which the colonists seem to have offered no opposition, gave to the British manufacturers the immense advantage of an unrestricted supply of raw material to which no foreigner had access. It is among the curious ironies of history that the prosperity of Lancashire, which was afterwards to be identified with Free Trade, was originally founded upon this very drastic and successful form of Protection.

The more northerly colonies had no such natural advantages. The bulk of the population lived by ordinary farming, grew wheat and the hard cereals and raised cattle. But during the eighteenth century England herself was still an exporting country as regards these commodities, and with other nations the colonists were forbidden to trade. The Northern colonies had, therefore, no considerable export commerce, but on the seaboard they gradually built up a considerable trade as carriers, and Boston and New York merchant captains began to have a name on the Atlantic for skill and enterprise. Much of the transoceanic trade passed into their hands, and especially one most profitable if not very honourable trade of which, by the Treaty of Utrecht, England had obtained a virtual monopoly—the trade in Negro slaves.

The pioneer of this traffic had been Sir John Hawkins, one of the boldest of the great Elizabethan sailors. He seems to have been the first of the merchant adventurers to realize that it might prove profitable to kidnap Negroes from the West Coast of Africa and sell them into slavery in the American colonies. The cultivation of cotton and tobacco in the Southern plantations, as of sugar in the West Indies, offered a considerable demand for labour of a type suitable to the Negro. The attempt to compel the native Indians to such labour had failed; the Negro proved more tractable. By the time with which we are dealing the whole industry of the Southern colonies already rested upon servile coloured labour.

In the Northern colonies—that is, those north of Maryland—the Negro slave existed, but only casually, and, as it were, as a sort of accident. Slavery was legal in all the colonies—even in Pennsylvania, whose great founder had been almost alone in that age in disapproving of it. As for the New England Puritans, they had from the first been quite enthusiastic about the traffic, in which indeed they were deeply interested as middlemen; and Calvinist ministers of the purest orthodoxy held services of thanksgiving to God for cargoes of poor barbarians rescued from the darkness of heathendom and brought (though forcibly) into the gospel light. But though the Northerners had no more scruple about Slavery than the Southerners, they had far less practical use for it. The Negro was of no value for the sort of labour in which the New Englanders engaged; he died of it in the cold climate. Negro slaves there were in all the Northern States, but mostly employed as domestic servants or in casual occupations. They were a luxury, not a necessity.

A final word must be said about the form of government under which the colonists lived. In all the colonies, though there were, of course, variations of detail, it was substantially the same. It was founded in every case upon Royal Charters granted at some time or other to the planters by the English king. In every case there was a Governor, who was assisted by some sort of elective assembly. The Governor was the representative of the King and was nominated by him. The legislature was in some form or other elected by the free citizens. The mode of election and the franchise varied from colony to colony—Massachusetts at one time based hers upon pew rents—but it was generally in harmony with the feeling and traditions of the colonists. It was seldom that any friction occurred between the King's representative and the burgesses, as they were generally called. While the relations between the colonies and the mother country remained tranquil the Governor had every motive for pursuing a conciliatory policy. His personal comfort depended upon his being popular in the only society which he could frequent. His repute with the Home Government, if he valued it, was equally served by the tranquility and contentment of the dominion he ruled.

In fact, the American colonists, during the eighteenth century, enjoyed what a simple society left to itself almost always enjoys, under whatever forms—the substance of democracy. That fact must be emphasized, because without a recognition of it the flaming response which met the first proclamation of theoretic democracy would be unintelligible. It is explicable only when we remember that to the unspoiled conscience of man as man democracy will ever be the most self- evident of truths. It is the complexity of our civilization that blinds us to its self-evidence, teaching us to acquiesce in irrational privilege as inevitable, and at last to see nothing strange in being ruled by a class, whether of nobles or of mere parliamentarians. But the man who looks at the world with the terrible eyes of his first innocence can never see an unequal law as anything but an iniquity, or government divorced from the general will as anything but usurpation.

Chapter 2

ARMS AND THE RIGHTS OF MAN

Such was roughly the position of the thirteen English colonies in North America when in the year 1764, shortly after the conclusion of the Seven Years' War, George Grenville, who had become the chief Minister of George III after the failure of Lord Bute, proposed to raise a revenue from these colonies by the imposition of a Stamp Act.

The Stamp Act and the resistance it met mark so obviously the beginning of the business which ended in the separation of the United States from Great Britain that Grenville and the British Parliament have been frequently blamed for the lightness of heart with which they entered upon so momentous a course. But in fact it did not seem to them momentous, nor is it easy to say why they should have thought it momentous. It is certain that Grenville's political opponents, many of whom were afterwards to figure as the champions of the colonists, at first saw its momentousness as little as he. They offered to his proposal only the most perfunctory sort of opposition, less than they habitually offered to all his measures, good or bad.

And, in point of fact, there was little reason why a Whig of the type and class that then governed England should be startled or shocked by a proposal to extend the English system of stamping documents to the English colonies. That Parliament had the legal right to tax the colonies was not seriously questionable. Under the British Constitution the power of

King, Lords and Commons over the King's subjects was and is absolute, and none denied that the colonists were the King's subjects. They pleaded indeed that their charters did not expressly authorize such taxation; but neither did they expressly exclude it, and on a strict construction it would certainly seem that a power which would have existed if there had been no charter remained when the charter was silent.

It might further be urged that equity as well as law justified the taxation of the colonies, for the expenditure which these taxes were raised to meet was largely incurred in defending the colonies first against the French and then against the Indians. The method of taxation chosen was not new, neither had it been felt to be specially grievous. Much revenue is raised in Great Britain and all European countries to-day by that method, and there is probably no form of taxation at which men grumble less. Its introduction into America had actually been recommended on its merits by eminent Americans. It had been proposed by the Governor of Pennsylvania as early as 1739. It had been approved at one time by Benjamin Franklin himself. To-day it must seem to most of us both less unjust and less oppressive than the Navigation Laws, which the colonists bore without complaint.

As for the suggestion sometimes made that there was something unprecedentedly outrageous about an English Parliament taxing people who were unrepresented there, it is, in view of the constitution of that Parliament, somewhat comic. If the Parliament of 1764 could only tax those whom it represented, its field of taxation would be somewhat narrow. Indeed, the talk about taxation without representation being tyranny, however honestly it might be uttered by an American, could only be conscious or unconscious hypocrisy in men like Burke, who were not only passing their lives in governing and taxing people who were unrepresented, but who were quite impenitently determined to resist any attempt to get them represented even in the most imperfect fashion.

All this is true; and yet it is equally true that the proposed tax at once excited across the Atlantic the most formidable discontent. Of this discontent we may perhaps summarize the immediate causes as follows. Firstly, no English minister or Parliament had, as a fact, ever before attempted to tax the colonies. That important feature of the case distinguished it from that of the Navigation Laws, which had prescription on their side. Then, if the right to tax were once admitted, no one could say how far it would be pushed. Under the Navigation Laws the colonists knew just how far they were restricted, and they knew that within the limits of such restrictions they could still prosper. But if once the claim of the British Parliament to tax were quietly accepted, it seemed likely enough that every British Minister who had nowhere else to turn for a revenue would turn to the unrepresented colonies, which would furnish supply after supply until they were "bled white." That was a perfectly sound, practical consideration, and it naturally appealed with especial force to mercantile communities like that of Boston.

But if we assume that it was the only consideration involved, we shall misunderstand all that followed, and be quite unprepared for the sweeping victory of a purely doctrinal political creed which brought about the huge domestic revolution of which the breaking of the ties with England was but an aspect. The colonists did feel it unjust that they should be taxed by an authority which was in no way responsible to them; and they so felt it because, as has already been pointed out, they enjoyed in the management of their everyday affairs a large measure of practical democracy. Therein they differed from the English, who, being habitually governed by an oligarchy, did not feel it extraordinary that the same oligarchy should tax them. The Americans for the most part governed themselves, and the oligarchy came in only as an alien and unnatural thing levying taxes. Therefore it was resisted.

The resistance was at first largely instinctive. The formulation of the democratic creed which should justify it was still to come. Yet already there were voices, especially in Virginia, which adumbrated the incomparable phrases of the greatest of Virginians. Already Richard Bland had appealed to "the law of Nature and those rights of mankind that flow from it." Already Patrick Henry had said, "Give me liberty or give me death!"

It was but a foreshadowing of the struggle to come. In 1766 the Rockingham Whigs, having come into power upon the fall of Grenville, after some hesitation repealed the Stamp Act, reaffirming at the same time the abstract right of Parliament to tax the colonies. America was for the time quieted. There followed in England a succession of weak Ministries, all, of course, drawn from the same oligarchical class, and all of much the same political temper, but all at issue with each other, and all more or less permanently at issue with the King. As a mere by-product of one of the multitudinous intrigues to which this situation gave rise, Charles Townshend, a brilliant young Whig orator who had become Chancellor of the Exchequer, revived in 1768 the project of taxing the American colonies. This was now proposed in the form of a series of duties levied on goods exported to those colonies—the one most obnoxious to the colonists and most jealously maintained by the Ministers being a duty on tea. The Opposition had now learnt from the result of the Stamp Act debate that American taxation was an excellent issue on which to challenge the Ministry, and the Tea Tax became at once a "Party Question"—that is, a question upon which the rival oligarchs divided themselves into opposing groups.

Meanwhile in America the new taxes were causing even more exasperation than the Stamp Act had caused—probably because they were more menacing in their form, if not much more severe in their effect. At any rate, it is significant that in the new struggle we find the commercial colony of Massachusetts very decidedly taking the lead. The taxed tea, on its arrival in Boston harbour, was seized and flung into the sea. A wise Government would have withdrawn when it was obvious that the enforcement of the taxes would cost far more than the taxes themselves were worth, the more so as they had already been so whittled down by concessions as to be worth practically nothing, and it is likely enough that the generally prudent and politic aristocrats who then directed the action of England would have reverted to the Rockingham policy had not the King made up his unfortunate German mind to the coercion and humiliation of the discontented colonists. It is true that the British Crown had long lost its power of independent action, and that George III had failed in his youthful attempts to recapture it. Against the oligarchy combined he was helpless; but his preference for one group of oligarchs over another was still an asset, and he let it clearly be understood that such influence as he possessed would be exercised unreservedly in favour of any group that would undertake to punish the American rebels. He found in Lord North a Minister willing, though not without considerable misgivings, to forward his policy and able to secure for it a majority in Parliament. And from that moment the battle between the Home Government and the colonists was joined.

The character and progress of that battle will best be grasped if we mark down certain decisive incidents which determine its course. The first of these was the celebrated "Boston Tea Party" referred to above. It was the first act of overt resistance, and it was followed on the English side by the first dispatch of an armed force—grossly inadequate for its purpose—to America, and on the American by the rapid arming and drilling of the local militias not yet avowedly against the Crown, but obviously with the ultimate intention of resisting the royal authority should it be pushed too far. The next turning-point is the decision of the British Government early in 1774 to revoke the Charter of Massachusetts. It is the chief event of the period during which war is preparing, and it leads directly to all that follows. For it raised a new controversy which could not be resolved by the old legal arguments, good or bad. Hitherto the colonists had relied upon their interpretation of existing charters, while the Government contented itself with putting forward a different interpretation. But the new action of that Government shifted the ground of debate from the question of the interpretation of the charters to that of the ultimate source of their authority. The Ministers said in effect, "You pretend that this document concedes to you the right of immunity from taxation. We deny it: but at any rate, it was a free gift from the British Crown, and whatever rights you enjoy under it you enjoy during His Majesty's pleasure. Since you insist on misinterpreting it, we will withdraw it, as we are perfectly entitled to do, and we will grant you a new charter about the terms of which no such doubts can arise."

It was a very direct and very fundamental challenge, and it inevitably produced two effects—the one immediate, the other somewhat deferred. Its practical first-fruit was the Continental Congress. Its ultimate but unmistakably logical consequence was the Declaration of Independence.

America was unified on the instant, for every colony felt the knife at its throat. In September a Congress met, attended by the representatives of eleven colonies. Peyton Randolph, presiding, struck the note of the moment with a phrase: "I am not a Virginian, but an American." Under Virginian leadership the Congress vigorously backed Massachusetts, and in October a "Declaration of Colonial Right" had been issued by the authority of all the colonies represented there.

The British Ministers seem to have been incomprehensibly blind to the seriousness of the situation. Since they were pledged not to concede what the colonists demanded, it was essential that they should at once summon all the forces at their command to crush what was already an incipient and most menacing rebellion. They did nothing of the sort. They slightly strengthened the totally inadequate garrison which would soon have to face a whole people in arms, and they issued a foolish proclamation merely provocative and backed by no power that could enforce it, forbidding the meeting of Continental Congresses in the future. That was in January. In April the skirmishes of Lexington and Concord had shown how hopelessly insufficient was their military force to meet even local sporadic and unorganized revolts. In May the second Continental Congress met, and in July appeared by its authority a general call to arms addressed to the whole population of America.

Up to this point the colonists, if rebellious in their practical attitude, had been strictly constitutional in their avowed aims. In the "Declaration of Colonial Right" of 1774, and even in the appeal to arms of 1775, all suggestion of breaking away from the Empire was repudiated. But now that the sword was virtually drawn there were practical considerations which made the most prudent of the rebels consider whether it would not be wiser to take the final step, and frankly repudiate the British Sovereignty altogether. For one thing, by the laws of England, and indeed of all civilized nations, the man who took part in an armed insurrection against the head of the State committed treason, and the punishment for treason was death. Men who levied war on the King's forces while still acknowledging him as their lawful ruler were really inviting the Government to hang them as soon as it could catch them. It might be more difficult for the British Government to treat as criminals soldiers who were fighting under the orders of an organized de facto government, which at any rate declared itself to be that of an independent nation. Again, foreign aid, which would not be given for the purpose of reforming the internal administration of British dominions, might well be forthcoming if it were a question of dismembering those dominions. These considerations were just and carried no little weight; yet it is doubtful if they would have been strong enough to prevail against the sentiments and traditions which still bound the colonies to the mother country had not the attack on the charters forced the controversy back to first principles, and so opened the door of history to the man who was to provide America with a creed and to convert the controversy from a legal to something like a religious quarrel.

Old Peyton Randolph, who had so largely guided the deliberations of the first Continental Congress, was at the last moment prevented by ill-health from attending the second. His place in the Virginian Delegation was taken by Thomas Jefferson.

Jefferson was not yet thirty when he took his seat in the Continental Congress, but he was already a notable figure in his native State. He belonged by birth to the slave-holding gentry of the South, though not to the richest and most exclusive section of that class. Physically he was long limbed and loose jointed, but muscular, with a strong ugly face and red hair. He was adept at the physical exercises which the Southerners cultivated most assiduously, a bold and tireless rider who could spend days in the saddle without fatigue, and a crack shot even among Virginians. In pursuit of the arts and especially of music he was equally eager, and his restless intelligence was keenly intrigued by the new wonders that physical science was beginning to reveal to men; mocking allusions to his interest in the habits of horned frogs will be found in American pasquinades of two generations. He had sat in the Virginian House of Burgesses and had taken a prominent part in the resistance of that body to the royal demands. As a speaker, however, he was never highly successful, and a just knowledge of his own limitations, combined perhaps with a temperamental dislike, generally led him to rely on his pen rather than his tongue in public debate. For as a writer he had a command of a pure, lucid and noble English unequalled in his generation and equalled by Corbett alone.

But for history the most important thing about the man is his creed. It was the creed of a man in the forefront of his age, an age when French thinkers were busy drawing from the heritage of Latin civilizations those fundamental principles of old Rome which custom and the corruptions of time had overgrown. The gospel of the new age had already been written: it had brought to the just mind of Jefferson a conviction which he was to communicate to all his countrymen, and through them to the new nation which the sword was creating. The Declaration of Independence is the foundation stone of the American Republic, and the Declaration of Independence in its essential part is but an incomparable translation and compression of the Contrat Social. The aid which France brought to America did not begin when a French fleet sailed into Chesapeake Bay. It began when, perhaps years before the first whisper of discontent, Thomas Jefferson sat down in his Virginian study to read the latest work of the ingenious M. Rousseau.

For now the time was rife for such intellectual leadership as Jefferson, armed by Rousseau, could supply. The challenge flung down by the British Government in the matter of the Charter of Massachusetts was to be taken up. The argument that whatever rights Americans might have they derived from Royal Charters was to be answered by one who held that their "inalienable rights" were derived from a primordial charter granted not by King George but by his Maker.

The second Continental Congress, after many hesitations, determined at length upon a complete severance with the mother country. A resolution to that effect was carried on the motion of Lee, the great Virginian gentleman, an ancestor of the noblest of Southern warriors. After much adroit negotiations a unanimous vote was secured for it. A committee was appointed to draft a formal announcement and defence of the step which had been taken. Jefferson was chosen a member of the committee, and to him was most wisely entrusted the drafting of the famous "Declaration."

The introductory paragraphs of the Declaration of Independence contain the whole substance of the faith upon which the new Commonwealth was to be built. Without a full comprehension of their contents the subsequent history of America would be unintelligible. It will therefore be well to quote them here verbatim, and I do so the more readily because, apart from their historic importance, it is a pity that more Englishmen are not acquainted with this masterpiece of English prose.

When in the course of human events it becomes necessary for one people to dissolve the political bands which have connected them with another and to assume among the powers of the earth the separate and equal station to which the laws of Nature and of Nature's God entitle them, a decent respect for the opinion of Mankind requires that they shall declare the cause that impels the separation.

We hold these truths to be self-evident: that all men are created equal; that they are endowed by their Creator with certain inalienable rights; that among these are life, liberty, and the pursuit of happiness; that to secure these rights governments are instituted among men, deriving their just powers from the consent of the governed; that whenever any form of government becomes destructive of those ends it is the right of the people to alter or to abolish it, and to reinstate a new government, laying its foundation on such principles and organizing its powers in such form as to them shall seem most likely to effect their safety and happiness.

The Declaration goes on to specify the causes of grievances which the colonists conceive themselves to have against the royal government, and concludes as follows:—

We, therefore, the representatives of the United States of America in General Congress assembled, appealing to the Supreme Judge of the World for the rectitude of our intentions, do in the name and by the authority of the good people of these colonies, solemnly publish and declare that these United Colonies are and of right ought to be Free and Independent States.

The first principles set out in the Declaration must be rightly grasped if American history is understood, for indeed the story of America is merely the story of the working out of those principles. Briefly the theses are two: first, that men are of right equal, and secondly, that the moral basis of the relations between governors and governed is contractual. Both doctrines have in this age had to stand the fire of criticisms almost too puerile to be noticed. It is gravely pointed out that men are of different heights and weights, that they vary in muscular power and mental cultivation—as if either Rousseau or Jefferson was likely to have failed to notice this occult fact! Similarly the doctrine of the contractual basis of society is met by a demand for the production of a signed, sealed, and delivered contract, or at least for evidence that such a contract was ever made. But Rousseau says—with a good sense and modesty which dealers in "prehistoric" history would do well to copy—that he does not know how government in fact arose. Nor does anyone else. What he maintains is that the moral sanction of government is contractual, or, as Jefferson puts it, that government "derives its just powers from the consent of the governed."

The doctrine of human equality is in a sense mystical. It is not apparent to the senses, nor can it be logically demonstrated as an inference from anything of which the senses can take cognizance. It can only be stated accurately, and left to make its appeal to men's minds. It may be stated theologically by saying, as the Christian theology says, that all men are equal before God. Or it may be stated in the form which Jefferson uses— that all men are equal in their "inalienable rights." But it must be accepted as a first principle or not at all. The nearest approach to a method of proving it is to take the alternative proposition and deduce its logical conclusion. Would those who would maintain that the "wisest and best" have rights superior to those of their neighbours, welcome a law which would enable any person demonstrably wiser or more virtuous than themselves to put them to death? I think that most of them have enough modesty (and humour) to shrink, as Huxley did, from such a proposition. But the alternative is the acceptance of Jefferson's doctrine that the fundamental rights of men are independent of adventitious differences, whether material or moral, and depend simply upon their manhood.

The other proposition, the contractual basis of human society and its logical consequences, the supremacy of the general will, can be argued in the same fashion. It is best defended by asking, like the Jesuit Suarez, the simple question: "If sovereignty is not in the People, where is it?" It is useless to answer that it is in the "wisest and best." Who are the wisest and best? For practical purposes the phrases must mean either those whom their neighbours think wisest and best—in which case the ultimate test of democracy is conceded—or those who think themselves wisest and best: which latter is what in the mouths of such advocates it usually does mean. Thus those to whom the Divine Right of the conceited makes no appeal are forced back on the Jeffersonian formula. Let it be noted that that formula does not mean that the people are always right or that a people cannot collectively do deliberate injustice or commit sins—indeed, inferentially it implies that possibility—but it means that there is on earth no temporal authority superior to the general will of a community.

It is, however, no part of the function of this book to argue upon the propositions contained in the Declaration of Independence. It is merely necessary to chronicle the historical fact that Jefferson, as mouthpiece of the Continental Congress, put forward these propositions as self-evident, and that all America, looking at them, accepted them as such. On that acceptance, the intensity and ardent conviction of which showed itself, as will presently be seen, in a hundred ways, the American Commonwealth is built. In the modern haze of doubt and amid the denial of all necessary things, there have been found plenty of sophists, even in America, to dispute these great truisms. But if the American nation as a whole ever ceases to believe in them, it will not merely decay, as all nations decay when they lose touch with eternal truths; it will drop suddenly dead.

We must now turn back a little in time in order to make clear the military situation as it stood when Jefferson's "Declaration" turned the war into a war of doctrines.

The summer of 1775 saw the first engagement which could well be dignified with the name of a battle. A small English force had been sent to Boston with the object of coercing the recalcitrant colony of Massachusetts. It was absolutely insufficient, as the event showed, even for that purpose, and before it had landed it was apparent that its real task would be nothing less than the conquest of America. The Massachusetts rebels wisely determined to avoid a combat with the guns of the British fleet; they abandoned the city and entrenched themselves in a strong position in the neighbourhood known as Bunker's Hill. The British troops marched out of Boston to dislodge them. This they eventually succeeded in doing; and those who regard war as a game like billiards to be settled by scoring points may claim Bunker's Hill as a British victory. But it produced all the consequences of a defeat. The rebel army was not destroyed; it was even less weakened than the force opposed to it. It retired in good order to a position somewhat further back, and the British force had no option but to return to Boston with its essential work undone. For some time England continued to hold Boston, but the State of Massachusetts remained in American hands. At last, in the absence of any hope of any effective action, the small English garrison withdrew, leaving the original prize of war to the rebels.

On the eve of this indecisive contest the American Congress met to consider the selection of a commander-in-chief for the revolutionary armies. Their choice fell on General George Washington, a Virginian soldier who, as has been remarked, had served with some distinction in the French wars.

The choice was a most fortunate one. America and England have agreed to praise Washington's character so highly that at the hands of the young and irreverent he is in some danger of the fate of Aristides. For the benefit of those who tend to weary of the Cherry Tree and the Little Hatchet, it may be well to say that Washington was a very typical Southern gentleman in his foibles as well as in his virtues. Though his temper was in large matters under strict control, it was occasionally formidable and vented itself in a free and cheerful profanity. He loved good wine, and like most eighteenth-century gentlemen, was not sparing in its use. He had a Southerner's admiration for the other sex—an admiration which, if gossip may be credited, was not always strictly confined within monogamic limits. He had also, in large measure, the high dignity and courtesy of his class, and an enlarged liberality of temper which usually goes with such good breeding. There is no story of him more really characteristic than that of his ceremoniously returning the salute of an aged Negro and saying to a friend who was disposed to deride his actions: "Would you have me let a poor ignorant coloured man say that he had better manners than I?" For the rest the traditional eulogy of his public character is not undeserved. It may justly be said of him, as it can be said of few of the great men who have moulded the destinies of nations, that history can put its fingers on no act of his and say: "Here this man was preferring his own interest to his country's."

As a military commander Washington ranks high. He had not, indeed, the genius of a Marlborough or a Napoleon. Rather he owed his success to a thorough grasp of his profession combined with just that remarkably level and unbiassed judgment which distinguished his conduct of civil affairs. He understood very clearly the conditions of the war in which he was to engage. He knew that Great Britain, as soon as she really woke up to the seriousness of her peril, would send out a formidable force of well-disciplined professional soldiers, and that at the hands of such a force no mere levy of enthusiastic volunteers could expect anything but defeat. The breathing space which the incredible supineness of the British Government allowed him enabled him to form something like a real army. Throughout the campaigns that followed his primary object was not to win victories, but to keep that army in being. So long as it existed, he knew that it could be continually reinforced by the enthusiasm of the colonials, and that the recruits so obtained could be consolidated into and imbued with the spirit of a disciplined body. The moment it ceased to exist Great Britain would have to deal simply with rebellious populations, and Washington was soldier enough to know that an army can always in time break up and keep down a mere population, however eager and courageous.

And now England at last did what, if she were determined to enforce her will upon the colonists, she ought to have done at least five years before. She sent out an army on a scale at least reasonably adequate to the business for which it was designed. It consisted partly of excellent British troops and partly of those mercenaries whom the smaller German princes let out for hire to those who chose to employ them. It was commanded by Lord Howe. The objective of the new invasion—for the procrastination of the British Government had allowed the war to assume that character—was the city of New York.

New York harbour possesses, as anyone who enters it can see, excellent natural defences. Manhattan Island, upon which the city is built, lies at the mouth of the Hudson between two arms of that river. At the estuary are a number of small islets well suited for the emplacement of powerful guns. The southern bank runs northward into a sharp promontory, at the end of which now stands the most formidable of American fortresses. The northern approach is covered by Long Island. The British command decided on the reduction of Long Island as a preliminary to an assault upon the city. The island is long and narrow, and a ridge of high ground runs down it like a backbone. This ridge Washington's army sought to hold against the attack of the British forces. It was the first real battle of the war, and it resulted in a defeat so overwhelming that it might well have decided the fate of America had not Washington, as soon as he saw how the day was going, bent all his energies to the tough task of saving his army. It narrowly escaped complete destruction, but ultimately a great part succeeded, though with great loss and not a little demoralization, in reaching Brooklyn in safety.

The Americans still held New York, the right bank of the Hudson; but their flank was dangerously threatened, and Washington, true to his policy, preferred the damaging loss of New York to the risk of his army. He retired inland, again offered battle, was again defeated and forced back into Pennsylvania. So decided did the superiority of the British army prove to be that eventually Philadelphia itself, then the capital of the Confederacy, had to be abandoned.

Meanwhile another British army under the command of General Burgoyne held Canada. That province had shown no disposition to join in the revolt; an early attempt on the part of the rebels to invade it had been successfully repelled. Besides English and German troops, Burgoyne had the aid of several tribes of Indian auxiliaries, whose aid the British Government had been at some pains to secure—a policy denounced by Chatham in a powerful and much-quoted speech. Burgoyne was a clever and imaginative though not a successful soldier. He conceived and suggested to his Government a plan of campaign which was sound in strategic principle, which might well have succeeded, and which, if it had succeeded, would have dealt a heavy and perhaps a decisive blow to American hopes. How far its failure is to be attributed to his own faulty execution, how far to the blunders of the Home Government, and how far to accidents which the best general cannot always avoid, is still disputed. But that failure was certainly the turning-point of the war.

Burgoyne's project was this: He proposed to advance from Canada and push across the belt of high land which forms the northern portion of what is now New York State, until he struck the upper Hudson. Howe was at the same time to advance northward up the Hudson, join hands with him and cut the rebellion in two.

It was a good plan. The cutting off and crushing of one isolated district after another is just the fashion in which widespread insurrectionary movements have most generally been suppressed by military force. The Government accepted it, but, owing as it would seem to the laziness or levity of the English Minister involved, instructions never reached Howe until it was too late for him to give effective support to his colleague. All, however, might have prospered had Burgoyne been able to move more rapidly. His first stroke promised well. The important fort of Ticonderoga was surprised and easily captured, and the road was open for his soldiers into the highlands. But that advance proved disastrously slow. Weeks passed before he approached the Hudson. His supplies were running short, and when he reached Saratoga, instead of joining hands with Howe he found himself confronted by strongly posted American forces, greatly outnumbering his own ill-sustained and exhausted army. Seeing no sign of the relief which he had expected to the south—though as a fact Howe had by this time learnt of the expedition and was hastening to his assistance—on October 6, 1777, he and his army surrendered to the American commander, General Gates.

The effect of Burgoyne's surrender was great in America; to those whose hopes had been dashed by the disaster of Long Island, the surrender of New York and Washington's enforced retreat it brought not only a revival of hope but a definite confidence in ultimate success. But that effect was even greater in Europe. Its immediate fruit was Lord North's famous "olive branch" of 1778; the decision of the British Government to accept defeat on the original issue of the war, and to agree to a surrender of the claim to tax the colonists on condition of their return to their allegiance. Such a proposition made three years earlier would certainly have produced immediate peace. Perhaps it might have produced peace even as it was—though it is unlikely, for the declaration had filled men's souls with a new hunger for pure democracy—if the Americans had occupied the same isolated position which was theirs when the war began. But it was not in London alone that Saratoga had produced its effect. While it decided the wavering councils of the British Ministry in favour of concessions, it also decided the wavering councils of the French Crown in favour of intervention.

As early as 1776 a mission had been sent to Versailles to solicit on behalf of the colonists the aid of France. Its principal member was Benjamin Franklin, the one revolutionary leader of the first rank who came from the Northern colonies. He had all the shrewdness and humour of the Yankee with an enlarged intelligence and a wide knowledge of men which made him an almost ideal negotiator in such a cause. Yet for some time his mission hung fire. France had not forgotten her expulsion from the North American continent twenty years before. She could not but desire the success of the colonists and the weakening or dismemberment of the British Empire. Moreover, French public opinion—and its power under the Monarchy, though insufficient, was far greater than is now generally understood—full of the new ideals which were to produce the Revolution, was warmly in sympathy with the rebellion. But, on the other hand, an open breach with England involved serious risks. France was only just recovering from the effects of a great war in which she had on the whole been worsted, and very decidedly worsted, in the colonial field. The revolt of the English colonies might seem a tempting opportunity for revenge; but suppose that the colonial resistance collapsed before effective aid could arrive? Suppose the colonists merely used the threat of French intervention to extort terms from England and then made common cause against the foreigner? These obvious considerations made the French statesmen hesitate. Aid was indeed given to the colonial rebels, especially in the very valuable form of arms and munitions, but it was given secretly and unofficially, with the satirist Beaumarchais, clever, daring, unscrupulous and ready to push his damaged fortunes in any fashion, as unaccredited go-between. But in the matter of open alliance with the rebels against the British Government France temporized, nor could the utmost efforts of Franklin and his colleagues extort a decision.

Saratoga extorted it. On the one hand it removed a principal cause of hesitation. After such a success it was unlikely that the colonists would tamely surrender. On the other it made it necessary to take immediate action. Lord North's attitude showed clearly that the British Government was ready to make terms with the colonists. It was clearly in the interests of France that those terms should be refused. She must venture something to make sure of such a refusal. With little hesitation the advisers of the French Crown determined to take the plunge. They acknowledged the revolted colonies as independent States, and entered into a defensive alliance with these States against Great Britain. That recognition and alliance immediately determined the issue of the war. What would have happened if it had been withheld cannot be certainly determined. It seems not unlikely that the war would have ended as the South African War ended, in large surrenders of the substance of Imperial power in return for a theoretic acknowledgment of its authority. But all this is speculative. The practical fact is that England found herself, in the middle of a laborious, and so far on the whole unsuccessful, effort to crush the rebellion of her colonies, confronted by a war with France, which, through the close alliance then existing between the two Bourbon monarchies, soon became a war with both France and Spain. This change converted the task of subjugation from a difficult but practicable one, given sufficient time and determination, to one fundamentally impossible.

Yet, so far as the actual military situation was concerned, there were no darker days for the Americans than those which intervened between the promise of French help and its fulfilment. Lord Cornwallis had appeared in the South and had taken possession of Charleston, the chief port of South Carolina. In that State the inhabitants were less unanimous than elsewhere. The "Tories," as the local adherents of the English Crown were called, had already attempted a rebellion against the rebellion, but had been forced to yield to the Republican majority backed by the army of Washington. The presence of Cornwallis revived their courage. They boasted in Tarleton, able, enterprising and imperious, an excellent commander for the direction of irregular warfare, whose name and that of the squadron of horse which he raised and organized became to the rebels what the names of Claverhouse and his dragoons were to the Covenanters. Cornwallis and Tarleton between them completely reduced the Carolinas, save for the strip of mountainous country to the north, wherein many of those families that Tarleton had "burnt out" found refuge, and proceeded to overrun Georgia. Only two successes encouraged the rebels. At the Battle of the Cowpens Tarleton having, with the recklessness which was the defeat of his qualities as a leader, advanced too far into the hostile country, was met and completely defeated by Washington. The defeat produced little immediate result, but it was the one definite military success which the American general achieved before the advent of the French, and it helped to keep up the spirit of the insurgents. Perhaps even greater in its moral effect was the other victory, which from the military point of view was even more insignificant. In Sumter and Davie the rebels found two cavalry leaders fully as daring and capable as Tarleton himself. They formed from among the refugees who had sought the shelter of the Carolinian hills a troop of horse with which they made a sudden raid upon the conquered province and broke the local Tories at the Battle of the Hanging Rock. It was a small affair so far as numbers went, and Davie's troopers were a handful of irregulars drawn as best might be from the hard-riding, sharp-shooting population of the South. Many of them were mere striplings; indeed, among them was a boy of thirteen, an incorrigible young rebel who had run away from school to take part in the fighting. In the course of this narration it will be necessary to refer to that boy again more than once. His name was Andrew Jackson.

While there was so little in the events of the Southern campaign to bring comfort to the rebels, in the North their cause suffered a moral blow which was felt at the moment to be almost as grave as any military disaster. Here the principal American force was commanded by one of the ablest soldiers the Rebellion had produced, a man who might well have disputed the pre-eminent fame of Washington if he had not chosen rather to challenge—and with no contemptible measures of success—that of Iscariot. Benedict Arnold was, like Washington, a professional soldier whose talent had been recognized before the war. He had early embraced the revolutionary cause, and had borne a brilliant part in the campaign which ended in the surrender of Burgoyne. There seemed before him every prospect of a glorious career. The motives which led him to the most inexpiable of human crimes were perhaps mixed, though all of them were poisonous. He was in savage need of money to support the extravagance of his private tastes: the Confederacy had none to give, while the Crown had plenty. But it seems also that his ravenous vanity had been wounded, first by the fact that the glory of Burgoyne's defeat had gone to Gates and not to him, and afterwards by a censure, temperate and tactful enough and accompanied by a liberal eulogy of his general conduct, which Washington had felt obliged to pass on certain of his later military proceedings. At any rate, the "ingratitude" of his country was the reason he publicly alleged for his treason; and those interested in the psychology of infamy may give it such weight as it may seem to deserve. For history the important fact is that Arnold at this point in the campaign secretly offered his services to the English, and the offer was accepted.

Arnold escaped to the British camp and was safe. The unfortunate gentleman on whom patriotic duty laid the unhappy task of trafficking with the traitor was less fortunate. Major André had been imprudent enough to pay a visit to a spot behind the American lines, and, at Arnold's suggestion, to do so in plain clothes. He was taken, tried, and hanged as a spy. Though espionage was not his intention, the Americans cannot fairly be blamed for deciding that he should die. He had undoubtedly committed an act which was the act of a spy in the eyes of military law. It is pretty certain that a hint was given that the authorities would gladly exchange him for Arnold, and it is very probable that the unslaked thirst for just vengeance against Arnold was partly responsible for the refusal of the American commanders to show mercy. André's courage and dignity made a profound impression on them, and there was a strong disposition to comply with his request that he should at least be shot instead of hanged.

But to that concession a valid and indeed irresistible objection was urged. Whatever the Americans did was certain to be scanned with critical and suspicious eyes. Little could be said in the face of the facts if they treated André as a spy and inflicted on him the normal fate of a spy. But if they showed that they scrupled to hang him as a spy, it would be easy to say that they had shot a prisoner of war.

Arnold was given a command in the South, and the rage of the population of that region was intensified into something like torment when they saw their lands occupied and their fields devastated no longer by a stranger from overseas who was but fulfilling his military duty, but by a cynical and triumphant traitor. Virginia was invaded and a bold stroke almost resulted in the capture of the author of the Declaration of Independence himself, who had been elected Governor of that State. In the course of these raids many abominable things were done which it is unnecessary to chronicle here. The regular English troops, on the whole, behaved reasonably well, but Tarleton's native "Tories" were inflamed by a fanaticism far fiercer than theirs, while atrocity was of course normal to the warfare of the barbarous mercenaries of England, whether Indian or German. It is equally a matter of course that such excesses provoked frequent reprisals from the irregular colonial levies.

But aid was at last at hand. Already Lafayette, a young French noble of liberal leanings, had appeared in Washington's camp at the head of a band of volunteers, and the accession, small as it was, led to a distinct revival of the fortunes of the revolution in the South. It was, however, but a beginning. England, under pressure of the war with France and Spain, lost that absolute supremacy at sea which has ever been and ever will be necessary to her conduct of a successful war. A formidable French armament was able to cross the Atlantic. A French fleet threatened the coasts. Cornwallis, not knowing at which point the blow would fall, was compelled to withdraw his forces from the country they had overrun, and to concentrate them in a strong position in the peninsula of Yorktown. Here he was threatened on both sides by Washington and Rochambeau, while the armada of De Grasse menaced him from the sea. The war took on the character of a siege. His resources were speedily exhausted, and on September 19, 1781, he surrendered.

It was really the end of the war so far as America was concerned, though the struggle between England and France continued for a time with varying fortunes in other theatres, and the Americans, though approached with tempting offers, wisely as well as righteously refused to make a separate peace at the expense of their Allies. But the end could no longer be in doubt. The surrender of Burgoyne had forced North to make concessions; the surrender of Cornwallis made his resignation inevitable. A new Ministry was formed under Rockingham pledged to make peace. Franklin again went to Paris as representative of the Confederation and showed himself a diplomatist of the first rank. To the firmness with which he maintained the Alliance against the most skillful attempts to dissolve it must largely be attributed the successful conclusion of a general peace on terms favourable to the Allies and especially favourable to America. Britain recognized the independence of her thirteen revolted colonies, and peace was restored.

I have said that England recognized her thirteen revolted colonies. She did not recognize the American Republic, for as yet there was none to recognize. The war had been conducted on the American side nominally by the Continental Congress, an admittedly ad hoc authority not pretending to permanency; really by Washington and his army which, with the new flag symbolically emblazoned with thirteen stars and thirteen stripes, was the one rallying point of unity. That also was now to be dissolved. The States had willed to be free, and they were free. Would they, in their freedom, will effectively to be a nation? That was a question which not the wisest observer could answer at the time, and which was not perhaps fully answered until well within the memory of men still living. Its solution will necessarily form the main subject of this book.

Chapter 3

"We, the People"

An account of the American Revolution which took cognizance only of the armed conflict with England would tell much less than half the truth, and even that half would be misleading. If anyone doubts that the real inspiration which made America a nation was drawn, not from Whiggish quarrels about taxes, but from the great dogmas promulgated by Jefferson, it is sufficient to point out that the States did not even wait till their victory over England was assured before effecting a complete internal revolution on the basis of those dogmas. Before the last shot had been fired almost the last privilege had disappeared.

The process was a spontaneous one, and its fruits appear almost simultaneously in every State. They can be followed best in Virginia, where Jefferson himself took the lead in the work of revolutionary reform.

Hereditary titles and privileges went first. On this point public feeling became so strong that the proposal to form after the war a society to be called "the Cincinnati," which was to consist of those who had taken a prominent part in the war and afterwards of their descendants, was met, in spite of the respect in which Washington and the other military heroes were held, with so marked an expression of public disapproval that the hereditary part of the scheme had to be dropped. Franchises were simplified, equalized, broadened, so that in practically every State the whole adult male population of European race received the suffrage. Social and economic reforms having the excellent aim of securing and maintaining a wide distribution of property, especially of land, were equally prominent among the achievements of that time. Jefferson himself carried in Virginia a drastic code of Land Laws, which anticipated many of the essential provisions which through the Code Napoleon revolutionized the system of land-owning in Europe. As to the practical effect of such reforms we have the testimony of a man whose instinct for referring all things to practice was, if anything, an excess, and whose love for England was the master passion of his life. "Every object almost that strikes my view," wrote William Cobbett many years later, "sends my mind and heart back to England. In viewing the ease and happiness of this people the contrast fills my soul with indignation, and makes it more and more the object of my life to assist in the destruction of the diabolical usurpation which has trampled on king as well as people."

Another principle, not connected by any direct logic with democracy and not set forth in the Declaration of Independence, was closely associated with the democratic thesis by the great French thinkers by whom that thesis was revived, and had a strong hold upon the mind of Jefferson—the principle of religious equality, or, as it might be more exactly defined, of the Secular State.

So many loose and absurd interpretations of this principle have been and are daily being propounded, that it may be well to state succinctly what it does and does not mean.

It does not mean that anyone may commit any anti-social act that appeals to him, and claim immunity from the law on the ground that he is impelled to that act by his religion; can rob as a conscientious communist, murder as a conscientious Thug, or refuse military service as a conscientious objector. None understood better than Jefferson—it was the first principle of his whole political system—that there must be some basis of agreement amongst citizens as to what is right and what is wrong, and that what the consensus of citizens regards as wrong must be punished by the law. All that the doctrine of the Secular State asserted was that such general agreement among citizens need not include, as in most modern States it obviously does not include, an agreement on the subject of religion. Religion is, so to speak, left out of the Social Contract, and consequently each individual retains his natural liberty to entertain and promulgate what views he likes concerning it, so long as such views do not bring him into conflict with those general principles of morality, patriotism and social order upon which the citizens of the State are agreed, and which form the basis of its laws.

The public mind of America was for the most part well prepared for the application of this principle. We have already noted how the first experiment in the purely secular organization of society had been made in the Catholic colony of Maryland and the Quaker colony of Pennsylvania. The principle was now applied in its completeness to one State after another. The Episcopalian establishment of Jefferson's own State was the first to fall; the other States soon followed the example of Virginia.

At the same time penalties or disabilities imposed as a consequence of religious opinions were everywhere abrogated. Only in New England was there any hesitation. The Puritan States did not take kindly to the idea of tolerating Popery. In the early days of the revolution their leaders had actually made it one of the counts of their indictment against the British Government that that Government had made peace with Anti-Christ in French Canada—a fact remembered to the permanent hurt of the Confederacy when the French Canadians were afterwards invited to make common cause with the American rebels. But the tide was too strong even for Calvinists to resist; the equality of all religions before the law was recognized in every State, and became, as it remains to-day, a fundamental part of the American Constitution.

It may be added that America affords the one conspicuous example of the Secular State completely succeeding. In France, where the same principles were applied under the same inspiration, the ultimate result was something wholly different: an organized Atheism persecuting the Christian Faith. In England the principle has never been avowedly applied at all. In theory the English State still professes the form of Protestant Christianity defined in the Prayer-book, and "tolerates" dissenters from it as the Christian States of the middle ages tolerated the Jews, and as in France, during the interval between the promulgation of the Edict of

Nantes and its revocation, a State definitely and even pronouncedly Catholic tolerated the Huguenots. Each dissentient religious body claims its right to exist in virtue of some specific Act of Parliament. Theoretically it is still an exception, though the exceptions have swallowed the rule.

Moreover, even under this rather hazy toleration, those who believe either more or less than the bulk of their fellow-countrymen and who boldly proclaim their belief usually find themselves at a political disadvantage. In America it never seems to have been so. Jefferson himself, a Deist (the claim sometimes made that he was a "Christian" seems to rest on nothing more solid than the fact that, like nearly all the eighteenth-century Deists, he expressed admiration for the character and teaching of Jesus Christ), never for a moment forfeited the confidence of his countrymen on that account, though attempts were made, notably by John Adams, to exploit it against him. Taney, a Catholic, was raised without objection on that score to the first judicial post in America, at a date when such an appointment would have raised a serious tumult in England. At a later date Ingersoll was able to vary the pastime of "Bible-smashing" with the profession of an active Republican wire-puller, without any of the embarrassments which that much better and honester man, Charles Bradlaugh, had to encounter. The American Republic has not escaped the difficulties and problems which are inevitable to the Secular State, when some of its citizens profess a religion which brings them into conflict with the common system of morals which the nation takes for granted; the case of the Mormons is a typical example of such a problem. But there is some evidence that, as the Americans have applied the doctrine far more logically than we, they have also a keener perception of the logic of its limitations. At any rate, it is notable that Congress has refused, in its Conscription Act, to follow our amazing example and make the conscience of the criminal the judge of the validity of legal proceedings against him.

Changes so momentous, made in so drastic and sweeping a fashion in the middle of a life and death struggle for national existence, show how vigorous and compelling was the popular impulse towards reform. Yet all the great things that were done seem dwarfed by one enormous thing left undone; the heroic tasks which the Americans accomplished are forgotten in the thought of the task which stared them in the face, but from which they, perhaps justifiably, shrank. All the injustices which were abolished in that superb crusade against privilege only made plainer the shape of the one huge privilege, the one typical injustice which still stood—the blacker against such a dawn—Negro Slavery.

It has already been mentioned that Slavery was at one time universal in the English colonies and was generally approved by American opinion, North and South. Before the end of the War of Independence it was almost as generally disapproved, and in all States north of the borders of Maryland it soon ceased to exist.

This was not because democratic ideals were more devotedly cherished in the North than in the South; on the whole the contrary was the case. But the institution of Slavery was in no way necessary to the normal life and industry of the North; its abrogation made little difference, and the rising tide of the new ideas to which it was necessarily odious easily swept it away. In their method of dealing with it the Northerners, it must be owned, were kinder to themselves than to the Negroes. They declared Slavery illegal within their own borders, but they generally gave the slave-holder time to dispose of his human property by selling it in the States where Slavery still existed. This fact is worth noting, because it became a prime cause of resentment and bitterness when, at a later date, the North began to reproach the South with the guilt of slave-owning. For the South was faced with no such easy and manageable problem. Its coloured population was almost equal in number to its white colonists; in some districts it was even greatly preponderant. Its staple industries were based on slave labour. To abolish Slavery would mean an industrial revolution of staggering magnitude of which the issue could not be foreseen. And even if that were faced, there remained the sinister and apparently insoluble problem of what to do with the emancipated Negroes. Jefferson, who felt the reproach of Slavery keenly, proposed to the legislature of Virginia a scheme so radical and comprehensive in its character that it is not surprising if men less intrepid than he refused to adopt it. He proposed nothing less than the wholesale repatriation of the blacks, who were to set up in Africa a Negro

Republic of their own under American protection. Jefferson fully understood the principles and implications of democracy, and he was also thoroughly conversant with Southern conditions, and the fact that he thought (and events have certainly gone far to justify him) that so drastic a solution was the only one that offered hope of a permanent and satisfactory settlement is sufficient evidence that the problem was no easy one. For the first time Jefferson failed to carry Virginia with him; and Slavery remained an institution sanctioned by law in every State south of the Mason-Dixon line.

While the States were thus dealing with the problems raised by the application to their internal administration of the principles of the new democratic creed, the force of mere external fact was compelling them to attempt some sort of permanent unity. Those who had from the first a specific enthusiasm for such unity were few, though Washington was among them, and his influence counted for much. But what counted for much more was the pressure of necessity. It was soon obvious to all clear-sighted men that unless some authoritative centre of union were created the revolutionary experiment would have been saved from suppression by arms only to collapse in mere anarchic confusion. The Continental Congress, the only existing authority, was moribund, and even had it been still in its full vigour, it had not the powers which the situation demanded. It could not, for instance, levy taxes on the State; its revenues were completely exhausted and it had no power to replenish them. The British Government complained that the conditions of peace were not observed on the American side, and accordingly held on to the positions which it had occupied at the conclusion of the war. The complaint was perfectly just, but it did not arise from deliberate bad faith on the part of those who directed (as far as anyone was directing) American policy, but from the simple fact that there was no authority in America capable of enforcing obedience and carrying the provisions of the treaty into effect. The same moral was enforced by a dozen other symptoms of disorder. The Congress had disbanded the soldiers, as had been promised, on the conclusion of peace, but, having no money, could not keep its at least equally important promise to pay them. This led to much casual looting by men with arms in their hands but nowhere to turn for a meal, and the trouble culminated in a rebellion raised in New England by an old soldier of the Continental Army called Shay. Such incidents as these were the immediate cause of the summoning at Philadelphia of a Convention charged with the task of framing a Constitution for the United States.

Of such a Convention Washington was the only possible President; and he was drawn from a temporary and welcome retirement in his Virginian home to re-enter in a new fashion the service of his country. Under his presidency disputed and compromised a crowd of able men representative of the widely divergent States whose union was to be attempted. There was Alexander Hamilton, indifferent or hostile to the democratic idea but intensely patriotic, and bent above all things upon the formation of a strong central authority; Franklin with his acute practicality and his admirable tact in dealing with men; Gerry, the New Englander, Whiggish and somewhat distrustful of the populace; Pinckney of South Carolina, a soldier and the most ardent of the Federalists, representing, by a curious irony, the State which was to be the home of the most extreme dogma of State Rights; Madison, the Virginian, young, ardent and intellectual, his head full of the new wine of liberty. One great name is lacking. Jefferson had been chosen to represent the Confederacy at the French Court, where he had the delight of watching the first act of that tremendous drama, whereby his own accepted doctrine was to re-shape France, as it had already re-shaped America. The Convention, therefore, lacked the valuable combination of lucid thought on the philosophy of politics and a keen appreciation of the direction of the popular will which he above all men could have supplied.

The task before the Convention was a hard and perilous one, and nothing about it was more hard and perilous than its definition. What were they there to do? Were they framing a treaty between independent Sovereignties, which, in spite of the treaty, would retain their independence, or were they building a nation by merging these Sovereignties in one general Sovereignty of the American people? They began by proceeding on the first assumption, re-modelling the Continental Congress—avowedly a mere alliance—and adding only such powers as it was plainly essential to add. They soon found that such a plan would not meet the difficulties of the hour. But they dared not openly adopt the alternative theory: the States would not have borne it. Had it, for example, been specifically laid down that a State once entering the Union might never after withdraw from it, quite half the States would have refused to enter it. To that extent the position afterwards taken up by the Southern Secessionists was historically sound. But there was a complementary historical truth on the other side. There can be little doubt that in this matter the founders of the Republic desired and intended more than they ventured to attempt. The fact that men of unquestionable honesty and intelligence were in after years so sharply and sincerely divided as to what the Constitution really was, was in truth the result of a divided mind in those who framed the Constitution. They made an alliance and hoped it would grow into a nation. The preamble of the Constitution represents the aspirations of the American Fathers; the clauses represent the furthest they dared towards those aspirations. The preamble was therefore always the rallying point of those who wished to see America one nation. Its operative clause ran: "We, the People of the United States, in order to form a more perfect Union, ... do ordain and establish this Constitution for the United States of America." That such language was a strong point in favour of the Federalist interpreters of the Constitution was afterwards implicitly admitted by the extreme exponents of State Sovereignty themselves, for when they came to frame for their own Confederacy a Constitution reflecting their own views they made a most significant alteration. The corresponding clause in the Constitution of the Southern Confederacy ran, "We, the deputies of the Sovereign and Independent States, ... do ordain," etc., etc.

For the rest two great practical measures which involved no overbold challenge to State Sovereignty were wisely planned to buttress the Union and render it permanent. A clause in the Constitution forbade tariffs between the States and established complete Free Trade within the limits of the Union. An even more important step was that by which the various States which claimed territory in the as yet undeveloped interior were induced to surrender such territory to the collective ownership of the

Federation. This at once gave the States a new motive for unity, a common inheritance which any State refusing or abandoning union must surrender.

Meanwhile it would be unjust to the supporters of State Rights to deny the excellence and importance of their contribution to the Constitutional settlement. To them is due the establishment of local liberties with safeguards such as no other Constitution gives. And, in spite of the military victory which put an end to the disputes about State Sovereignty and finally established the Federalist interpretation of the Constitution, this part of their work endures. The internal affairs of every State remain as the Constitution left them, absolutely in its own control. The Federal Government never interferes save for purposes of public taxation, and, in the rare case of necessity, of national defence. For the rest nine-tenths of the laws under which an American citizen lives, nearly all the laws that make a practical difference to his life, are State laws. Under the Constitution, as framed, the States were free to form their separate State Constitutions according to their own likings, and to arrange the franchise and the test of citizenship, even for Federal purposes, in their own fashion. This, with the one stupid and mischievous exception made by the ill-starred Fifteenth Amendment, remains the case to this day, with the curious consequence, among others, that it is now theoretically possible for a woman to become President of the United States, if she is the citizen of a State where female suffrage is admitted.

Turning to the structure of the central authority which the Constitution sought to establish, the first thing that strikes us—in the teeth of the assertion of most British and some American writers—is that it was emphatically not a copy of the British Constitution in any sense whatever. It is built on wholly different principles, drawn mostly from the French speculations of that age. Especially one notes, alongside of the careful and wise separation of the judiciary from the executive, the sound principle enunciated by Montesquieu and other French thinkers of the eighteenth century, but rejected and contemned by England (to her great hurt) as a piece of impracticable logic—the separation of the executive and legislative powers. It was this principle which made possible the later transformation of the Presidency into a sort of Elective Monarchy.

This result was not designed or foreseen; or rather it was to an extent foreseen, and deliberately though unsuccessfully guarded against. The American revolutionists were almost as much under the influence of classical antiquity as the French. From it they drew the noble conception of "the Republic," the public thing acting with impersonal justice towards all citizens. But with it they also drew an exaggerated dread of what they called "Cæsarism," and with it they mixed the curious but characteristic illusion of that age—an illusion from which, by the way, Rousseau himself was conspicuously free—that the most satisfactory because the most impersonal organ of the general will is to be found in an elected assembly. They had as yet imperfectly learnt that such an assembly must after all consist of persons, more personal because less public than an acknowledged ruler. They did not know that, while a despot may often truly represent the people, a Senate, however chosen, always tends to become an oligarchy. Therefore they surrounded the presidential office with checks which in mere words made the President seem less powerful than an English King. Yet he has always in fact been much more powerful. And the reason is to be found in the separation of the executive from the legislature. The President, while his term lasted, had the full powers of a real executive. Congress could not turn him out, though it could in various ways check his actions. He could appoint his own Ministers (though the Senate must ratify the choice) and they were wisely excluded from the legislature. An even wiser provision limited the appointment of Members of Congress to positions under the executive. Thus both executive and legislature were kept, so far as human frailty permitted, pure in their normal functions. The Presidency remained a real Government. Congress remained a real check.

In England, where the opposite principle was adopted, the Ministry became first the committee of an oligarchical Parliament and later a close corporation nominating the legislature which is supposed to check it.

The same fear of arbitrary power was exhibited, and that in fashion really inconsistent with the democratic principles which the American statesmen professed, in the determination that the President should be chosen by the people only in an indirect fashion, through an Electoral

College. This error has been happily overruled by events. Since the Electoral College was to be chosen ad hoc for the single purpose of choosing a President, it soon became obvious that pledges could easily be exacted from its members in regard to their choice. By degrees the pretence of deliberate action by the College wore thinner and thinner. Finally it was abandoned altogether, and the President is now chosen, as the first magistrate of a democracy ought to be chosen, if election is resorted to at all, by the direct vote of the nation. At the time, however, it was supposed that the Electoral College would be an independent deliberative assembly. It was further provided that the second choice of the Electoral College should be Vice-President, and succeed to the Presidency in the event of the President dying during his term of office. If there was a "tie" or if no candidate had an absolute majority in the College, the election devolved on the House of Representatives voting in this instance by States.

In connection with the election both of Executive and Legislature, the old State Rights problem rose in another form. Were all the States to have equal weight and representation, as had been the case in the old Continental Congress, or was their weight and representation to be proportional to their population? On this point a compromise was made. The House of Representatives was to be chosen directly by the people on a numerical basis, and in the Electoral College which chose the President the same principle was adopted. In the Senate all States were to have equal representation; and the Senators were to be chosen by the legislatures of the States; they were regarded rather as ambassadors than as delegates. The term of a Senator was fixed for six years, a third of the Senate resigning in rotation every two years. The House of Representatives was to be elected in a body for two years. The President was elected for four years, at the end of which time he could be re-elected.

Such were the main lines of the compromises which were effected between the conflicting views of the extreme Federalists and extreme State Rights advocates, and the conflicting interests of the larger and smaller States. But there was another threatened conflict, more formidable and, as the event proved, more enduring, with which the framers of the

Constitution had to deal. Two different types of civilization had grown up on opposite sides of the Mason-Dixon line. How far Slavery was the cause and how far a symptom of this divergence will be discussed more fully in future chapters. At any rate it was its most conspicuous mark or label. North and South differed so conspicuously not only in their social organization but in every habit of life and thought that neither would tamely bear to be engulfed in a union in which the other was to be predominant. To keep an even balance between them was long the principal effort of American statesmanship. That effort began in the Convention which framed the Constitution. It did not cease till the very eve of the Civil War.

The problem with which the Convention had to deal was defined within certain well-understood limits. No one proposed that Slavery should be abolished by Federal enactment. It was universally acknowledged that Slavery within a State, however much of an evil it might be, was an evil with which State authority alone had a right to deal. On the other hand, no one proposed to make Slavery a national institution. Indeed, all the most eminent Southern statesmen of that time, and probably the great majority of Southerners, regarded it as a reproach, and sincerely hoped that it would soon disappear. There remained, however, certain definite subjects of dispute concerning which an agreement had to be reached if the States were to live in peace in the same household. First, not perhaps in historic importance, but in the insistence of its demand for an immediate settlement, was the question of representation. It had been agreed that in the House of Representatives and in the Electoral College this should be proportionate to population. The urgent question at once arose: should free white citizens only be counted, or should the count include the Negro slaves? When it is remembered that these latter numbered something like half the population of the Southern States, the immediate political importance of the issue will at once be recognized. If they were omitted the weight of the South in the Federation would be halved. In the opposite alternative it would be doubled. By the compromise eventually adopted it was agreed that the whole white population should be counted and three-fifths of the slaves.

The second problem was this: if Slavery was to be legal in one State and illegal in another, what was to be the status of a slave escaping from a Slave State into a free? Was such an act to be tantamount to an emancipation? If such were to be the case, it was obvious that slave property, especially in the border States, would become an extremely insecure investment. The average Southerner of that period was no enthusiast for Slavery. He was not unwilling to listen to plans of gradual and compensated emancipation. But he could not be expected to contemplate losing in a night property for which he had perhaps paid hundreds of dollars, without even the hope of recovery. On this point it was found absolutely necessary to give way to the Southerners, though Franklin, for one, disliked this concession more than any other. It was determined that "persons held to service or labour" escaping into another State should be returned to those "to whom such service or labour may be due."

The last and on the whole the least defensible of the concessions made in this matter concerned the African Slave Trade. That odious traffic was condemned by almost all Americans—even by those who were accustomed to domestic slavery, and could see little evil in it. Jefferson, in the original draft of the Declaration of Independence, had placed amongst the accusations against the English King the charge that he had forced the slave trade on reluctant colonies. The charge was true so far at any rate as Virginia was concerned, for both that State and its neighbour, Maryland, had passed laws against the traffic and had seen them vetoed by the Crown. But the extreme South, where the cotton trade was booming, wanted more Negro labour; South Carolina objected, and found an expected ally in Massachusetts. Boston had profited more by the Slave Trade than any other American city. She could hardly condemn King George without condemning herself. And, though her interest in the traffic had diminished, it had not wholly ceased. The paragraph in question was struck out of the Declaration, and when the Convention came to deal with the question the same curious alliance thwarted the efforts of those who demanded the immediate prohibition of the trade. Eventually the Slave Trade was suffered to continue for twenty years, at the end of which time Congress might forbid it. This was done in 1808, when the term of suffrance had expired.

Thus was Negro Slavery placed under the protection of the Constitution. It would be a grave injustice to the founders of the American Commonwealth to make it seem that any of them liked doing this. Constrained by a cruel necessity, they acquiesced for the time in an evil which they hoped that time would remedy. Their mind is significantly mirrored by the fact that not once in the Constitution are the words "slave" or "slavery" mentioned. Some euphemism is always used, as "persons held to service or labour," "the importation of persons," "free persons," contrasted with "other persons," and so on. Lincoln, generations later, gave what was undoubtedly the true explanation of this shrinking from the name of the thing they were tolerating and even protecting. They hoped that the Constitution would survive Negro Slavery, and they would leave no word therein to remind their children that they had spared it for a season. Beyond question they not only hoped but expected that the concession which for the sake of the national unity they made to an institution which they hated and deplored would be for a season only. The influence of time and the growth of those great doctrines which were embodied in the Declaration of Independence could not but persuade all men at last; and the day, they thought, could not be far distant when the Slave States themselves would concur in some prudent scheme of emancipation, and make of Negro Slavery an evil dream that had passed away. None the less not a few of them did what they had to do with sorrowful and foreboding hearts, and the author of the Declaration of Independence has left on record his own verdict, that he trembled for his country when he remembered that God was just.

Chapter 4

THE MANTLE OF WASHINGTON

The compromises of the Constitution, on whatever grounds they may be criticized, were so far justified that they gained their end. That end was the achievement of union; and union was achieved. This was not done easily nor without opposition. In some cities anti-Constitutional riots took place. Several States refused to ratify. The opposition had the support of the great name of Patrick Henry, who had been the soul of the resistance to the Stamp Act, and who now declared that under the specious name of "Federation" Liberty had been betrayed. The defence was conducted in a publication called the Federalist largely by two men afterwards to be associated with fiercely contending parties, Alexander Hamilton and James Madison. But more persuasive than any arguments that the ablest advocate could use were the iron necessities of the situation. The Union was an accomplished fact. For any State, and especially for a small State—and it was the small States that hesitated most—to refuse to enter it would be so plainly disastrous to its interests that the strongest objections and the most rooted suspicions had eventually to give way. Some States hung back long: some did not ratify the Constitution until its machinery was actually working, until the first President had been chosen and the first Congress had met. But all ratified it at last, and before the end of Washington's first Presidency the complement of Stars and Stripes was made up.

The choice of a President was a foregone conclusion. Everyone knew that Washington was the man whom the hour and the nation demanded. He was chosen without a contest by the Electoral College, and would undoubtedly have been chosen with the same practical unanimity by the people had the choice been theirs. So long as he retained his position he retained along with it the virtually unchallenged pre-eminence which all men acknowledged. There had been cabals against him as a general, and there were signs of a revival of them when his Presidency was clearly foreshadowed. The impulse came mostly from the older and wealthier gentry of his own State—the Lees for example—who tended to look down upon him as a "new man." Towards the end of his political life he was to some extent the object of attack from the opposite quarter; his fame was assailed by the fiercer and less prudent of the Democratic publicists. But, throughout, the great mass of the American people trusted him as their representative man, as those who abused him or conspired against him did so to their own hurt. A less prudent man might easily have worn out his popularity and alienated large sections of opinion, but Washington's characteristic sagacity, which had been displayed so constantly during the war, stood him in as good stead in matters of civil government. He propitiated Nemesis and gave no just provocation to any party to risk its popularity by attacking him. While he was President the mantle of his great fame was ample enough to cover the deep and vital divisions which were appearing even in his own Cabinet, and were soon to convulse the nation in a dispute for the inheritance of his power.

His Secretary to the Treasury was Alexander Hamilton. This extraordinary man presents in more than one respect a complex problem to the historian. He has an unquestionable right to a place and perhaps to a supreme place among the builders of the American Republic, and much of its foundation-laying was his work. Yet he shows in history as a defeated man, and for at least a generation scarcely anyone dared to give him credit for the great work that he really did. To-day the injustice is perhaps the other way. In American histories written since the Civil War he is not only acclaimed as a great statesman, but his overthrow at the hands of the Jeffersonians is generally pointed at as a typical example of the folly and ingratitude of the mob. This version is at least as unjust to the American people as the depreciation of the Democrats was to him. The fact is that Hamilton's work had a double aspect. In so far as it was directed to the cementing of a permanent union and the building of a strong central authority it was work upon the lines along which the nation was moving, and towards an end which the nation really, if subconsciously, desired. But closely associated with this object in Hamilton's mind was another which the nation did not desire and which was alien to its instincts and destiny. All this second part of his work failed, and involved him in its ruin.

Hamilton had fought bravely in the Revolutionary War, but for the ideals which had become more and more the inspiration of the Revolution he cared nothing, and was too honest to pretend to care. He had on the other hand a strong and genuine American patriotism. Perhaps his origin helped him to a larger view in this matter than was common among his contemporaries. He was not born in any of the revolted colonies, but in Bermuda, of good blood but with the bar sinister stamped upon his birth. He had migrated to New York to seek his fortune, but his citizenship of that State remained an accident. He had no family traditions tying him to any section, and, more than any public man that appeared before the West began to produce a new type, he felt America as a whole. He had great administrative talents of which he was fully conscious, and the anarchy which followed the conclusion of peace was hateful to his instinct for order and strong government. But the strong government which he would have created was of a different type from that which America ultimately developed. Theoretically he made no secret of his preference for a Monarchy over a Republic, but the suspicion that he meditated introducing monarchical institutions into America, though sincerely entertained by Jefferson and others, was certainly false. Whatever his theoretic preferences, he was intensely alive to the logic of facts, and must have known that a brand-new American monarchy would have been as impossible as it would have been ludicrous. In theory and practice, however, he really was anti-democratic. Masses of men seemed to him incapable alike of judgment and of action, and he thought no enduring authority could be based upon the instincts of the "great beast," as he called the mob. He looked for such authority and what seemed to him the example of history, and especially to the example of England. He knew how powerful both at home and abroad was the governing machine which the English aristocracy had established after the Revolution of 1689; and he realized more fully than most men of that age, or indeed of this, that its strength lay in a small but very national governing class wielding the people as an instrument. Such a class he wished to create in America, to connect closely, as the English oligarchy had connected itself closely, with the great moneyed interests, and to entrust with the large powers which in his judgment the central government of the Federation needed. Jefferson came back from France in the winter of 1789, and was at once offered by Washington the Secretaryship of State. The offer was not a very welcome one, for he was hot with the enthusiasm of the great French struggle, and would gladly have returned to Paris and watched its progress. He felt, however, that the President's insistence laid upon him the duty of giving the Government the support of his abilities and popularity. He had accepted the Constitution which he had no share in framing, not perhaps as exactly what he would have desired, but certainly in full good faith and without reserve. It probably satisfied him at least as well as it satisfied Hamilton, who had actually at one time withdrawn from the Convention in protest against its refusal to accept his views. Jefferson's criticisms, such as they were, related mostly to matters of detail: some of them were just and some were subsequently incorporated in amendments. But there is ample evidence that for none of them was he prepared to go the length of opposing or even delaying the settlement. It is also worth noting that none of them related to the balance of power between the Federal and State Governments, upon which Jefferson is often loosely accused of holding extreme particularist views. As a fact he never held such views. His formula that "the States are independent as to everything within themselves and united as to everything respecting foreign nations" is really a very good summary of the principles upon which the Constitution is based, and states substantially the policy which all the truest friends of the Union have upheld. But he was committed out and out to the principle of popular government, and when it became obvious that the Federalists under

Hamilton's leadership were trying to make the central government oligarchical, and that they were very near success, Jefferson quite legitimately invoked and sought to confirm the large powers secured by the Constitution itself to the States for the purpose of obstructing their programme.

It was some time, however, before the antagonism between the two Secretaries became acute, and meanwhile the financial genius of Hamilton was reducing the economic chaos bequeathed by the war to order and solvency. All of his measures showed fertility of invention and a thorough grasp of his subject; some of them were unquestionably beneficial to the country. But a careful examination will show how closely and deliberately he was imitating the English model which we know to have been present to his mind. He established a true National Debt similar to that which Montague had created for the benefit of William of Orange. In this debt he proposed to merge the debts of the individual States contracted during the War of Independence. Jefferson saw no objection to this at the time, and indeed it was largely through his favour that a settlement was made which overcame the opposition of certain States.

This settlement had another interest as being one of the perennial geographical compromises by means of which the Union was for so long preserved. The support of Hamilton's policy came mainly from the North; the opposition to it from the South. It so happened that coincidentally North and South were divided on another question, the position of the projected Capital of the Federation. The Southerners wanted it to be on the Potomac between Virginia and Maryland; the Northerners would have preferred it further north. At Jefferson's house Hamilton met some of the leading Southern politicians, and a bargain was struck. The Secretary's proposal as to the State debts was accepted, and the South had its way in regard to the Capital. Hamilton probably felt that he had bought a solid advantage in return for a purely sentimental concession. Neither he nor anyone else could foresee the day of peril when the position of Washington between the two Southern States would become one of the gravest of the strategic embarrassments of the Federal Government.

Later, when Hamilton's policy and personality had become odious to him, Jefferson expressed remorse for his conduct of the occasion, and blamed his colleague for taking advantage of his ignorance of the question. His sincerity cannot be doubted, but it will appear to the impartial observer that his earlier judgment was the wiser of the two. The assumption of State debts had really nothing "monocratic" or anti-popular about it—nothing even tending to infringe the rights and liberties of the several States—while it was clearly a statesmanlike measure from the national standpoint, tending at once to restore the public credit and cement the Union. But Jefferson read backwards into this innocuous and beneficent stroke of policy the spirit which he justly perceived to inform the later and more dubious measures which proceeded from the same author.

Of these the most important was the creation of the first United States Bank. Here Hamilton was quite certainly inspired by the example of the English Whigs. He knew how much the stability of the settlement made in 1689 had owed to the skill and foresight with which Montague, through the creation of the Bank of England, had attached to it the great moneyed interests of the City. He wished, through the United States Bank, to attach the powerful moneyed interests of the Eastern and Middle States in the same fashion to the Federal Government. This is how he and his supporters would have expressed it. Jefferson said that he wished to fill Congress with a crowd of mercenaries bound by pecuniary ties to the Treasury and obliged to lend it, through good and evil repute, a perennial and corrupt support. The two versions are really only different ways of stating the same thing. To a democrat such a standing alliance between the Government and the rich will always seem a corrupt thing—nay, the worst and least remediable form of corruption. To a man of Hamilton's temper it seemed merely the necessary foundation of a stable political equilibrium. Thus the question of the Bank really brought the two parties which were growing up in the Cabinet and in the nation to an issue which revealed the irreconcilable antagonism of their principles.

The majority in Congress was with Hamilton; but his opponents appealed to the Constitution. They denied the competency of Congress under that instrument to establish a National Bank. When the Bill was in due course sent to Washington for signature he asked the opinions of his Cabinet on the constitutional question, and both Hamilton and Jefferson wrote very able State Papers in defence of their respective views. After some hesitation Washington decided to sign the Bill and to leave the question of constitutional law to the Supreme Court. In due course it was challenged there, but Marshal, the Chief Justice, was a decided Federalist, and gave judgment in favour of the legality of the Bank.

The Federalists had won the first round. Meanwhile the party which looked to Jefferson as leader was organizing itself. It took the name of "Republican," as signifying its opposition to the alleged monarchical designs of Hamilton and his supporters. Later, when it appeared that such a title was really too universal to be descriptive, the Jeffersonians began to call themselves by the more genuinely characteristic title of "Democratic Republicans," subsequently abbreviated into "Democrats." That name the party which, alone among American parties, can boast an unbroken historic continuity of more than a century, retains to this day.

At the end of his original term of four years, Washington was prevailed upon to give way to the universal feeling of the nation and to accept a second term. No party thought of opposing him, but a significant division appeared over the Vice-Presidency. The Democrats ran Clinton against John Adams of Massachusetts, and though they failed there appeared in the voting a significant alliance, which was to determine the politics of a generation. New York State, breaking away from her Northern neighbours, voted with the Democratic South for Clinton. And the same year saw the foundation in New York City of that dubious but very potent product of democracy, which has perhaps become the best abused institution in the civilized world, yet has somehow or other contrived to keep in that highly democratic society a power which it could never retain for a day without a genuine popular backing—Tammany Hall.

Meanwhile the destinies of every nation of European origin, and of none perhaps more, in spite of their geographical remoteness, than of the United States, were being profoundly influenced by the astonishing events that were shaping themselves in Western Europe. At first all America was enthusiastic for the French Revolution. Americans were naturally grateful for the aid given them by the French in their own struggle for freedom, and saw with eager delight the approaching liberation of their liberators. But as the drama unrolled itself a sharp, though very unequal, division of opinion appeared. In New England, especially, there were many who were shocked at the proceedings of the French, at their violence, at their Latin cruelty in anger, and, above all perhaps, at that touch of levity which comes upon the Latin when he is face to face with death. Massacres and carmagnoles did not strike the typical Massachusetts merchant as the methods by which God-fearing men should protest against oppression. The strict military government which succeeded to, controlled and directed in a national fashion the violent mood of the people—that necessary martial law which we call "the Terror"—seemed even less acceptable to his fundamentally Whiggish political creed. Yet—and it is a most significant fact—the bulk of popular American opinion was not shocked by these things. It remained steadily with the French through all those events which alienated opinion—even Liberal opinion—in Europe. It was perhaps because European opinion, especially English opinion, even when Liberal, was at bottom aristocratic, while the American people were already a democracy. But the fact is certain. By the admission of those American writers who deplore it and fail to comprehend it, the great mass of the democracy of America continued, through good and evil repute, to extend a vivid and indulgent sympathy to the democracy of France.

The division of sympathies which had thus become apparent was converted into a matter of practical politics by the entry of England into the war which a Coalition was waging against the French Republic. That intervention at once sharpened the sympathies of both sides and gave them a practical purpose. England and France were now arrayed against each other, and Americans, though their Government remained neutral, arrayed themselves openly as partisans of either combatant. The division followed almost exactly the lines of the earlier quarrel which had begun to appear as the true meaning of Hamilton's policy discovered itself. The Hamiltonians were for England. The Jeffersonians were for France.

A war of pamphlets and newspapers followed, into the details of which it is not necessary to go. The Federalists, with the tide going steadily against them, had the good luck to secure the aid of a pen which had no match in Europe. The greatest master of English controversial prose that ever lived was at that time in America. Normally, perhaps, his sympathies would have been with the Democrats. But love of England was ever the deepest and most compelling passion of the man who habitually abused her institutions so roundly. The Democrats were against his fatherland, and so the supporters of Hamilton found themselves defended in a series of publications over the signature of "Peter Porcupine" with all the energy and genius which belonged only to William Cobbett.

A piquancy of the contest was increased by the fact that it was led on either side by members of the Administration. Washington had early put forth a Declaration of Neutrality, drawn up by Randolph, who, though leaning if anything to Jefferson's side, took up a more or less intermediate position between the parties. Both sides professed to accept the principle of neutrality, but their interpretations of it were widely different. Jefferson did not propose to intervene in favour of France, but he did not think that Americans were bound to disguise their moral sympathies. They would appear, he thought, both ungrateful and false to the first principles of their own commonwealth if, whatever limitation prudence might impose in their action, they did not desire that France should be victorious over the Coalition of Kings. The great majority of the American people took the same view. When Genet, the envoy of the newly constituted Republic, arrived from France, he received an ovation which Washington himself at the height of his glory could hardly have obtained. Nine American citizens out of ten hastened to mount the tricolour cockade, to learn the "Marseillaise," and to take their glasses to the victory of the sister Republic. So strong was the wave of popular enthusiasm that the United States might perhaps have been drawn into active co-operation with France had France been better served by her Minister.

Genet was a Girondin, and the Girondins, perhaps through that defect in realism which ruined them at home, were not good diplomatists. It is likely enough that the warmth of his reception deranged his judgment; at any rate he misread its significance. He failed to take due account of that sensitiveness of national feeling in a democracy which, as a Frenchman of that time, he should have been specially able to appreciate. He began to treat the resources of the United States as if they had already been placed at the disposal of France, and, when very properly rebuked, he was foolish enough to attempt to appeal to the nation against its rulers. The attitude of the Secretary of State ought to have warned him of the imprudence of his conduct. No man in America was a better friend to France than Jefferson; but he stood up manfully to Genet in defence of the independent rights of his country, and the obstinacy of the ambassador produced, as Jefferson foresaw that it must produce, a certain reaction of public feeling by which the Anglophil party benefited.

At the close of the year 1793, Jefferson, weary of endless contests with Hamilton, whom he accused, not without some justification, of constantly encroaching on his colleague's proper department, not wholly satisfied with the policy of the Government and perhaps feeling that Genet's indiscretions had made his difficult task for the moment impossible, resigned his office. He would have done so long before had not Washington, sincerely anxious throughout these troubled years to hold the balance even between the parties, repeatedly exerted all his influence to dissuade him. The following year saw the "Whiskey Insurrection" in Pennsylvania—a popular protest against Hamilton's excise measures. Jefferson more than half sympathized with the rebels. Long before, on the occasion of Shay's insurrection, he had expressed with some exaggeration a view which has much more truth in it than those modern writers who exclaim in horror at his folly could be expected to understand—the view that the readiness of people to rebel against their rulers is no bad test of the presence of democracy among them. He had even added that he hoped the country would never pass ten years without a rebellion of some sort. In the present case he had the additional motives for sympathy that he himself disapproved of the law against which Pennsylvania was in revolt, and detested its author. Washington could not be expected to take the same view. He was not anti-democratic like Hamilton; he sincerely held the theory of the State set forth in the Declaration of Independence. But he was something of an aristocrat, and very much of a soldier. As an aristocrat he was perhaps touched with the illusion which was so fatal to his friend

Lafayette, the illusion that privilege can be abolished and yet the once privileged class partially retain its ascendancy by a sort of tacit acknowledgment by others of its value. As a soldier he disliked disorder and believed in discipline. As a commander in the war he had not spared the rod, and had even complained of Congress for mitigating the severity of military punishments. It may be that the "Whiskey Insurrection," which he suppressed with prompt and drastic energy, led him for the first time to lean a little to the Hamiltonian side. At any rate he was induced, though reluctantly and only under strong pressure, to introduce into a Message to Congress a passage reflecting on the Democratic Societies which were springing up everywhere and gaining daily in power; and in return found himself attacked, sometimes with scurrility, in the more violent organs of the Democracy.

Washington's personal ascendancy was, however, sufficient to prevent the storm from breaking while he was President. It was reserved for his successor. In 1797 his second term expired. He had refused a third, thereby setting an important precedent which every subsequent President has followed, and bade farewell to politics in an address which is among the great historical documents of the Republic. The two points especially emphasized were long the acknowledged keynotes of American policy: the avoidance at home of "sectional" parties—that is, of parties following geographical lines—and abroad the maintenance of a strict independence of European entanglements and alliances.

Had a Presidential election then been what it became later, a direct appeal to the popular vote, it is probable that Jefferson would have been the second President of the United States. But the Electoral College was still a reality, and its majority leant to Federalism. Immeasurably the ablest man among the Federalists was Hamilton, but for many reasons he was not an "available" choice. He was not a born American. He had made many and formidable personal enemies even within the party. Perhaps the shadow on his birth was a drawback; perhaps also the notorious freedom of his private life—for the strength of the party lay in Puritan New England. At any rate the candidate whom the Federalists backed and succeeded in electing was John Adams of Massachusetts. By the curiously unworkable rule, soon repealed, of the original Constitution, which gave the Vice-Presidency to the candidate who had the second largest number of votes, Jefferson found himself elected to that office under a President representing everything to which he was opposed.

John Adams was an honest man and sincerely loved his country. There his merits ended. He was readily quarrelsome, utterly without judgment and susceptible to that mood of panic in which mediocre persons are readily induced to act the "strong man." During his administration a new quarrel arose with France—a quarrel in which once again those responsible for that country's diplomacy played the game of her enemies. Genet had merely been an impracticable and impatient enthusiast. Talleyrand, who under the Directory took charge of foreign affairs, was a scamp; and, clever as he was, was unduly contemptuous of America, where he had lived for a time in exile. He attempted to use the occasion of the appearance of an American Mission in Paris to wring money out of America, not only for the French Treasury, but for his own private profit and that of his colleagues and accomplices. A remarkable correspondence, which fully revealed the blackmailing attempt made by the agents of the French Government on the representatives of the United States, known as the "X.Y.Z." letters, was published and roused the anger of the whole country. "Millions for defence but not a cent for tribute" was the universal catchword. Hamilton would probably have seized the opportunity to go to war with France with some likelihood of a national backing. Adams avoided war and thereby split his party, but he did not avoid steps far more certain than a war to excite the hostility of democratic America. His policy was modelled upon the worst of the panic-bred measures by means of which Pitt and his colleagues were seeking to suppress "Jacobinism" in England. Such a policy was odious anywhere; in a democracy it was also insane. Further the Aliens Law and the Sedition Law which he induced Congress to pass were in flagrant and obvious violation of the letter and spirit of the Constitution. They were barely through Congress when the storm broke on their authors. Jefferson, in retirement at Monticello, saw that his hour was come. He put himself at the head of the opposition and found a whole nation behind him.

Kentucky, carved out of the western territory and newly grown to Statehood, took the lead of resistance. For her legislature Jefferson drafted the famous "Kentucky Resolutions," which condemned the new laws as unconstitutional (which they were) and refused to allow them to be administered within her borders. On the strength of these resolutions Jefferson has been described as the real author of the doctrine of "Nullification": and technically this may be true. Nevertheless there is all the difference in the world between the spirit of the Kentucky Resolutions and that of "Nullification," as South Carolina afterwards proclaimed its legitimacy. About the former there was nothing sectional. It was not pretended that Kentucky had any peculiar and local objection to the Sedition Law, or was standing against the other States in resisting it. She was vindicating a freedom common to all the States, valued by all and menaced in all. She claimed that she was making herself the spokesman of the other States in the same fashion as Hampden made himself the spokesman of the other great landed proprietors in resisting taxation by the Crown.

The event amply justified her claim. The oppression laws which the Federalists had induced Congress to pass were virtually dead letters from the moment of their passing. And when the time came for the nation to speak, it rose as one man and flung Adams from his seat. The Federalist Party virtually died of the blow. The dream of an oligarchical Republic was at an end, and the will of the people, expressed with unmistakable emphasis, gave the Chief Magistracy to the author of the Declaration of Independence.

Chapter 5

THE VIRGINIAN DYNASTY

I have spoken of Jefferson's election as if it had been a direct act of the people; and morally it was so. But in the actual proceedings there was a certain hitch, which is of interest not only because it illustrated a peculiar technical defect in the original Constitution and so led to its amendment, but because it introduces here, for the first time, the dubious but not unfascinating figure of Aaron Burr.

Burr was a politician of a type which democracies will always produce, and which those who dislike democracy will always use for its reproach. Yet the reproach is evidently unjust. In all societies, most of those who meddle with the government of men will do so in pursuit of their own interests, and in all societies the professional politician will reveal himself as a somewhat debased type. In a despotism he will become a courtier and obtain favour by obsequious and often dishonourable services to a prince. In an old-fashioned oligarchy he will adopt the same attitude towards some powerful noble. In a parliamentary plutocracy, like our own, he will proceed in fashion with which we are only too familiar, will make himself the paid servant of those wealthy men who finance politicians, and will enrich himself by means of "tips" from financiers and bribes from Government contractors. In a democracy, the same sort of man will try to obtain his ends by flattering and cajoling the populace. It is not obvious that he is more mischievous as demagogue than he was as courtier, lackey, or parliamentary intriguer. Indeed, he is almost certainly less so, for he must at least in some fashion serve, even if only that he may deceive them, those whose servant he should be. At any rate, the purely self-seeking demagogue is certainly a recurrent figure in democratic politics, and of the self-seeking demagogue Aaron Burr was an excellent specimen.

He had been a soldier not without distinction, and to the last he retained a single virtue—the grand virtue of courage. For the rest, he was the Tammany Boss writ large. An able political organizer, possessed of much personal charm, he had made himself master of the powerful organization of the Democratic Party in New York State, and as such was able to bring valuable support to the party which was opposing the administration of Adams. As a reward for his services, it was determined that he should be Democratic candidate for the Vice-Presidency. But here the machinery devised by the Convention played a strange trick. When the votes of the Electoral College came to be counted, it was found that instead of Jefferson leading and yet leaving enough votes to give Burr the second place, the votes for the two were exactly equal. This, under the Constitution, threw the decision into the hands of the House of Representatives, and in that House the Federalists still held the balance of power. They could not choose their own nominee, but they could choose either Jefferson or Burr, and many of them, desiring at the worst to frustrate the triumph of their great enemy, were disposed to choose Burr; while Burr, who cared only for his own career, was ready enough to lend himself to such an intrigue.

That the intrigue failed was due mainly to the patriotism of Hamilton. All that was best and worst in him concurred in despising the mere flatterer of the mob. Jefferson was at least a gentleman. And, unfairly as he estimated him both morally and intellectually, he knew very well that the election of Jefferson would not be a disgrace to the Republic, while the election of Burr would. His patriotism overcame his prejudices. He threw the whole weight of his influence with the Federalists against the intrigue, and he defeated it. It is the more to his honour that he did this to the advantage of a man whom he could not appreciate and who was his enemy.

It was the noblest and purest act of his public career. It probably cost him his life.

Jefferson was elected President and Burr Vice-President, as had undoubtedly been intended by the great majority of those who had voted the Democratic ticket at the elections. But the anomaly and disaster of Burr's election had been so narrowly avoided that a change in the Constitution became imperative. It was determined that henceforward the votes for President and Vice-President should be given separately. The incident had another consequence. Burr, disappointed in hopes which had almost achieved fulfilment, became from that moment a bitter enemy of Jefferson and his administration. Also, attributing the failure of his promising plot to Hamilton's intervention, he hated Hamilton with a new and insatiable hatred. Perhaps in that hour he already determined that his enemy should die.

Jefferson's inauguration was full of that deliberate and almost ceremonial contempt of ceremony in which that age found a true expression of its mood, though later and perhaps more corrupt times have inevitably found such symbolism merely comic. It was observed as striking the note of the new epoch that the President rejected all that semi-regal pomp which Washington and Adams had thought necessary to the dignity of their office. It is said that he not only rode alone into Washington (he was the first President to be inaugurated in the newly built capital), dressed like any country gentleman, but, when he dismounted to take the oath, tethered his horse with his own hands. More really significant was the presence of the populace that elected him—the great heaving, unwashed crowd elbowing the dainty politicians in the very presence chamber. The President's inaugural address was full of a generous spirit of reconciliation. "We are all Republicans," he said, "we are all Federalists." Every difference of opinion was not a difference of principle, nor need such differences interfere with "our attachment, to our Union and to representative government."

Such liberality was the more conspicuous by contrast with the petty rancour of his defeated rival, who not only refused to perform the customary courtesy of welcoming his successor at the White House, but spent his last hours there appointing Federalists feverishly to public offices solely in order to compel Jefferson to choose between the humiliation of retaining such servants and the odium of dismissing them. The new President very rightly refused to recognize nominations so made, and this has been seized upon by his detractors to hold him up as the real author of what was afterwards called "the Spoils System." It would be far more just to place that responsibility upon Adams.

The most important event of Jefferson's first administration was the Louisiana Purchase. The colony of Louisiana at the mouth of the Mississippi, with its vast hinterland stretching into the heart of the American continent, had, as we have seen, passed in 1762 from French into Spanish hands. Its acquisition by the United States had been an old project of Jefferson's. When Secretary of State under Washington, he had mooted it when settling with the Spanish Government the question of the navigation of the Mississippi. As President he revived it; but before negotiations could proceed far the whole situation was changed by the retrocession of Louisiana to France as part of the terms dictated by Napoleon to a Spain which had fallen completely under his control. The United States could not, in any case, have regarded the transfer without uneasiness, and to all schemes of purchase it seemed a death-blow, for it was believed that the French Emperor had set his heart upon the resurrection of French Colonial power in America. But Jefferson was an excellent diplomatist, at once conciliatory and unyielding: he played his cards shrewdly, and events helped him. The Peace of Amiens was broken, and, after a very brief respite, England and France were again at war. Napoleon's sagacity saw clearly enough that he could not hope to hold and develop his new colony in the face of a hostile power which was his master on the sea. It would suit his immediate purpose better to replenish his treasury with good American dollars which might soon be urgently needed. He became, therefore, as willing to sell as Jefferson was to buy, and between two men of such excellent sense a satisfactory bargain was soon struck. The colony of Louisiana and all the undeveloped country which lay behind it became the inheritance of the American Federation.

Concerning the transaction, there is more than one point to be noted of importance to history. One is the light which it throws on Jefferson's personal qualities. Because this man held very firmly an abstract and reasoned theory of the State, could define and defend it with extraordinary lucidity and logic, and avowedly guided his public conduct by its light, there has been too much tendency to regard him as a mere theorist, a sort of Girondia, noble in speculation and rhetoric, but unequal to practical affairs and insufficiently alive to concrete realities. He is often contrasted unfavourably with Hamilton in this respect: and yet he had, as events proved, by far the acuter sense of the trend of American popular opinion and the practical requirements of a government that should command its respect; and he made fewer mistakes in mere political tactics than did his rival. But his diplomacy is the best answer to the charge. Let anyone who entertains it follow closely the despatches relating to the Louisiana purchase, and observe how shrewdly this supposed visionary can drive a good bargain for his country, even when matched against Talleyrand with Bonaparte behind him. One is reminded that before he entered politics he enjoyed among his fellow-planters a reputation for exceptional business acumen.

Much more plausible is the accusation that Jefferson in the matter of Louisiana forgot his principles, and acted in a manner grossly inconsistent with his attitude when the Federalists were in power. Certainly, the purchase can only be defended constitutionally by giving a much larger construction to the powers of the Federal authority than even Hamilton had ever promulgated. If the silence of the Constitution on the subject must, as Jefferson had maintained, be taken as forbidding Congress and the Executive to charter a bank, how much more must a similar silence forbid them to expend millions in acquiring vast new territories beyond the borders of the Confederacy. In point of fact, Jefferson himself believed the step he and Congress were taking to be beyond their present powers, and would have preferred to have asked for a Constitutional Amendment to authorize it. But he readily gave way on this to those who represented that such a course would give the malcontent minority their chance, and perhaps jeopardize the whole scheme. The fact is, that "State Rights" were not to Jefferson a first principle, but a weapon which he used for the single purpose of resisting oligarchy. His first principle, in which he never wavered for a moment, was that laid down in the "Declaration"—the sovereignty of the General Will. To him Federalism was nothing and State Sovereignty was nothing but the keeping of the commandments of the people. Judged by this test, both his opposition to Hamilton's bank and his purchase of the Louisiana territory were justified; for on both occasions the nation was with him.

Jefferson's inconsistency, therefore, if inconsistency it were, brought him little discredit. It was far otherwise with the inconsistency of the Federalists. For they also changed sides, and of their case it may be said that, like Milton's Satan, they "rode with darkness." The most respectable part of their original political creed was their nationalism, their desire for unity, and their support of a strong central authority. Had this been really the dominant sentiment of their connection, they could not but have supported Jefferson's policy, even though they might not too unfairly have reproached him with stealing their thunder. For not only was Jefferson's act a notable example of their own theory of "broad construction" of the Constitution, but it was perhaps a more fruitful piece of national statesmanship than the best of Hamilton's measures, and it had a direct tendency to promote and perpetuate that unity which the Federalists professed to value so highly, for it gave to the States a new estate of vast extent and incalculable potentialities, which they must perforce rule and develop in common. But the Federalists forgot everything, even common prudence, in their hatred of the man who had raised the people against them. To injure him, most of them had been ready to conspire with a tainted adventurer like Burr. They were now ready for the same object to tear up the Union and all their principles with it. One of their ablest spokesmen, Josiah Quincey, made a speech against the purchase, in which he anticipated the most extreme pronouncements of the Nullifiers of 1832 and the Secessionists of 1860, declared that his country was not America but Massachusetts, that to her alone his ultimate allegiance was due, and that if her interests were violated by the addition of new Southern territory in defiance of the Constitution, she would repudiate the Union and take her stand upon her rights as an independent Sovereign State.

By such an attitude the Federalists destroyed only themselves. Some of the wiser among them left the party on this issue, notably John Quincey Adams, son of the second President of the United States, and himself to be raised later, under somewhat disastrous circumstances, to the same position. The rump that remained true, not to their principles but rather to their vendetta, could make no headway against a virtually unanimous nation. They merely completed and endorsed the general judgment on their party by an act of suicide.

But the chief historical importance of the Louisiana purchase lies in the fact that it gave a new and for long years an unlimited scope to that irresistible movement of expansion westward which is the key to all that age in American history. In the new lands a new kind of American was growing up. Within a generation he was to come by his own; and a Westerner in the chair of Washington was to revolutionize the Commonwealth.

Of the governing conditions of the West, two stand out as of especial importance to history.

One was the presence of unsubdued and hostile Indian tribes. Ever since that extraordinary man, Daniel Boone (whose strange career would make an epic for which there is no room in this book), crossed the Alleghanies a decade before the beginning of the Revolution and made an opening for the white race into the rich valleys of Kentucky, the history of the western frontier of European culture had been a cycle of Indian wars. The native race had not yet been either tamed or corrupted by civilization. Powerful chiefs still ruled great territories as independent potentates, and made peace and war with the white men on equal terms. From such a condition it followed that courage and skill in arms were in the West not merely virtues and accomplishments to be admired, but necessities which a man must acquire or perish. The Westerner was born a fighter, trained as a fighter, and the fighting instinct was ever dominant in him. So also was the instinct of loyalty to his fellow-citizens, a desperate, necessary loyalty as to comrades in a besieged city—as, indeed, they often were.

The other condition was the product partly of natural circumstances and partly of that wise stroke of statesmanship which had pledged the new lands in trust to the whole Confederacy. The Westerner was American—perhaps he was the first absolutely instinctive American. The older States looked with much pride to a long historical record which stretched back far beyond the Union into colonial times. The Massachusetts man would still boast of the Pilgrim Fathers. The Virginian still spoke lovingly of the "Old Plantation." But Kentucky and Tennessee, Ohio and Indiana were children of the Union. They had grown to statehood within it, and they had no memories outside it. They were peopled from all the old States, and the pioneers who peopled them were hammered into an intense and instinctive homogeneity by the constant need of fighting together against savage nature and savage man. Thus, while in the older settlements one man was conscious above all things that he was a New Englander, and another that he was a Carolinian, the Western pioneer was primarily conscious that he was a white man and not a Red Indian, nay, often that he was a man and not a grizzly bear. Hence grew up in the West that sense of national unity which was to be the inspiration of so many celebrated Westerners of widely different types and opinions, of Clay, of Jackson, of Stephen Douglas, and of Abraham Lincoln.

But this was not to take place until the loyalty of the West had first been tried by a strange and sinister temptation.

Aaron Burr had been elected Vice-President coincidently with Jefferson's election as President; but his ambition was far from satisfied. He was determined to make another bid for the higher place, and as a preliminary he put himself forward as candidate for the Governorship of New York State. It was as favourable ground as he could find to try the issue between himself and the President, for New York had been the centre of his activities while he was still an official Democrat, and her favour had given him his original position in the party. But he could not hope to succeed without the backing of those Federalist malcontents who had nearly made him President in 1800. To conciliate them he bent all his energies and talents, and was again on the point of success when Hamilton, who also belonged to New York State, again crossed his path. Hamilton urged all the Federalists whom he could influence to have nothing to do with Burr, and, probably as a result of his active intervention, Burr was defeated.

Burr resolved that Hamilton must be prevented from thwarting him in the future, and he deliberately chose a simple method of removing him. He had the advantage of being a crack shot. He forced a private quarrel on Hamilton, challenged him to a duel, and killed him.

He can hardly have calculated the effect of his action: it shocked the whole nation, which had not loved Hamilton, but knew him for a better man than Burr. Duelling, indeed, was then customary among gentlemen in the United States, as it is to-day throughout the greater part of the civilized world; but it was very rightly felt that the machinery which was provided for the vindication of outraged honour under extreme provocation was never meant to enable one man, under certain forms, to kill another merely because he found his continued existence personally inconvenient. That was what Burr had done; and morally it was undoubtedly murder. Throughout the whole East Burr became a man marked with the brand of Cain. He soon perceived it, but his audacity would not accept defeat. He turned to the West, and initiated a daring conspiracy which, as he hoped, would make him, if not President of the United States, at least President of something.

What Burr's plan, as his own mind conceived it, really was it is extremely difficult to say; for he gave not only different but directly opposite accounts to the various parties whom he endeavoured to engage in it. To the British Ambassador, whom he approached, he represented it as a plan for the dismemberment of the Republic from which England had everything to gain. Louisiana was to secede, carrying the whole West with her, and the new Confederacy was to become the ally of the Mother Country. For the Spanish Ambassador he had another story. Spain was to recover predominant influence in Louisiana by detaching it from the American Republic, and recognizing it as an independent State. To the French-Americans of Louisiana he promised complete independence of both America and Spain. To the Westerners, whom he tried to seduce, exactly the opposite colour was given to the scheme. It was represented as a design to provoke a war with Spain by the invasion and conquest of Mexico; and only if the Federal Government refused to support the filibusters was the West to secede. Even this hint of hypothetical secession was only whispered to those whom it might attract. To others all thought of disunion was disclaimed; and yet another complexion was put on the plot. The West was merely to make legitimate preparations for the invasion of Mexico and Florida in the event of certain disputes then pending with Spain resulting in war. It was apparently in this form that the design was half disclosed to the most influential citizen and commander of the militia in the newly created State of Tennessee, Andrew Jackson, the same that we saw as a mere school-boy riding and fighting at Hanging Rock.

Jackson had met Burr during the brief period when he was in Congress as representative of his State. He had been entertained by him and liked him, and when Burr visited Tennessee he was received by Jackson with all the hospitality of the West. Jackson was just the man to be interested in a plan for invading Mexico in the event of a Spanish war, and he would probably not have been much shocked—for the West was headstrong, used to free fighting, and not nice on points of international law—at the idea of helping on a war for the purpose. But he loved the Union as he loved his own life. Burr said nothing to him of his separatist schemes. When later he heard rumours of them, he wrote peremptorily to Burr for an explanation. Burr, who, to do him justice, was not the man to shuffle or prevaricate, lied so vigorously and explicitly that Jackson for the moment believed him. Later clearer proof came of his treason, and close on it followed the President's proclamation apprehending him, for Burr had been betrayed by an accomplice to Jefferson. Jackson at once ordered out the militia to seize him, but he had already passed westward out of his control. The Secretary for War, who, as it happened, was a personal enemy of Jackson's, thinking his connection with Burr might be used against him, wrote calling in sinister tone for an account of his conduct. Jackson's reply is so characteristic of the man that it deserves to be quoted. After saying that there was nothing treasonable in Burr's communications to him personally, he adds: "But, sir, when proofs showed him to be a Treator" (spelling was never the future President's strong point), "I would cut his throat with as much pleasure as I would cut yours on equal testimony."

The whole conspiracy fizzled out. Burr could get no help from any of the divergent parties he had attempted to gain. No one would fight for him. His little band of rebels was scattered, and he himself was seized, tried for treason, and acquitted on a technical point. But his dark, tempestuous career was over. Though he lived to an unlovely old age, he appears no more in history.

Jefferson was re-elected President in 1804. He was himself doubtful about the desirability of a second tenure, but the appearance at the moment of a series of particularly foul attacks upon his private character made him feel that to retire would amount to something like a plea of guilty.

Perhaps it would have served his permanent fame better if he had not accepted another term, for, owing to circumstances for which he was only partly to blame, his second Presidency appears in history as much less successful than his first.

Its chief problem was the maintenance of peace and neutrality during the colossal struggle between France under Napoleon and the kings and aristocracies of Europe who had endeavoured to crush the French Revolution, and who now found themselves in imminent peril of being crushed by its armed and amazing child.

Jefferson sincerely loved peace. Moreover, the sympathy for France, of which he had at one time made no disguise, was somewhat damped by the latest change which had taken place in the French Government. Large as was his vision compared with most of his contemporaries, he was too much soaked in the Republican tradition of antiquity, which was so living a thing in that age, to see in the decision of a nation of soldiers to have a soldier for their ruler and representative the fulfilment of democracy and not its denial. But his desire for peace was not made easier of fulfilment by either of the belligerent governments. Neither thought the power of the United States to help or hinder of serious account, and both committed constant acts of aggression against American rights. Nor was his position any stronger in that he had made it a charge against the Federalists that they had provided in an unnecessarily lavish fashion for the national defence. In accordance with his pledges he had reduced the army. His own conception of the best defensive system for America was the building of a large number of small but well-appointed frigates to guard her coasts and her commerce. It is fair to him to say that when war came these frigates of his gave a good account of themselves. Yet his own position was a highly embarrassing one, anxious from every motive to avoid war and yet placed between an enemy, or rather two enemies, who would yield nothing to his expostulations, and the rising clamour, especially in the West, for the vindication of American rights by an appeal to arms.

Jefferson attempted to meet the difficulty by a weapon which proved altogether inadequate for the purpose intended, while it was bound to react almost as seriously as a war could have done on the prosperity of America. He proposed to interdict all commerce with either of the belligerents so long as both persisted in disregarding American rights, while promising to raise the interdict in favour of the one which first showed a disposition to treat the United States fairly. Such a policy steadily pursued by such an America as we see to-day would probably have succeeded. But at that time neither combatant was dependent upon American products for the essentials of vitality. The suppression of the American trade might cause widespread inconvenience, and even bring individual merchants to ruin, but it could not hit the warring nations hard enough to compel governments struggling on either side for their very lives in a contest which seemed to hang on a hair to surrender anything that might look like a military advantage. On the other hand, the Embargo, as it was called, hit the Americans themselves very hard indeed. So great was the outcry of the commercial classes, that the President was compelled to retrace his steps and remove the interdict. The problem he handed over unsolved to his successor.

That successor was James Madison, another Virginian, Jefferson's lieutenant ever since the great struggle with the Federalists and his intimate friend from a still earlier period. His talents as a writer were great; he did not lack practical sagacity, and his opinions were Jefferson's almost without a single point of divergence. But he lacked Jefferson's personal prestige, and consequently the policy followed during his Presidency was less markedly his own than that of his great predecessor had been.

Another turn of the war-wheel in Europe had left America with only one antagonist in place of two. Trafalgar had destroyed, once and for all, the power of France on the sea, and she was now powerless to injure American interests, did she wish to do so. England, on the other hand, was stronger for that purpose than ever, and was less restrained than ever in the exercise of her strength. A new dispute, especially provocative to the feelings of Americans, had arisen over the question of the impressment of seamen. The press-gang was active in England at the time, and pursued its victims on the high seas. It even claimed the right to search the ships of neutrals for fugitives. Many American vessels were violated in this fashion, and it was claimed that some of the men thus carried off to forced service, though originally English, had become American citizens. England was clearly in the wrong, but she refused all redress. One Minister, sent by us to Washington, Erskine, did indeed almost bring matters to a satisfactory settlement, but his momentary success only made the ultimate anger of America more bitter, for he was disowned and recalled, and, as if in deliberate insult, was replaced by a certain Jackson who, as England's Ambassador to Denmark in 1804, had borne a prominent part in the most sensational violation of the rights of a neutral country that the Napoleonic struggle had produced.

There seemed no chance of peace from any conciliatory action on the part of Great Britain. The sole chance hung on the new President's inheritance of Jefferson's strong leaning in that direction. But Madison was by no means for peace at any price; and indeed Jefferson himself, from his retreat at Monticello, hailed the war, when it ultimately came, as unmistakably just. For a long time, however, the President alone held the nation back from war. The War Party included the Vice-President Monroe, who had been largely instrumental in bringing about the Louisiana purchase. But its greatest strength was in the newly populated West, and its chief spokesman in Congress was Henry Clay of Kentucky.

This man fills so large a space in American politics for a full generation that some attempt must be made to give a picture of him. Yet a just account of his character is not easy to give. It would be simple enough to offer a superficial description, favourable or hostile, but not one that would account for all his actions. Perhaps the best analysis would begin by showing him as half the aboriginal Westerner and half the Washington politician. In many ways he was very Western. He had a Westerner's pugnacity, and at the same time a Westerner's geniality and capacity for comradeship with men. He had to the last a Westerner's private tastes—especially a taste for gambling—and a Westerner's readiness to fight duels. Above all, from the time that he entered Congress as the fiercest of the "war hawks" who clamoured for vengeance on England, to the time when, an old and broken man, he expended the last of his enormous physical energy in an attempt to bridge the widening gulf between North and South, he showed through many grievous faults and errors that intense national feeling and that passion for the Union which were growing so vigorously in the fertile soil beyond the Alleghanies. But he was a Western shoot early engrafted on the political society of Washington—the most political of all cities, for it is a political capital and nothing else. He entered Congress young and found there exactly the atmosphere that suited his tastes and temperament. He was as much the perfect parliamentarian as Gladstone. For how much his tact and instinct for the tone of the political assembly in which he moved counted may be guessed from this fact: that while there is no speech of his that has come down to us that one could place for a moment beside some of extant contemporary speeches of Webster and Calhoun, yet it is unquestionable that he was considered fully a match for either Webster or Calhoun in debate, and in fact attained an ascendancy over Congress which neither of those great orators ever possessed. At the management of the minds of men with whom he was actually in contact he was unrivalled. No man was so skillful in harmonizing apparently irreconcilable differences and choosing the exact line of policy which opposing factions could agree to support. Three times he rode what seemed the most devastating political storms, and three times he imposed a peace. But with the strength of a great parliamentarian he had much of the weakness that goes with it. He thought too much as a professional; and in his own skilled work of matching measures, arranging parties and moving politicians about like pawns, he came more and more to forget the silent drive of the popular will. All this, however, belongs to a later stage of Clay's development. At the moment, we have to deal with him as the ablest of those who were bent upon compelling the President to war.

Between Clay and the British Government Madison's hand was forced, and war was declared. In America there were widespread rejoicings and high hopes of the conquest of Canada and the final expulsion of England from the New World. Yet the war, though on the whole justly entered upon, and though popular with the greater part of the country, was not national in the fullest sense. It did not unite, rather it dangerously divided, the Federation, and that, unfortunately, on geographical lines. New England from the first was against it, partly because most of her citizens sympathized with Great Britain in her struggle with Napoleon, and partly because her mercantile prosperity was certain to be hard hit, and might easily be ruined by a war with the greatest of naval powers. When, immediately after the declaration of war, in 1812, Madison was put forward as Presidential candidate for a second term, the contest showed sharply the line of demarcation. North-east of the Hudson he did not receive a vote.

The war opened prosperously for the Republic, with the destruction by Commander Perry of the British fleet on Lake Ontario—an incident which still is held in glorious memory by the American Navy and the American people. Following on this notable success, an invasion of Canada was attempted; but here Fortune changed sides. The invasion was a complete failure, the American army was beaten, forced to fall back, and attacked, in its turn, upon American soil. Instead of American troops occupying Quebec, English troops occupied a great part of Ohio.

Meanwhile, Jefferson's frigates were showing their metal. In many duels with English cruisers they had the advantage, though we in this country naturally hear most—indeed, it is almost the only incident of this war of which we ever do hear—of one of the cases in which victory went the other way—the famous fight between the Shannon and the Chesapeake. On the whole, the balance of such warfare leant in favour of the American sea-captains. But it was not by such warfare that the issue could be settled. England, summoning what strength she could spare from her desperate struggle with the French Emperor, sent an adequate fleet to convoy a formidable army to the American coast. It landed without serious opposition at the mouth of the Chesapeake, and marched straight on the national capital, which the Government was forced to abandon.

No Englishman can write without shame of what followed. All the public buildings of Washington were deliberately burnt. For this outrage the Home Government was solely responsible. The general in command received direct and specific orders, which he obeyed unwillingly. No pretence of military necessity, or even of military advantage, can be pleaded. The act, besides being a gross violation of the law of nations, was an exhibition of sheer brutal spite, such as civilized war seldom witnessed until Prussia took a hand in it. It had its reward. It burnt deep into the soul of America; and from that incident far more than from anything that happened in the War of Independence dates that ineradicable hatred of England which was for generations almost synonymous with patriotism in most Americans, and which almost to the hour of President Wilson's intervention made many in that country doubt whether, even as against Prussia, England could really be the champion of justice and humanity.

Things never looked blacker for the Republic than in those hours when the English troops held what was left of Washington. Troubles came thicker and thicker upon her. The Creek Nation, the most powerful of the independent Indian tribes, instigated partly by English agents, partly by the mysterious native prophet Tecumseh, suddenly descended with fire and tomahawk on the scattered settlements of the South-West, while at the same time a British fleet appeared in the Gulf of Mexico, apparently meditating either an attack on New Orleans or an invasion through the Spanish territory of Western Florida, and in that darkest hour when it seemed that only the utmost exertions of every American could save the United States from disaster, treason threatened to detach an important section of the Federation from its allegiance.

The discontent of New England is intelligible enough. No part of the Union had suffered so terribly from the war, and the suffering was the bitterer for being incurred in a contest which was none of her making, which she had desired to avoid, and which had been forced on her by other sections which had suffered far less. Her commerce, by which she largely lived, had been swept from the seas. Her people, deeply distressed, demanded an immediate peace. Taking ground as discontented sections, North and South, always did before 1864, on the doctrine of State Sovereignty, one at least, and that the greatest of the New England States, began a movement which seemed to point straight to the dilemma of surrender to the foreigner or secession and dismemberment from within.

Massachusetts invited representatives of her sister States to a Convention at Hartford. The Convention was to be consultative, but its direct and avowed aim was to force the conclusion of peace on any terms. Some of its promoters were certainly prepared, if they did not get their way, to secede and make a separate peace for their own State. The response of New England was not as unanimous as the conspirators had hoped. Vermont and New Hampshire refused to send delegates. Rhode Island consented, but qualified her consent with the phrase "consistently with her obligations"—implying that she would be no party to a separate peace or to the break-up of the Union. Connecticut alone came in without reservation. Perhaps this partial failure led the plotters to lend a more moderate colour to their policy. At any rate, secession was not directly advocated at Hartford. It was hinted that if such evils as those of which the people of New England complained proved permanent, it might be necessary; but the members of the Convention had the grace to admit that it ought not to be attempted in the middle of a foreign war. Their good faith, however, is dubious, for they put forward a proposal so patently absurd that it could hardly have been made except for the purpose of paving the way for a separate peace. They declared that each State ought to be responsible for its own defences, and they asked that their share of the Federal taxes should be paid over to them for the purpose. With that and a resolution to meet again at Boston and consider further steps if their demands were not met, they adjourned. They never reassembled.

In the South the skies were clearing a little. Jackson of Tennessee, vigorous and rapid in movement, a master of Indian warfare, leading an army of soldiers who worshipped him as the Old Guard worshipped

Napoleon, by a series of quick and deadly strokes overthrew the Creeks, followed them to their fastnesses, and broke them decisively at Tohopeka in the famous "hickory patch" which was the holy place of their nation.

He was rewarded in the way that he would have most desired: by a commission against the English, who had landed at Pensacola in Spanish territory, perhaps with the object of joining hands with their Indian allies. They found those allies crushed by Jackson's energy, but they still retained their foothold on the Florida coast, from which they could menace Georgia on the one side and New Orleans on the other. Spain was the ally of England in Europe, but in the American War she professed neutrality. As, however, she made no effort to prevent England using a Spanish port as a base of operations, she could not justly complain when Jackson seized the neighbouring port of Mobile, from which he marched against the British and dislodged them. But the hardest and most glorious part of his task was to come. The next blow was aimed at New Orleans itself. Jackson hastened to its defence. The British landed in great force at the mouth of the Mississippi and attacked the city from both sides. Jackson's little army was greatly outnumbered, but the skill with which he planned the defence and the spirit which he infused into his soldiers (the British themselves said that Jackson's men seemed of a different stuff from all other American troops they had encountered) prevailed against heavy odds. Three times Jackson's lines were attacked: in one place they were nearly carried, but his energy just repaired the disaster. At length the British retired with heavy losses and took to their ships. New Orleans was saved.

Before this last and most brilliant of American victories had been fought and won, peace had been signed at Ghent. News travelled slowly across the Atlantic, and neither British nor American commanders knew of it for months later. But early in the year negotiations had been opened, and before Christmas they reached a conclusion. Great Britain was more weary of the war than her antagonist. If she had gone on she might have won a complete victory, or might have seen fortune turn decisively against her. She had no wish to try the alternative. Napoleon had abdicated at Fontainebleau, and been despatched to Elba, and there were many who urged that the victorious army of the Peninsula under Wellington himself should be sent across the Atlantic to dictate terms. But England was not in the mood for more fighting. After twenty years of incessant war she saw at last the hope of peace. She saw also that the capture of Washington had not, as had been hoped, put an end to American resistance, but had rather put new life into it. To go on meant to attempt again the gigantic task which she had let drop as much from weariness as from defeat a generation before. She preferred to cry quits. The Peace, which was signed on behalf of a Republic by Clay—once the most vehement of "war-hawks"—was in appearance a victory for neither side. Frontiers remained exactly as they were when the first shot was fired. No indemnity was demanded or paid by either combatant. The right of impressment—the original cause of war, was neither affirmed nor disclaimed, though since that date England has never attempted to use it. Yet there is no such thing in history as "a drawn war." One side or the other must always have attempted the imposition of its will and failed. In this case it was England. America will always regard the war of 1812 as having ended in victory; and her view is substantially right. The new Republic, in spite of, or, one might more truly say, because of the dark reverses she had suffered and survived, was strengthened and not weakened by her efforts. The national spirit was raised and not lowered. The mood of a nation after a war is a practically unfailing test of victory or defeat; and the mood of America after 1814 was happy, confident, creative—the mood of a boy who has proved his manhood.

In 1816 Madison was succeeded by Monroe. Monroe, though, like his successor, a Virginian and a disciple of Jefferson, was more of a nationalist, and had many points of contact with the new Democracy which had sprung up first in the West, and was daily becoming more and more the dominant sentiment of the Republic. "Federalism" had perished because it was tainted with oligarchy, but there had been other elements in it which were destined to live, and the "National Republicans," as they came to call themselves, revived them. They were for a vigorous foreign policy and for adequate preparations for war. They felt the Union as a whole, and were full of a sense of its immense undeveloped possibilities. They planned expensive schemes of improvement by means of roads, canals, and the like to be carried out at the cost of the Federal Government, and they cared little for the protests of the doctrinaires of "State Right." To them America owes, for good or evil, her Protective system. The war had for some years interrupted commerce with the Old World, and native industries had, perforce, grown up to supply the wants of the population. These industries were now in danger of destruction through the reopening of foreign trade, and consequently of foreign competition. It was determined to frame the tariff hitherto imposed mainly, if not entirely, with a view to revenue in such a way as to shelter them from such peril. The exporting Cotton States, which had nothing to gain from Protection, were naturally hostile to it; but they were overborne by the general trend of opinion, especially in the West. One last development of the new "national" policy—the most questionable of its developments and opposed by Clay at the time, though he afterwards made himself its champion—was the revival, to meet the financial difficulties created by the war, of Hamilton's National Bank, whose charter, under the Jeffersonian régime, had been suffered to expire.

But the Western expansion, though it did much to consolidate the Republic, contained in it a seed of dissension. We have seen how, in the Convention, the need of keeping an even balance between Northern and Southern sections was apparent. That need was continually forced into prominence as new States were added. The presence or absence of Negro Slavery had become the distinguishing badge of the sections; and it became the apple of discord as regards the development of the West. Jefferson had wished that Slavery should be excluded from all the territory vested in the Federal authority, but he had been overruled, and the prohibition had been applied only to the North-Western Territory out of which the States of Ohio, Indiana, and Illinois were carved. The South-West had been left open to Slavery, and it had become the custom, with the purpose of preserving the balance in the Senate, to admit Slave States and Free in pairs. This worked satisfactorily enough so long as the States claiming admission were within a well-defined geographical area. But when Missouri became sufficiently populated to be recognized as a State, there was a keen contest. Her territory lay across the line which had hitherto divided the sections. She must be either a Northern promontory projecting into the south or a Southern promontory projecting into the north. Neither section would yield, and matters were approaching a domestic crisis when Clay intervened. He was in an excellent position to arbitrate, for he came from the most northern of Southern States, and had ties with both sections. Moreover, as has been said, his talents were peculiarly suited to such management as the situation required. He proposed a settlement which satisfied moderate men on both sides, was ratified by a large majority in Congress, and accepted on all hands as final. Missouri was to enter the Union, as she apparently desired to do, as a Slave State, but to the west of her territory the line 36° 30' longitude, very little above her southern border, was to be the dividing line of the sections. This gave the South an immediate advantage, but at a heavy ultimate price, for it left her little room for expansion. But one more Slave State could be carved out of the undeveloped Western Territory—that of Arkansas. Beyond that lay the lands reserved by treaty to the Indian tribes, which extended to the frontier of the Western dominions of Mexico. Clay, who, though by no means disposed to be a martyr on the question, sincerely desired to bring about the gradual extinction of Slavery, may well have deliberately planned this part of his compromise to accomplish that end. At the same time, Maine—a territory hitherto attached to Connecticut—was admitted as a Free State to balance Missouri.

Such was the great Missouri Compromise which kept the peace between the sections for a generation, and which gradually acquired an almost religious sanction in the minds of Americans devoted to the Union. It struck the note of the new era, which is called in American history "the era of good feeling." Sectional differences had been settled, political factions were in dissolution. Monroe's second election was, for the first time since Washington's retirement, without opposition. There were no longer any organized parties, such as Hamilton and Jefferson and even Clay had led. There were, of course, still rivalries and differences, but they were personal or concerned with particular questions. Over the land there was a new atmosphere of peace.

Abroad, America had never been stronger. To this period belongs the acquisition of Florida from Spain, an acquisition carried through by purchase, but by a bargain rather leonine in character. It cannot, however, be said that the United States had no reasonable grievance in the matter. Spain had not been able—or said that she had not been able—to prevent the British from taking forcible possession of one of her principal ports during a war in which she was supposed to be neutral. She declared herself equally unable to prevent the Creek and Seminole Indians from taking refuge in her territory and thence raiding the American lands over the border. Monroe had a good case when he pressed on her the point that she must either maintain order in her dominions or allow others to do so. Jackson, who was in command against the Seminoles, insisted—not unreasonably—that he could not deal with them unless he was allowed to follow them across the Spanish frontier and destroy their base of operations. Permission was given him, and he used it to the full, even to the extent of occupying important towns in defiance of the edicts of their Spanish governors. Monroe's Cabinet was divided in regard to the defensibility of Jackson's acts, but these acts probably helped to persuade Spain to sell while she could still get a price. The bargain was struck: Florida became American territory, and Jackson was appointed her first governor.

But the best proof that the prestige of America stood higher since the war of 1812 was the fact that the Power which had then been her rather contemptuous antagonist came forward to sue for her alliance. The French Revolution, which had so stirred English-speaking America, had produced an even greater effect on the Latin colonies that lay further south. Almost all the Spanish dominions revolted against the Spanish Crown, and after a short struggle successfully established their independence. Naturally, the rebels had the undivided sympathy of the United States, which was the first Power to recognize their independence. Now, however, the Holy Alliance was supreme in Europe, and had reinstated the Bourbons on the Spanish as on the French throne. It was rumoured that the rulers of the Alliance meditated the further step of re-subjugating Spain's American empire. Alexander I. of Russia was credited with being especially eager for the project, and with having offered to dispatch a Russian army from Siberia for the purpose: it was further believed that he proposed to reward himself by extending his own Alaskan dominions as far south as California. England, under Canning's leadership, had separated herself from the Holy Alliance, and had almost as much reason as the United States to dread and dislike such a scheme as the Czar was supposed to meditate. Canning sent for the American Ambassador, and suggested a joint declaration against any adventures by European powers on the American Continent. The joint declaration was declined, as seeming to commit the United States too much to one of those "entangling alliances" against which Washington had warned his fellow-countrymen; but the hint was taken.

Monroe put forth a proclamation in which he declared that America was no longer a field for European colonization, and that any attempt on the part of a European power to control the destiny of an American community would be taken as a sign of "an unfriendly disposition towards the United States."

Canning let it be understood that England backed the declaration, and that any attempt to extend the operations of the Holy Alliance to America would have to be carried out in the teeth of the combined opposition of the two great maritime powers so recently at war with each other. The plan was abandoned, and the independence of the South American Republics was successfully established.

But much more was established. The "Monroe Doctrine" became, and remains to-day, the corner- stone of American foreign policy. It has been greatly extended in scope, but no American Government has ever, for a moment, wavered in its support. None could afford to do so. To many Englishmen the doctrine itself, and still more the interpretation placed upon it by the United States in later times, seems arrogant—just as to many Americans the British postulate of unchallengeable supremacy at sea seems arrogant. But both claims, arrogant or no, are absolutely indispensable to the nation that puts them forward. If the American Republic were once to allow the principle that European Powers had the right, on any pretext whatever, to extend their borders on the American Continent, then that Republic would either have to perish or to become in all things a European Power, armed to the teeth, ever careful of the balance of power, perpetually seeking alliances and watching rivals. The best way to bring home to an honest but somewhat puzzled American—and there are many such—why we cannot for a moment tolerate what is called by some "the freedom of the seas," is to ask him whether he will give us in return the "freedom" of the American Continent. The answer in both cases is that sane nations do not normally, and with their eyes open, commit suicide.

Chapter 6

THE JACKSONIAN REVOLUTION

During the "era of good feeling" in which the Virginian dynasty closed, forces had been growing in the shadow which in a few short years were to transform the Republic. The addition to these forces of a personality completed the transformation which, though it made little or no change in the laws, we may justly call a revolution.

The government of Jefferson and his successors was a government based on popular principles and administered by democratically minded gentlemen. The dreams of an aristocratic republic, which had been the half-avowed objective of Hamilton, were dissipated forever by the Democratic triumph of 1800. The party which had become identified with such ideas was dead; no politician any longer dared to call himself a Federalist. The dogmas of the Declaration of Independence were everywhere recognized as the foundation of the State, recognized and translated into practice in that government was by consent, and in the main faithfully reflected the general will. But the administration, in the higher branches at least, was exclusively in the hands of gentlemen. When a word is popularly used in more than one sense, the best course is perhaps to define clearly the sense in which one uses it, and then to use it unvaryingly in that sense. The word "gentleman," then, will here always be used in its strictly impartial class significance without thought of association with the idea of "Good man" or "Quietly conducted person," and without any more intention of compliment than if one said "peasant" or "mechanic." A gentleman is one who has that kind of culture and habit of life which usually go with some measure of inheritance in wealth and status. That, at any rate, is what is meant when it is here said that Jefferson and his immediate successors were gentlemen, while the growing impulses to which they appealed and on which they relied came from men who were not gentlemen.

This peculiar position endured because the intense sincerity and single-mindedness of Jefferson's democracy impressed the populace and made them accept him as their natural leader, while his status as a well-bred Virginian squire, like Washington, veiled the revolution that was really taking place. The mantle of his prestige was large enough to cover not only his friend Madison, but Madison's successor Monroe. But at that point the direct inheritance failed. Among Monroe's possible successors there was no one plainly marked out as the heir of the Jeffersonian tradition. Thus—though no American public man saw it at the time—America had come to a most important parting of the ways. The Virginian dynasty had failed; the chief power in the Federation must now either be scrambled for by the politicians or assumed by the people.

Among the politicians who must be considered in the running for the presidency, the ablest was Henry Clay of Kentucky. He was the greatest parliamentary leader that America has known. He was unrivalled in the art of reconciling conflicting views and managing conflicting wills. We have already seen him as the triumphant author of the Missouri Compromise. He was a Westerner, and was supposed to possess great influence in the new States. Politically he stood for Protection, and for an interpretation of the Constitution which leaned to Federalism and away from State Sovereignty. Second only to Clay—if, indeed, second to him—in abilities was John Caldwell Calhoun of South Carolina. Calhoun was not yet the Calhoun of the 'forties, the lucid fanatic of a fixed political dogma. At this time he was a brilliant orator, an able and ambitious politician whose political system was unsettled, but tended at the time rather in a nationalist than in a particularist direction. The other two candidates were of less intellectual distinction, but each had something in his favour. William Crawford of

Georgia was the favourite candidate of the State Rights men; he was supposed to be able to command the support of the combination of Virginia and New York, which had elected every President since 1800, and there lingered about him a sort of shadow of the Jeffersonian inheritance. John Quincey Adams of Massachusetts was the grandson of Washington's successor, but a professed convert to Democratic Republicanism—a man of moderate abilities, but of good personal character and a reputation for honesty. He was Monroe's Secretary of State, and had naturally a certain hereditary hold on New England.

Into the various intrigues and counter-intrigues of these politicians it is not necessary to enter here, for from the point of view of American history the epoch-making event was the sudden entry of a fifth man who was not a politician. To the confusion of all their arrangements the great Western State of Tennessee nominated as her candidate for the Presidency General Andrew Jackson, the deliverer of New Orleans.

Jackson was a frontiersman and a soldier. Because he was a frontiersman he tended to be at once democratic in temper and despotic in action. In the rough and tumble of life in the back blocks a man must often act without careful inquiry into constitutional privileges, but he must always treat men as men and equals. It has already been noted that men left to themselves always tend to be roughly democratic, and that even before the Revolution the English colonies had much of the substance of democracy; they had naturally more of it after the Revolution. But even after the Revolution something like an aristocracy was to be noted in the older States, North and South, consisting in the North of the old New England families with their mercantile wealth and their Puritan traditions, in the South of the great slave-owning squires. In the new lands, in the constant and necessary fight with savage nature and savage man, such distinctions were obliterated. Before a massacre all men are equal. In the presence of a grizzly bear "these truths" are quite unmistakably self-evident. The West was in a quite new and peculiar sense democratic, and was to give to America the great men who should complete the work of democracy.

The other side of Jackson's character, as it influenced his public life, was the outlook which belonged to him as a soldier. He had the soldier's special virtue of loyalty. He was, throughout his long life, almost fanatically loyal in word and deed to his wife, to his friends, to his country. But above all he was loyal to the Jeffersonian dogma of popular sovereignty, which he accepted quite simply and unquestioningly, as soldiers are often found to accept a religion. And, accepting it, he acted upon it with the same simplicity. Sophistications of it moved him to contempt and anger.

Sovereignty was in the people. Therefore those ought to rule whom the people chose; and these were the servants of the people and ought to act as the people willed. All of which is quite unassailable; but anyone who has ever mixed in the smallest degree in politics will understand how appalling must have been the effect of the sudden intrusion in that atmosphere of such truisms by a man who really acted as if they were true. With this simplicity of outlook Jackson possessed in an almost unparalleled degree the quality which makes a true leader—the capacity to sum up and interpret the inarticulate will of the mass. His eye for the direction of popular feeling was unerring, perhaps largely because he snared or rather incarnated the instincts, the traditions—what others would call the prejudices—of those who followed him. As a military leader his soldiers adored him, and he carried into civil politics a good general's capacity for identifying himself with the army he leads.

He had also, of course, the advantage of a picturesque personality and of a high repute acquired in arms. The populace called him "Old Hickory"—a nickname originally invented by the soldiers who followed him in the frontier wars of Tennessee. They loved to tell the tale of his victories, his duels, his romantic marriage, and to recall and perhaps exaggerate his soldier's profanity of speech. But this aspect of Jackson's personality has been too much stressed. It was stressed by his friends to advertise his personality and by his enemies to disparage it. It is not false, but it may lead us to read history falsely. Just as Danton's loud voice, large gesture and occasional violence tend to produce a portrait of him which ignores the lucidity of his mind and the practicality of his instincts, making him a mere chaotic demagogue, so the "Old Hickory" legend makes Jackson too much the peppery old soldier and ignores his sagacity, which was in essential matters remarkable. His strong prejudices and his hasty temper often led him wrong in his estimate of individuals, but he was hardly ever at fault in his judgment of masses of men—presenting therein an almost exact contrast to his rival and enemy, Clay. With all his limitations, Jackson stands out for history as one of the two or three genuine creative statesmen that America has produced, and you cannot become a creative statesman merely by swearing and fighting duels.

Jackson accepted the nomination for the Presidency. He held, in strict accordance with his democratic creed, that no citizen should either seek or refuse popular election. But there seems no reason to think that at this time he cared much whether he were elected or no. He was not an ambitious man, he made no special efforts to push his cause, and he indignantly refused to be involved in any of the intrigues and bargains with which Washington was buzzing, or to give any private assurances to individuals as to the use which he would make of his power and patronage if chosen. But when the votes were counted it was clear that he was the popular favourite. He had by far the largest number of votes in the Electoral College, and these votes came from all parts of the Republic except New England, while so far as can be ascertained the popular vote showed a result even more decidedly in his favour. But in the College no candidate had an absolute majority, and it therefore devolved, according to the Constitution, upon the House of Representatives, voting by States, to choose the President from among the three candidates whose names stood highest on the list.

The House passed over Jackson and gave the prize to Adams, who stood next to him—though at a considerable interval. That it had a constitutional right to do so cannot be disputed: as little can it be disputed that in doing so it deliberately acted against the sentiment of the country. There was no Congressman who did not know perfectly well that the people wanted Jackson rather than Adams. This, however, was not all. The main cause of the decision to which the House came was the influence of Clay. Clay had been last on the list himself, for the West, where his main strength lay, had deserted him for Jackson, but his power in Congress was great, and he threw it all into Adams' scale. It is difficult to believe that a man of such sagacity was really influenced by the reasons he gave at the time—that he "would not consent by contributing to the election of a military chieftain to give the strongest guarantee that the Republic will march in the fatal road which has conducted every Republic to ruin." Jackson was a soldier, but he had no army, nor any means of making himself a Cæsar if he had wished to do so. Yet Clay may reasonably have felt, and was even right in feeling, that Jackson's election would be a blow to Republican Institutions as he understood them. He was really a patriot, but he was above all things a Parliamentarian, and the effect of Jacksonian democracy really was to diminish the importance of Parliamentarianism. Altogether Clay probably honestly thought that Adams was a fitter man to be President than Jackson.

Only he had another motive; and the discovery of this motive moved not only Jackson but the whole country to indignation. Adams had no sooner taken the oath than, in accordance with a bargain previously made between the backers of the two men, unofficially but necessarily with their knowledge, he appointed Clay Secretary of State.

Jackson showed no great resentment when he was passed over for Adams: he respected Adams, though he disliked and distrusted Clay. But when, in fulfilment of rumours which had reached him but which he had refused to credit, Clay became Secretary, he was something other than angry: he was simply shocked, as he would have been had he heard of an associate caught cheating at cards. He declared that the will of the people had been set aside as the result of a "corrupt bargain." He was not wrong. It was in its essence a corrupt bargain, and its effect was certainly to set aside the will of the people. Where Jackson was mistaken was in deducing that Adams and Clay were utterly dishonourable and unprincipled men. He was a soldier judging politicians. But the people judged them in the same fashion.

From that moment Jackson drew the sword and threw away the scabbard. He and his followers fought the Adams administration step by step and hour by hour, and every preparation was made for the triumphant return of Jackson at the next election. If there was plenty of scurrility against Adams and Clay in the journals of the Jacksonian party, it must be owned that the scribblers who supported the Administration stooped lower when they sought to attack Jackson through his wife, whom he had married under circumstances which gave a handle to slander. The nation was overwhelmingly with Jackson, and the Government of Quincey Adams was almost as much hated and abused as that of old John Adams had been. The tendency of recent American writers has been to defend the unpopular President and to represent the campaign against him and his Secretary as grossly unjust. The fact is that many of the charges brought against both were quite unfounded, but that the real and just cause of the popular anger against the Administration was its tainted origin.

The new elections came in 1828, and the rejected of Congress carried the whole country. The shadowy figment of the "Electoral College," already worn somewhat thin, was swept away and Jackson was chosen as by a plebiscite. That was the first and most important step in the Jacksonian Revolution. The founders of the Republic, while acknowledging the sovereignty of the people, had nevertheless framed the Constitution with the intention of excluding the people from any direct share in the election of the Chief Magistrate. The feeble check which they had devised was nullified. The Sovereign People, baulked in 1824, claimed its own in 1828, and Jackson went to the White House as its direct nominee.

His first step was to make a pretty thorough clearance of the Departmental Offices from the highest to the lowest. This action, which inaugurated what is called in America the "Spoils System" and has been imitated by subsequent Presidents down to the present time, is legitimately regarded as the least defensible part of Jackson's policy. There can be little doubt that the ultimate effect was bad, especially as an example; but in Jackson's case there were extenuating circumstances. He was justly conscious of a mandate from the people to govern. He had against him a coalition of the politicians who had till that moment monopolized power, and the public offices were naturally full of their creatures. He knew that he would have a hard fight in any case with the Senate against him and no very certain majority in the House of Representation. If the machinery of the Executive failed him he could not win, and, from his point of view, the popular mandate would be betrayed.

For the most drastic measures he could take to strengthen himself and to weaken his enemies left those enemies still very formidable. Of the leading politicians, only Calhoun, who had been chosen as Vice-President, was his ally, and that alliance was not to endure for long. The beginning of the trouble was, perhaps, the celebrated "Eaton" affair, which is of historic importance only as being illustrative of Jackson's character. Of all his Cabinet, Eaton, an old Tennessee friend and comrade in arms, probably enjoyed the highest place in the President's personal affections. Eaton had recently married the daughter of an Irish boarding-house keeper at whose establishment he stayed when in Washington. She had previously been the wife of a tipsy merchant captain who committed suicide, some said from melancholia produced by strong drink, others from jealousy occasioned by the levity of his wife's behaviour. There seems no real evidence that she was more than flirtatious with her husband's guests, but scandal had been somewhat busy with her name, and when Eaton married her the ladies of Washington showed a strong disposition to boycott the bride. The matrons of the South were especially proud of the unblemished correctitude of their social code, and Calhoun's wife put herself ostentatiously at the head of the movement. Jackson took the other side with fiery animation. He was ever a staunch friend, and Eaton had appealed to his friendship. Moreover, his own wife, recently dead, had received Mrs. Eaton and shown a strong disposition to be friends with her, and he considered the reflections on his colleague's wife were a slur on her, whose memory he honoured almost as that of a saint, but who, as he could not but remember, had herself not been spared by slanderers. He not only extended in the most conspicuous manner the protection of his official countenance to his friend's wife, but almost insisted upon his Cabinet taking oath, one by one, at the point of the sword, that they believed Mrs. Eaton to be "as chaste as a virgin." But the Ministers, even when overborne by their chivalrous chief, could not control the social behaviour of their wives, who continued to cold-shoulder the Eatons, to the President's great indignation and disgust. Van Buren, who regarded Calhoun as his rival, and who, as a bachelor, was free to pay his respects to Mrs. Eaton without prejudice or hindrance, seems to have suggested to Jackson that Calhoun had planned the whole campaign to ruin Eaton. Jackson hesitated to believe this, but close on the heels of the affair came another cause of quarrel, arising from the disclosure of the fact that Calhoun, when Secretary for War in Monroe's Cabinet, had been one of those who wished to censure Jackson for his proceedings in Florida—a circumstance which he had certainly withheld, and, according to Jackson, deliberately lied about in his personal dealings with the general. Private relations between the two men were completely broken off, and they were soon to be ranged on opposite sides in the public quarrel of the utmost import to the future of the Republic.

We have seen how the strong Nationalist movement which had sprung from the war of 1812 had produced, among other effects, a demand for the protection of American industries. The movement culminated in the Tariff of 1828, which the South called the "Tariff of Abominations." This policy, popular in the North and West, was naturally unpopular in the Cotton States, which lived by their vast export trade and had nothing to gain by a tariff. South Carolina, Calhoun's State, took the lead in opposition, and her representatives, advancing a step beyond the condemnation of the taxes themselves, challenged the constitutional right of Congress to impose them. The argument was not altogether without plausibility. Congress was undoubtedly empowered by the Constitution to raise a revenue, nor was there any stipulation as to how this revenue was to be raised. But it was urged that no power was given to levy taxes for any other purpose than the raising of such revenue. The new import duties were, by the admission of their advocates, intended to serve a wholly different purpose not mentioned in the Constitution—the protection of native industries. Therefore, urged the Carolinian Free Traders, they were unconstitutional and could not be lawfully imposed.

This argument, though ingenious, was not likely to convince the Supreme Court, the leanings of which were at this time decidedly in favour of Nationalism. The Carolinians therefore took their stand upon another principle, for which they found a precedent in the Kentucky Resolutions.

They declared that a State had, in virtue of its sovereignty, the right to judge as an independent nation would of the extent of its obligations under the Treaty of Union, and, having arrived at its own interpretation, to act upon it regardless of any Federal authority. This was the celebrated doctrine of "Nullification," and in pursuance of it South Carolina announced her intention of refusing to allow the protective taxes in question to be collected at her ports.

Calhoun was not the originator of Nullification. He was Vice-President when the movement began, and could with propriety take no part in it. But after his quarrel with Jackson he resigned his office and threw in his lot with his State. The ablest and most lucid statements of the case for Nullification are from his pen, and when he took his seat in the Senate he was able to add to his contribution the weight of his admirable oratory.

Much depended upon the attitude of the new President, and the Nullifiers did not despair of enlisting him on their side. Though he had declared cautiously in favour of a moderate tariff (basing his case mainly on considerations of national defence), he was believed to be opposed to the high Protection advocated by Clay and Adams. He was himself a Southerner and interested in the cotton industry, and at the late election he had had the unanimous backing of the South; its defection would be very dangerous for him. Finally, as an ardent Democrat he could hardly fail to be impressed by the precedent of the Kentucky Resolutions, which had Jefferson's authority behind them, and, perhaps to enforce this point, Jefferson's birthday was chosen as the occasion when the President was to be committed to Nullification.

A Democratic banquet was held at Washington in honour of the founder of the party. Jackson was present, and so were Calhoun and the leading Nullifiers. Speeches had to be made and toasts given, the burden of which was a glorification of State Sovereignty and a defence of Nullification. Then Jackson rose and gave his famous toast: "Our Union: it must be preserved." Calhoun tried to counter it by giving: "Our Union, next to our liberties most dear." But everyone understood the significance of the President's toast. It was a declaration of war.

The Nullifiers had quite miscalculated Jackson's attitude. He was a Southerner by birth, but a frontiersman by upbringing, and all the formative influences of his youth were of the West. It has been noted how strongly the feeling of the West made for the new unity, and in no Westerner was the national passion stronger than in Jackson. In 1814 he had told Monroe that he would have had the leaders of the Hartford Convention hanged, and he applied the same measure to Southern as to Northern sectionalism. To the summoning of the Nullifying Convention in South Carolina, he replied by a message to Congress asking for powers to coerce the recalcitrant State. He further told his Cabinet that if Congress refused him the powers he thought necessary he should have no hesitation in assuming them. He would call for volunteers to maintain the Union, and would soon have a force at his disposal that should invade South Carolina, disperse the State forces, arrest the leading Nullifiers and bring them to trial before the Federal Courts.

If the energy of Jackson was a menace to South Carolina, it was a grave embarrassment to the party regularly opposed to him in Congress and elsewhere. That this party could make common cause with the Nullifiers seemed impossible. The whole policy of high Protection against which South Carolina had revolted was Clay's. Adams had signed the Tariff of Administrations. Daniel Webster of Massachusetts, the leading orator of the party and the greatest forensic speaker that America has produced, had at one time been a Free Trader. But he was deeply committed against the Nullifiers, and had denounced the separatist doctrines which found favour in South Carolina in a speech the fine peroration of which American schoolboys still learn by heart. Webster, indeed, whether from shame or from conviction, separated himself to some extent from his associates and gave strenuous support to the "Force Bill" which the President had demanded.

But Clay was determined that Jackson should not have the added power and prestige which would result from the suppression of Nullification by the strong hand of the Executive. His own bias was in favour of a strong and unified Federal authority, but he would have made Congress that authority rather than the President—a policy even less favourable than Jackson's to State Rights, but more favourable to the Parliamentarianism in which Clay delighted and in which his peculiar talents shone. At all costs the Kentucky politician resolved to discount the intervention of the President, and his mind was peculiarly fertile in devising and peculiarly skillful in executing such manœuvres as the situation required. The sacrifice of his commercial policy was involved, but he loved Protection less than he hated Jackson, and less, to do him justice, than he loved the Union. Negotiations were opened with Calhoun, and a compromise tariff proposed, greatly modified in the direction of Free Trade and free of the "abominations" of which South Carolina specially complained. This compromise the Nullifiers, awed perhaps by the vigour of Jackson, and doubtful of the issue if matters were pushed too far, accepted.

Jackson did not like the Clay-Calhoun compromise, which seemed to him a surrender to treason; but in such a matter he could not control Congress. On one thing he insisted: that the Force Bill should take precedence over the new Tariff. On this he carried his point. The two Bills were passed by Congress in the order he demanded, and both were signed by him on the same day. Upon this the South Carolinian Convention repealed its ordinance nullifying the Tariff, and agreed to the collection of the duties now imposed. It followed this concession by another ordinance nullifying the Force Bill. The practical effect of this was nil, for there was no longer anything to enforce. It was none the less important. It meant that South Carolina declined to abandon the weapon of Nullification. Indeed, it might plausibly be urged that that weapon had justified itself by success. It had been defended as a protection against extreme oppression, and the extreme oppression complained of had actually ceased in consequence of its use. At any rate, the effect was certainly to strengthen rather than to weaken extreme particularism in the South. On this point Jackson saw further than Clay or any of his contemporaries. While all America was rejoicing over the peaceful end of what had looked like an ugly civil quarrel, the President was writing to a friend and supporter: "You have Nullifiers amongst you. Frown upon them.... The Tariff was a mere excuse and a Southern Confederacy the real object. The next excuse will be the Negro or Slavery Question. "

The controversy with the Nullifiers had exhibited Jackson's patriotism and force of character in a strong and popular light, but it had lost him what support he could still count upon among the politicians. Calhoun was now leagued with Clay and Webster, and the "front bench" men (as we should call them) were a united phalanx of opposition. It is characteristic of his courage that in face of such a situation Jackson ventured to challenge the richest and most powerful corporation in America.

The first United States Bank set up by Alexander Hamilton as part of his scheme for creating a powerful governing class in America was, as we have seen, swept away by the democratic reaction which Jefferson led to victory. The second, springing out of the financial embarrassments which followed the war with Great Britain, had been granted a charter of twenty years which had now nearly expired. The renewal of that charter seemed, however, to those who directed the operations of the Bank and to those who were deep in the politics of Washington, a mere matter of course.

The Bank was immensely powerful and thoroughly unpopular. The antinomy would hardly strike a modern Englishman as odd, but it was anomalous in what was already a thoroughly democratic state. It was powerful because it had on its side the professional politicians, the financiers, the rich of the great cities generally—in fact, what the Press which such people control calls "the intelligence of the nation." But it was hated by the people, and it soon appeared that it was hated as bitterly by the President. Writers who sympathize with the plutocratic side in the quarrel had no difficulty in convicting Jackson of a regrettable ignorance of finance. Beyond question he had not that intimate acquaintance with the technique of usury which long use alone can give. But his instincts in such a matter were as keen and true as the instincts of the populace that supported him. By the mere health of his soul he could smell out the evil of a plutocracy. He knew that the bank was a typical monopoly, and he knew that such monopolies ever grind the faces of the poor and fill politics with corruption. And the corruption with which the Bank was filling America might have been apparent to duller eyes. The curious will find ample evidence in the records of the time, especially in the excuses of the Bank itself, the point at which insolence becomes comic being reached when it was gravely pleaded that loans on easy terms were made to members of Congress because it was in the public interest that such persons should have practical instruction in the principles of banking! Meanwhile everything was done to corner the Press. Journals favourable to the Bank were financed with loans issued on the security of their plant. Papers on the other side were, whenever possible, corrupted by the same method. As for the minor fry of politics, they were of course bought by shoals.

It is seldom that such a policy, pursued with vigour and determination by a body sufficiently wealthy to stick at nothing, fails, to carry a political assembly. With Congress the Bank was completely successful. A Bill to re-charter that institution passed House and Senate by large majorities. It was immediately vetoed by the President.

Up to this point, though his private correspondence shows that his mind had long been made up, there had been much uncertainty as to what Jackson would do. Biddle, the cunning, indefatigable and unscrupulous chairman of the Bank, believed up to the last moment that, if Congress could be secured, he would not dare to interpose. To do so was an enterprise which certainly required courage. It meant fighting at the same time an immensely strong corporation representing two- thirds of the money power of the nation, and with tentacles in every State in the Union, and a parliamentary majority in both Houses led by a coalition of all the most distinguished politicians of the day. The President had not in his Cabinet any man whose name carried such public weight as those of Clay, Webster, or Calhoun, all now in alliance in support of the Bank; and his Cabinet, such as it was, was divided. The cleverest and most serviceable of his lieutenants, Van Buren, was unwilling to appear prominently in the matter. He feared the power of the Bank in New York State, where his own influence lay. McLane, his Secretary of the Treasury, was openly in favour of the Bank, and continued for some time to assure Biddle of his power to bring the President round to his views.

But, as a fact, the attitude of Jackson was never really in doubt. He knew that the Bank was corrupting public life; the very passage of the Bill, against the pledges given by any Congressmen to their constituents, was evidence of this, if any were needed. He knew further that it was draining the productive parts of the country, especially the South and West, for the profit of a lucky financial group in the Eastern States. He knew also that such financial groups are never national: he knew that the Bank had foreign backers, and he showed an almost startling prescience as to the evils that were to follow in the train of cosmopolitan finance, "more formidable and more dangerous than the naval and military power of an enemy." But above all he knew that the Bank was odious to the people, and he was true to his political creed, whereby he, as the elect of the people, was bound to enforce its judgment without fear or favour.

Jackson's Veto Message contained a vigorous exposition of his objections to the Bank on public grounds, together with a legal argument against its constitutionality. It was admitted that the Supreme Court had declared the chartering of the Bank to be constitutional, but this, it was urged, could not absolve the President of the duty of following his own conscience in interpreting the Constitution he had sworn to maintain. The authority of the Supreme Court must not, therefore, be permitted to control the Congress or the Executive, but have only such influence as the force of its reasoning may discover. It is believed that this part of the message, which gave scandal to legalists, was supplied by Taney, the Attorney-General. It is a curious coincidence, if this be so, that more than twenty years later we shall find another great President, though bred in the anti-Jacksonian Whig tradition, compelled to take up much the same attitude in regard to a Supreme Court decision delivered by Taney himself.

Biddle and his associates believed that the Message would be fatal to the President. So did the leaders of the political opposition, and none more than Clay. Superlatively skillful in managing political assemblies, he was sometimes strangely at fault in judging the mind of the mass—a task in which Jackson hardly ever failed. He had not foreseen the anger which his acceptance of a place for Adams would provide; and he now evidently believed that the defence of the Bank would be a popular cry in the country. He forced the "Whig" Convention—for such was the name which the very composite party opposed to Jackson had chosen—to put it in the forefront of their programme, and he seems to have looked forward complacently to a complete victory on that issue.

His complacency could not last long. Seldom has a nation spoken so directly through the complex and often misleading machinery of elections as the American nation spoke in 1832 against the bank. North, south, east and west the Whigs were routed. Jackson was re-elected President by such an overwhelming expression of the popular choice as made the triumph of 1828 seem a little thing. Against all the politicians and all the interests he had dared to appeal to Cæsar, and the people, his unseen ally, had in an instant made his enemies his footstool.

It was characteristic of the man that he at once proceeded to carry the war into Africa. Biddle, though bitterly disappointed, was not yet resigned to despair. It was believed—and events in the main confirm the belief—that he contemplated a new expedient, the use of what still remained of the financial power of the Bank to produce deliberate scarcity and distress, in the hope that a reaction against the President's policy would result. Jackson resolved to strike the Bank a crippling blow before such juggling could be attempted. The Act of Congress which had established the Bank gave him power to remove the public deposits at will; and that power he determined to exercise.

A more timid man would have had difficulty with his Cabinet. Jackson overcame the difficulty by accepting full personal responsibility for what he was about to do. He did not dismiss the Ministers whose opinion differed from his, he brought no pressure to bear on their consciences; but neither did he yield his view an inch to theirs. He acted as he had resolved to act, and made a minute in the presence of his Cabinet that he did so on his own initiative. It was essential that the Secretary of the Treasury, through whom he must act, should be with him. McLane had already been transferred to the State Department, and Jackson now nominated Taney, a strong-minded lawyer, who was his one unwavering supporter in the struggle. Taney removed the public deposits from the United States Bank. They were placed for safe keeping in the banks of the various States. The President duly reported to Congress his reasons for taking this action.

In the new House of Representatives, elected at the same time as the President, the Democrats were now predominant; but the Senate changes its complexion more slowly, and there the "Whigs" had still a majority. This majority could do nothing but exhibit impotent anger, and that they most unwisely did. They refused to confirm Taney's nomination as Secretary to the Treasury, as a little later they refused to accept him as a Judge of the High Court. They passed a solemn vote of censure on the President, whose action they characterized, in defiance of the facts, as unconstitutional. But Jackson, strong in the support of the nation, could afford to disregard such natural ebullitions of bad temper. The charter of the Bank lapsed and was not renewed, and a few years later it wound up its affairs amid a reek of scandal, which sufficed to show what manner of men they were who had once captured Congress and attempted to dictate to the President. The Whigs were at last compelled to drink the cup of humiliation to the dregs. Another election gave Jackson a majority even in the Senate, and in spite of the protests of Clay, Webster and Calhoun the censure on the President was solemnly expunged from its records.

After the triumphant termination of the Bank, Jackson's second term of office was peaceful and comparatively uneventful. There were indeed some important questions of domestic and foreign policy with which it fell to him to deal. One of these was the position of the Cherokee Indians, who had been granted territory in Georgia and the right to live on their own lands there, but whom the expansion of civilization had now made it convenient to displace. It is impossible for an admirer of Jackson to deny that his attitude in such a matter was too much that of a frontiersman. Indeed, it is a curious irony that the only American statesman of that age who showed any disposition to be careful of justice and humanity in dealing with the native race was John C. Calhoun, the uncompromising defender of Negro Slavery. At any rate, the Indians were, in defiance, it must be said, of the plain letter of the treaty, compelled to choose between submission to the laws of Georgia and transplantation beyond the Mississippi. Most of them were in the event transplanted. Jackson's direction of foreign policy was not only vigorous but sagacious. Under his Presidency long-standing disputes with both France and England were brought to a peaceful termination on terms satisfactory to the Republic. To an Englishman it is pleasant to note that the great President, though he had fought against the English—perhaps because he had fought against them—was notably free from that rooted antipathy to Great Britain which was conspicuous in most patriotic Americans of that age and indeed down to very recent times. "With Great Britain, alike distinguished in peace and war," he wrote in a message to Congress, "we may look forward to years of peaceful, honourable, and elevated competition. Everything in the condition and history of the two nations is calculated to inspire sentiments of mutual respect and to carry conviction to the minds of both that it is their policy to preserve the most cordial relations." It may also be of some interest to quote the verdict of an English statesman, who, differing from Jackson in all those things in which an aristocratic politician must necessarily differ from the tribune of a democracy, had nevertheless something of the same symbolic and representative national character and something of the same hold upon his fellow-countrymen. A letter from Van Buren, at that time representing the United States at the Court of St. James's, to Jackson reports Palmerston as saying to him that "a very strong impression had been made here of the dangers which this country had to apprehend from your elevation, but that they had experienced better treatment at your hands than they had done from any of your predecessors."

So enormous was Jackson's popularity that, if he had been the ambitious Cæsarist that his enemies represented, he could in all probability have safely violated the Washington-Jefferson precedent and successfully sought election a third time. But he showed no desire to do so. He had undergone the labours of a titan for twelve eventful and formative years. He was an old man; he was tired. He may well have been glad to rest for what years were left to him of life in his old frontier State, which he had never ceased to love. He survived his Presidency by nine years. Now and then his voice was heard on a public matter, and, whenever it was heard, it carried everywhere a strange authority as if it were the people speaking. But he never sought public office again.

Jackson's two periods of office mark a complete revolution in American institutions; he has for the Republic as it exists today the significance of a second founder. From that period dates the frank abandonment of the fiction of the Electoral College as an independent deliberative assembly, and the direct and acknowledged election of the nation's Chief Magistrate by the nation itself. In the constitution of the Democratic Party, as it grouped itself round him, we get the first beginnings of the "primary," that essential organ of direct democracy of which English Parliamentarism has no hint, but which is the most vital feature of American public life. But, most of all, from his triumph and the abasement of his enemies dates the concentration of power in the hands of the President as the real unifying centre of authority. His attitude towards his Cabinet has been imitated by all strong Presidents since. America does not take kindly to a President who shirks personal responsibility or hides behind his Ministers. Nothing helped Lincoln's popularity more than the story—apocryphal or no—of his taking the vote of his Cabinet on a proposition of his own and then remarking: "Ayes one; Noes six. The Ayes have it." Even the "Spoils System," whatever its evils, tended to strengthen the Elect of the People. It made the power of an American President more directly personal than that of the most despotic rulers of Continental Europe; for they are always constrained by a bureaucracy, while his bureaucracy even down to its humblest members is of his own appointment and dependent on him.

The party, or rather coalition, which opposed these changes, selected for itself, as has been seen, the name of "Whig." The name was, perhaps, better chosen than the American Whigs realized. They meant—and it was true as far as it went—that, like the old English Whigs, they stood for free government by deliberative assemblies against arbitrary personal power. They were not deep enough in history to understand that they also stood, like the old English Whigs, for oligarchy against the instinct and tradition of the people. There is a strange irony about the fate of the parties in the two countries. In the Monarchy an aristocratic Parliamentarism won, and the Crown became a phantom. In the Republic a popular sovereignty won, and the President became more than a king.

Chapter 7

THE SPOILS OF MEXICO

The extent of Jackson's more than monarchical power is well exemplified by the fact that Van Buren succeeded him almost as a king is succeeded by his heir. Van Buren was an apt master of electioneering and had a strong hold upon the democracy of New York. He occupied in the new Democratic Party something of the position which Burr had occupied in the old. But while Burr had sought his own ends and betrayed, Van Buren was strictly loyal to his chief. He was a sincere democrat and a clever man; but no one could credit him with the great qualities which the wielding of the immense new power created by Jackson seemed to demand. None the less he easily obtained the Presidency as Jackson's nominee. Since the populace, whose will Jackson had made the supreme power in the State, could not vote for him, they were content to vote for the candidate he was known to favour.

Indeed, in some ways the coalition which called itself the Whig Party was weakened rather than strengthened by the substitution of a small for a great man at the head of the Democracy. Antagonism to Jackson was the real cement of the coalition, and some of its members did not feel called upon to transfer their antagonism unabated to Van Buren.

The most eminent of these was Calhoun, who now broke away from the Whigs and appeared prepared to give a measure of independent support to the Administration. He did not, however, throw himself heartily into the

Democratic Party or seek to regain the succession to its leadership which had once seemed likely to be his. From the moment of his quarrel with Jackson the man changes out of recognition: it is one of the most curious transformations in history, like an actor stripping off his stage costume and appearing as his very self. Political compromises, stratagems, ambitions drop from him, and he stands out as he appears in that fine portrait whose great hollow eyes look down from the walls of the Capitol at Washington, the enthusiast, almost the fanatic, of a fixed idea and purpose. He is no longer national, nor pretends to be. His one thought is the defence of the type of civilization which he finds in his own State against the growing power of the North, which he perceives with a tragic clearness and the probable direction of which he foresees much more truly than did any Northerner of that period. He maintains continually, and without blurring its lines by a word of reservation or compromise, the dogma of State Sovereignty in its most extreme and almost parricidal form. His great pro-Slavery speeches belong to the same period. They are wonderful performances, full of restrained eloquence, and rich in lucid argument and brilliant illustration. Sincerity shines in every sentence. They serve to show how strong a case an able advocate can make out for the old pre-Christian basis of European society; and they will have a peculiar interest if ever, as seems not improbable, the industrial part of Northern Europe reverts to that basis.

Van Buren, on the whole, was not an unsuccessful President. He had many difficulties to contend with. He had to face a serious financial panic, which some consider to have been the result of Jackson's action in regard to the Bank, some of the machinations of the Bank itself. He surmounted it successfully, though not without a certain loss of popularity. We English have some reason to speak well of him in that he resisted the temptation to embroil his country with ours when a rebellion in Canada offered an opportunity which a less prudent man might very well have taken. For the rest, he carried on the government of the country on Jacksonian lines with sufficient fidelity not to forfeit the confidence of the old man who watched and advised him, sympathetically but not without anxiety, from his "Hermitage" in Tennessee.

One singular episode may conveniently be mentioned here, though the incident in which it originated rather belongs to the Jacksonian epoch. This is not the place to discuss the true nature of that curious institution called Freemasonry. Whatever its origin, whether remote and derived from Solomon's Temple as its devotees assert, or, as seems more intrinsically probable, comparatively modern and representing one of the hundreds of semi-mystical fads which flourished in the age of Cagliostro, it had acquired considerable importance in Europe at the end of the eighteenth century. At some unknown date it was carried across the Atlantic, and sprouted vigorously in America; but it does not seem to have been taken particularly seriously, until the States were startled by an occurrence which seemed more like part in what is known in that country as "a dime novel" than a piece of history.

A journalist named Morgan, who had been a Freemason, announced his intention of publishing the inviolable secrets of the Society. The announcement does not seem to have created any great sensation; probably the majority of Americans were as sceptical as is the present writer as to the portentous nature of the awful Unspeakabilities which so many prosperous stock-brokers and suburban builders keep locked in their bosoms. But what followed naturally created a sensation of the most startling kind. For on the morrow of his announcement Morgan disappeared and never returned. What happened to him is not certainly known. A body was found which may or may not have been his. The general belief was that he had been kidnapped and murdered by his fellow-Craftsmen, and, indeed, it really seems the natural inference from the acknowledged facts that at least some one connected with the Brotherhood was responsible for his fate. A violent outcry against Masonry was the natural result, and, as some of the more prominent politicians of the day, including President Jackson himself, were Masons, the cry took a political form. An Anti-Masonic Party was formed, and at the next Presidential election was strong enough to carry one State and affect considerably the vote of others. The movement gradually died down and the party disappeared; but the popular instinct that secret societies, whether murderous or not, have no place in a Free State was none the less a sound one.

I have said that Van Buren's election was a sign of Jackson's personal influence. But the election of 1840 was a more startling sign of the completeness of his moral triumph, of the extent to which his genius had transformed the State. In 1832 the Whigs pitted their principles against his and lost. In 1840 they swallowed their principles, mimicked his, and won.

The Whig theory—so far as any theory connected the group of politicians who professed that name—was that Congress and the political class which Congress represented should rule, or at least administer, the State. From that theory it seemed to follow that some illustrious Senator or Congressman, some prominent member of that political class, should be chosen as President. The Whigs had acted in strict accord with their theory when they had selected as their candidate their ablest and most representative politician, Clay. But the result had not been encouraging. They now frankly abandoned their theory and sought to imitate the successful practice of their adversaries. They looked round for a Whig Jackson, and they found him in an old soldier from Ohio named Harrison, who had achieved a certain military reputation in the Indian wars. Following their model even more closely, they invented for him the nickname of "Old Tippercanoe," derived from the name of one of his victories, and obviously suggested by the parallel of "Old Hickory." Jackson, however, really had been called "Old Hickory" by his soldiers long before he took a leading part in politics, while it does not appear that Harrison was ever called "Tippercanoe" by anybody except for electioneering purposes. However, the name served its immediate purpose, and—

"Tippercanoe, And Tyler too!"

became the electoral war-cry of the Whigs. Tyler, a Southern Whig from Virginia, brought into the ticket to conciliate the Southern element in the party, was their candidate for the Vice-Presidency. Unfortunately for themselves, the Democrats played the Whig game by assailing Harrison with very much the same taunts which had previously been used by the Whigs against Jackson. The ignorance of the old soldier, his political inexperience, even his poverty and obscurity of origin, were exploited in a hundred Democratic pamphlets by writers who forgot that every such reflection made closer the parallel between Harrison and Jackson, and so brought to the former just the sort of support for which the Whigs were angling.

"Tippercanoe" proved an excellent speculation for the Whig leaders. It was "Tyler too," introduced to meet the exigencies of electioneering (and rhyme) that altogether disconcerted all their plans. Tyler was a Southerner and an extreme Particularist. He had been a Nullifier, and his quarrel with Jackson's Democracy had simply been a quarrel with his Unionism. His opinions on all subjects, political, administrative, and fiscal, were as remote from those of a man like Clay as any opinions could be. This was perfectly well known to those who chose him for Vice-President. But while the President lives and exercises his functions the Vice-President is in America a merely ornamental figure. He has nothing to say in regard to policy. He is not even a member of the Administration. He presides over the Senate, and that is all. Consequently there has always been a strong temptation for American wire-pullers to put forward as candidate for the Vice-Presidency a man acceptable to some more or less dubious and detached group of their possible supporters, whose votes it is desired to obtain, but who are not intended to have any control over the effective policy of the Government. Yet more than one example has shown how perilous this particular electioneering device may turn out to be. For if the President should die before the expiration of his term, the whole of his almost despotic power passes unimpaired to a man who represents not the party, but a more or less mutinous minority in the party.

It was so in this case. Harrison was elected, but barely lived to take the oath. Tyler became President. For a short time things went comparatively smoothly. Harrison had chosen Webster as Secretary of State, and Tyler confirmed his appointment. But almost at once it became apparent that the President and his Secretary differed on almost every important question of the day, and that the Whig Party as a whole was with the Secretary. The

President's views were much nearer to those of the Democratic opposition, but that opposition, smarting under its defeat, was not disposed to help either combatant out of the difficulties and humiliations which had so unexpectedly fallen on both in the hour of triumph. Yet, if Webster were dismissed or driven to resign, someone of note must be found to take his place. Personal followers the President had none. But in his isolation he turned to the one great figure in American politics that stood almost equally alone. It was announced that the office vacated by Webster had been offered to and accepted by John Caldwell Calhoun.

Calhoun's acceptance of the post is sometimes treated as an indication of the revival of his ambitions for a national career. It is suggested that he again saw a path open to him to the Presidency which he had certainly once coveted. But though his name was mentioned in 1844 as a possible Democratic candidate, it was mentioned only to be found wholly unacceptable, and indeed Calhoun's general conduct when Secretary was not such as to increase his chances of an office for which no one could hope who had not a large amount of Northern as well as Southern backing. It seems more likely that Calhoun consented to be Secretary of State as a means to a definite end closely connected with what was now the master-passion of his life, the defence of Southern interests. At any rate, the main practical fruit of his administration of affairs was the annexation of Texas.

Texas had originally been an outlying and sparsely peopled part of the Spanish province of Mexico, but even before the overthrow of Spanish rule a thin stream of immigration had begun to run into it from the South-Western States of America. The English-speaking element became, if not the larger part of the scant population, at least the politically dominant one. Soon after the successful assertion of Mexican independence against Spain, Texas, mainly under the leadership of her American settlers, declared her independence of Mexico. The occasion of this secession was the abolition of Slavery by the native Mexican Government, the Americans who settled in Texas being mostly slave-owners drawn from the Slave States. Some fighting took place, and ultimately the independence of Texas seems to have been recognized by one of the many governments which military and popular revolutions and counter-revolutions rapidly set up and pulled down in Mexico proper. The desire of the Texans—or at least of that governing part of them that had engineered the original secession—was to enter the American Union, but there was a prolonged hesitation at Washington about admitting them, so that Texas remained for a long time the "Lone Star State," independent alike of Mexico and the United States. This hesitation is difficult at first sight to understand, for Texas was undoubtedly a valuable property and its inhabitants were far more willing to be incorporated than, say, the French colonists of Louisiana had been. The key is, no doubt, to be found in the internecine jealousies of the sections. The North—or at any rate New England—had been restive over the Louisiana purchase as tending to strengthen the Southern section at the expense of the Northern. If Texas were added to Louisiana the balance would lean still more heavily in favour of the South. But what was a cause of hesitation to the North and to politicians who looked for support to the North was a strong recommendation to Calhoun. He had, as he himself once remarked, a remarkable gift of foresight—an uncomfortable gift, for he always foresaw most clearly the things he desired least. He alone seems to have understood fully how much the South had sacrificed by the Missouri Compromise. He saw her hemmed in and stationary while the North added territory to territory and State to State. To annex Texas would be, to an extent at least, to cut the bonds which limited her expansion. When the population should have increased sufficiently it was calculated that at least four considerable States could be carved out of that vast expanse of country.

But, though Calhoun's motive was probably the political strengthening of the South, his Texan policy could find plenty of support in every part of the Union. Most Northerners, especially in the new States of the North-West, cared more for the expansion of the United States than for the sectional jealousies. They were quite prepared to welcome Texas into the Union; but, unfortunately for Calhoun, they had a favourite project of expansion of their own for which they expected a corresponding support.

The whole stretch of the Pacific slope which intervenes between Alaska and California, part of which is now represented by the States of Washington and Oregon and part by British Columbia, was then known generally as "Oregon." Its ownership was claimed both by British and American Governments upon grounds of prior exploration, into the merits of which it is hardly necessary to enter here. Both claims were in fact rather shadowy, but both claimants were quite convinced that theirs was the stronger. For many years the dispute had been hung up without being settled, the territory being policed jointly by the two Powers. Now, however, there came from the Northern expansionists a loud demand for an immediate settlement and one decidedly in their favour. All territory south of latitude 47° 40' must be acknowledged as American, or the dispute must be left to the arbitrament of arms. "Forty-seven-forty or fight!" was the almost unanimous cry of the Democracy of the North and West.

The Secretary of State set himself against the Northern Jingoes, and though his motives may have been sectional, his arguments were really unanswerable. He pointed out that to fight England for Oregon at that moment would be to fight her under every conceivable disadvantage. An English army from India could be landed in Oregon in a few weeks. An American army sent to meet it must either round Cape Horn and traverse the Atlantic and Pacific oceans in the face of the most powerful navy in the world or March through what was still an unmapped wilderness without the possibility of communications or supports. If, on the other hand, the question were allowed to remain in suspense, time would probably redress the balance in favour of the United States. American expansion would in time touch the borders of Oregon, and then the dispute could be taken up and settled under much more favourable circumstances. It was a perfectly just argument, but it did not convince the "forty-seven-forty-or-fighters," who roundly accused the Secretary—and not altogether unjustly—of caring only for the expansion of his own section.

Calhoun was largely instrumental in averting a war with England, but he did not otherwise conduct himself in such a manner as to conciliate opinion in that country. England, possibly with the object of strengthening her hand in bargaining for Oregon, had intervened tentatively in relation to Texas. Lord Aberdeen, then Peel's Foreign Secretary, took up that question from the Anti-Slavery standpoint, and expressed the hope that the prohibition of Slavery by Mexico would not be reversed if Texas became part of the American Union. The intervention, perhaps, deserved a snub—for, after all, England had only recently emancipated the slaves in her own colonies—and a sharp reminder that by the Monroe Doctrine, to which she was herself a consenting party, no European Power had a right to interfere in the domestic affairs of an American State. Calhoun did not snub Lord Aberdeen: he was too delighted with his lordship for giving him the opportunity for which he longed. But he did a thing eminently characteristic of him, which probably no other man on the American continent would have done. He sat down and wrote an elaborate and very able State Paper setting forth the advantages of Slavery as a foundation for civilization and public liberty. It was this extraordinary dispatch that led Macaulay to say in the House of Commons that the American Republic had "put itself at the head of the nigger-driving interest throughout the world as Elizabeth put herself at the head of the Protestant interest." As regards Calhoun the charge was perfectly true; and it is fair to him to add that he undoubtedly believed in Slavery much more sincerely than ever Elizabeth did in Protestantism. But he did not represent truly the predominant feeling of America. Northern Democratic papers, warmly committed to the annexation of Texas, protested vehemently against the Secretary's private fad concerning the positive blessedness of Slavery being put forward as part of the body of political doctrine held by the United States. Even Southerners, who accepted Slavery as a more or less necessary evil, did not care to see it thus blazoned on the flag. But Calhoun was impenitent. He was proud of the international performance, and the only thing he regretted, as his private correspondence shows, was that Lord Aberdeen did not continue the debate which he had hoped would finally establish his favourite thesis before the tribunal of European opinion.

Texas was duly annexed, and Tyler's Presidency drew towards its close. He seems to have hoped that the Democrats whom he had helped to defeat in 1840 would accept him as their candidate for a second term in 1844; but they declined to do so, nor did they take kindly to the suggestion of nominating Calhoun. Instead, they chose one Polk, who had been a stirring though not very eminent politician in Jacksonian days. The choice is interesting as being the first example of a phenomenon recurrent in subsequent American politics, the deliberate selection of a more or less obscure man on the ground of what Americans call "availability."

It is the product of the convergence of two things—the fact of democracy as indicated by the election of a First Magistrate by a method already frankly plebiscitary, and the effect of a Party System, becoming, as all Party Systems must become if they endure, at once increasingly rigid and increasingly unreal.

The aim of party managers—necessarily professionals—was to get their party nominee elected. But the conditions under which they worked were democratic. They could not, as such professionals can in an oligarchy like ours, simply order the electors to vote for any nincompoop who was either rich and ambitious enough to give them, the professionals, money in return for their services, or needy and unscrupulous enough to be their hired servant. They were dealing with a free people that would not have borne such treatment. They had to consider as a practical problem for what man the great mass of the party would most readily and effectively vote. And it was often discovered that while the nomination of an acknowledged "leader" led, through the inevitable presence (in a democracy) of conflicts and discontents within the party, to the loss of votes, the candidate most likely to unite the whole party was one against whom no one had any grudge and who simply stood for the "platform" which was framed in a very democratic fashion by the people themselves voting in their "primaries." When this system is condemned and its results held up to scorn, it should be remembered that among other effects it is certainly responsible for the selection of Abraham Lincoln.

Polk was not a Lincoln, but he was emphatically an "available" candidate, and he won, defeating Clay, to whom the Whigs had once more reverted, by a formidable majority. He found himself confronted with two pressing questions of foreign policy. During the election the Democrats had played the "Oregon" card for all it was worth, and the new President found himself almost committed to the "forty-seven-forty-or-fight" position. But the practical objections to a war with England on the Oregon dispute were soon found to be just as strong as Calhoun had represented them to be. Moreover, the opportunity presented itself for a war at once much more profitable and much less perilous than such a contest was likely to prove, and it was obvious that the two wars could not be successfully undertaken at once.

The independence of Texas had been in some sort recognized by Mexico, but the frontier within which that independence formally existed was left quite undefined, and the Texan view of it differed materially from the Mexican. The United States, by annexing Texas, had shouldered this dispute and virtually made it their own.

It is seldom that historical parallels are useful; they are never exact. But there are certain real points of likeness between the war waged by the United States against Mexico in the 'forties and the war waged by Great Britain against the Boer Republics between 1899 and 1902. In both cases it could be plausibly represented that the smaller and weaker Power was the actual aggressor. But in both cases there can be little doubt that it was the stronger Power which desired or at least complacently contemplated war. In both cases, too, the defenders of the war, when most sincere, tended to abandon their technical pleas and to take their stand upon the principle that the interests of humanity would best be served by the defeat of a "backward" people by a more "progressive" one. It is not here necessary to discuss the merits of such a plea. But it may be interesting to note the still closer parallel presented by the threefold division of the opposition in both cases. The Whig Party was divided in 1847, almost exactly as was the "Liberal" Party in 1899. There was, especially in New England, an ardent and sincere minority which was violently opposed to the war and openly denounced it as an unjustifiable aggression. Its attitude has been made fairly familiar to English readers by the first series of Lowell's "Bigelow Papers." This minority corresponded roughly to those who in England were called "Pro-Boers." There was another section which warmly supported the war: it sought to outdo the Democrats in their patriotic enthusiasm, and to reap as much of the electoral harvest of the prevalent Jingoism as might be. Meanwhile, the body of the party took up an intermediate position, criticized the diplomacy of the President, maintained that with better management the war might have been avoided, but refused to oppose the war outright when once it had begun, and concurred in voting supplies for its prosecution.

The advocates of the war had, however, to face at its outset one powerful and unexpected defection, that of Calhoun. No man had been more eager than he for the annexation of Texas, but, Texas once annexed, he showed a marked desire to settle all outstanding questions with Mexico quickly and by a compromise on easy terms. He did all he could to avert war. When war actually came, he urged that even the military operations of the United States should be strictly defensive, that they should confine themselves to occupying the disputed territory and repelling attacks upon it, but should under no circumstances attempt a counter-invasion of Mexico. There can be little doubt that Calhoun's motive in proposing this curious method of conducting a war was, as usual, zeal for the interests of his section, and that he acted as he did because he foresaw the results of an extended war more correctly than did most Southerners. He had coveted Texas because Texas would strengthen the position of the South. Slavery already existed there, and no one doubted that if Texas came into the Union at all it must be as a Slave State. But it would be otherwise if great conquests were made at the expense of Mexico. Calhoun saw clearly that there would be a strong movement to exclude Slavery from such conquests, and, having regard to the numerical superiority of the North, he doubted the ability of his own section to obtain in the scramble that must follow the major part of the spoil.

Calhoun, however, was as unable to restrain by his warnings the warlike enthusiasm of the South as were the little group of Peace Whigs in New England to prevent the North from being swept by a similar passion. Even Massachusetts gave a decisive vote for war.

The brief campaign was conducted with considerable ability, mainly by Generals Taylor and Scott. Such army as Mexico possessed was crushingly defeated at Monterey. An invasion followed, and the fall of Mexico City completed the triumph of American arms. By the peace dictated in the captured capital Mexico had, of course, to concede the original point of dispute in regard to the Texan frontier. But greater sacrifices were demanded of her, though not without a measure of compensation. She was compelled to sell at a fixed price to her conqueror all the territory to which she laid claim on the Pacific slope north of San Diego. Thus Arizona, New Mexico, and, most important of all, California passed into American hands.

But before this conclusion had been reached a significant incident justified the foresight of Calhoun. Towards the close of the campaign, a proposal made in Congress to grant to the Executive a large supply to be expended during the recess at the President's discretion in purchasing Mexican territory was met by an amendment moved by a Northern Democrat named Wilmot, himself an ardent supporter of the war, providing that from all territory that might be so acquired from Mexico Slavery should be forever excluded. The proviso was carried in the House of Representatives by a majority almost exactly representative of the comparative strength of the two sections. How serious the issue thus raised was felt to be is shown by the fact that the Executive preferred dispensing with the money voted to allowing it to be pushed further. In the Senate both supply and condition were lost. But the "Wilmot Proviso" had given the signal for a sectional struggle of which no man could foresee the end.

Matters were further complicated by a startlingly unexpected discovery. On the very day on which peace was proclaimed, one of the American settlers who had already begun to make their way into California, in digging for water on his patch of reclaimed land, turned up instead a nugget of gold. It was soon known to the ends of the earth that the Republic had all unknowingly annexed one of the richest goldfields yet discovered. There followed all the familiar phenomena which Australia had already witnessed, which South Africa was later to witness, and which Klondyke has witnessed in our time. A stream of immigrants, not only from every part of the United States but from every part of the civilized world, began to pour into California drunk with the hope of immediate and enormous gains. Instead of the anticipated gradual development of the new territory, which might have permitted considerable delay and much cautious deliberation in the settlement of its destiny, one part of that territory at least found itself within a year the home of a population already numerous enough to be entitled to admission to the Union as a State, a population composed in great part of the most restless and lawless of mankind, and urgently in need of some sort of properly constituted government.

A Convention met to frame a plan of territorial administration, and found itself at once confronted with the problem of the admission or exclusion of Slavery. Though many of the delegates were from the Slave States, it was decided unanimously to exclude it. There was nothing sentimentally Negrophil about the attitude of the Californians; indeed, they proclaimed an exceedingly sensible policy in the simple formula: "No Niggers, Slave or Free!" But as regards Slavery their decision was emphatic and apparently irreversible.

The Southerners were at once angry and full of anxiety. It seemed that they had been trapped, that victories won largely by Southern valour were to be used to disturb still more the balance already heavily inclining to the rival section. In South Carolina, full of the tradition of Nullification, men already talked freely of Secession. The South, as a whole, was not yet prepared for so violent a step, but there was a feeling in the air that the type of civilization established in the Slave States might soon have to fight for its life.

On the top of all this vague unrest and incipient division came a Presidential election, the most strangely unreal in the whole history of the United States. The issue about which alone all men, North and South, were thinking was carefully excluded from the platforms and speeches of either party. Everyone of either side professed unbounded devotion to the Union, no one dared to permit himself the faintest allusion to the hot and human passions which were patently tearing it in two. The Whigs, divided on the late war, divided on Slavery, divided on almost every issue by which the minds of men were troubled, yet resolved to repeat the tactics which had succeeded in 1840. And the amazing thing is that they did in fact repeat them and with complete success. They persuaded Zachary Taylor, the victor of Monterey, to come forward as their candidate. Taylor had shown himself an excellent commander, but what his political opinions might be no-one knew, for it transpired that he had never in his life even recorded a vote. The Whigs, however, managed to extract from him the statement that if he had voted at the election of 1844—as, in fact, he had not—it would have been for Clay rather than for Polk; and this admission they proceeded, rather comically, to trumpet to the world as a sufficient guarantee from "a consistent and truth-speaking man" of the candidate's lifelong devotion to "Whig" principles. Nothing further than the above remark and the frank acknowledgment that he was a slave-owner could be extracted from Taylor in the way of programme or profession of faith. But the Convention adopted him with acclamation. Naturally such a selection did not please the little group of Anti-War Whigs—a group which was practically identical with the extreme Anti-Slavery wing of the party—and Lowell, in what is perhaps the most stinging of all his satires, turned Taylor's platform or absence of platform to ridicule in lines known to thousands of Englishmen who know nothing of their occasion:—

"Ez fer my princerples, I glory In hevin' nothin' of the sort. I ain't a Whig, I ain't a Tory, I'm jest a—Candidate in short."

"Monterey," however, proved an even more successful election cry than "Tippercanoe." The Democrats tried to play the same game by putting forward General Cass, who had also fought with some distinction in the Mexican War and had the advantage—if it were an advantage—of having really proved himself a stirring Democratic partisan as well. But Taylor was the popular favourite, and the Whigs by the aid of his name carried the election.

He turned out no bad choice. For the brief period during which he held the Presidential office he showed considerable firmness and a sound sense of justice, and seems to have been sincerely determined to hold himself strictly impartial as between the two sections into which the Union was becoming every day more sharply divided. Those who expected, on the strength of his blunt avowal of slave-owning, that he would show himself eager to protect and extend Slavery were quite at fault. He declared with the common sense of a soldier that California must come into the Union, as she wished to come in, as a Free State, and that it would be absurd as well as monstrous to try and compel her citizens to be slave-owners against their will. But he does not appear to have had any comprehensive plan of pacification to offer for the quieting of the distracted Union, and, before he could fully develop his policy, whatever it may have been, he died and bequeathed his power to Millard Filmore, the Vice-President, a typical "good party man" without originality or initiative.

The sectional debate had by this time become far more heated and dangerous than had been the debates which the Missouri Compromise had settled thirty years before. The author of the Missouri Compromise still lived, and, as the peril of the Union became desperate, it came to be said more and more, even by political opponents, that he and he alone could save the Republic. Henry Clay, since his defeat in 1844, had practically retired from the active practice of politics. He was an old man. His fine physique had begun to give way, as is often the case with such men, under the strain of a long life that had been at once laborious and self-indulgent. But he heard in his half-retirement the voice of the nation calling for him, and he answered. His patriotism had always been great, great also his vanity. It must have been strangely inspiring to him, at the end of a career which, for all its successes, was on the whole a failure—for the great stake for which he played was always snatched from him—to live over again the great triumph of his youth, and once more to bequeath peace, as by his last testament, to a distracted nation. God allowed him that not ignoble illusion, and mercifully sent him to his rest before he could know that he had failed.

The death of Taylor helped Clay's plans; for the soldier-President had discovered a strong vein of obstinacy. He had his own views on the question, and was by no means disposed to allow any Parliamentary leader to over-ride them. Filmore was quite content to be an instrument in the hands of a stronger man, and, after his succession, Clay had the advantage of the full support of the Executive in framing the lines of the last of his great compromises.

In the rough, those lines were as follows: California was to be admitted at once, and on her own terms, as a Free State, Arizona and New Mexico were to be open to Slavery if they should desire its introduction; their Territorial Governments, when formed, were to decide the question. This adjustment of territory was to be accompanied by two balancing measures dealing with two other troublesome problems which had been found productive of much friction and bitterness. The District of Columbia—that neutralized territory in which the city of Washington stood—having been carved out of two Slave States, was itself within the area of legalized Slavery. But it was more than that. It was what we are coming to call, in England, a "Labour Exchange." In fact, it was the principal slave mart of the South, and slave auctions were carried on at the very doors of the Capitol, to the disgust of many who were not violent in their opposition to Slavery as a domestic institution. To this scandal Clay proposed to put an end by abolishing the Slave Trade in the District of Columbia. Slavery was still to be lawful there, but the public sale and purchase of slaves was forbidden. In return for this concession to Anti-Slavery sentiment, a very large counter- concession was demanded. As has already been said, the Constitution had provided in general terms for the return of fugitive slaves who escaped from Slave States into the Free. But for reasons and in a fashion which it will be more convenient to examine in the next chapter, this provision of the Constitution had been virtually nullified by the domestic legislation of many Northern States. To put an end to this, Clay proposed a Fugitive Slave Law which imposed on the Federal Government the duty of recovering escaped slaves, and authorized the agents of that Government to do so without reference to the Courts or Legislature of the State in which the slave might be seized.

The character of the settlement showed that its author's hand had in no way forgotten its cunning in such matters. As in the Missouri Compromise, every clause shows how well he had weighed and judged the conditions under which he was working, how acutely he guessed the points upon which either side could be persuaded to give way, and the concessions for which either would think worth paying a high price. And in fact his settlement was at the time accepted by the great mass of Union-loving men, North and South. Some Northern States, and especially Massachusetts, showed a disposition to break away under what seemed to them the unbearable strain of the Fugitive Slave Law. But in dealing with Massachusetts Clay found a powerful ally in Webster. That orator was her own son, and a son of whom she was immensely proud. He had, moreover, throughout his public life, avowed himself a convinced opponent of Slavery. When, therefore, he lent the weight of his support to Clay's scheme he carried with him masses of Northern men whom no one else could have persuaded. He proclaimed his adhesion of the Compromise in his famous speech of the 10th of May—one of the greatest that he ever delivered. It was inevitable that his attitude should be assailed, and the clamour raised against him by the extreme Anti-Slavery men at the time has found an echo in many subsequent histories of the period. He is accused of having sold his principles in order that he might make an unscrupulous bid for the Presidency. That he desired to be President is true, but it is not clear that the 10th of May speech improved his chances of it; indeed, the reverse seems to have been the case. A candid examination of the man and his acts will rather lead to the conclusion that throughout his life he was, in spite of his really noble gift of rhetoric, a good deal more of the professional lawyer- politician than his admirers have generally been disposed to admit, but that his "apostacy" of 1850 was, perhaps, the one act of that life which was least influenced by professional motives and most by a genuine conviction of the pressing need of saving the Union.

The support of a Southern statesman of like authority might have done much to give finality to the settlement. But the one Southerner who carried weight comparable to that of Webster in the North was found among its opponents. A few days after Webster had spoken, the Senate listened to the last words of Calhoun. He was already a dying man. He could not even deliver his final protest with his own lips. He sat, as we can picture him, those great, awful eyes staring haggardly without hope into nothingness, while a younger colleague read that protest for him to the Assembly that he had so often moved, yet never persuaded. Calhoun rejected the settlement; indeed, he rejected the whole idea of a territorial settlement on Missouri lines. It is fair to his sagacity to remember that the mania for trying to force Slavery on unsuitable and unwilling communities which afterwards took possession of those who led the South to disaster could claim no authority from him. His own solution is to be found in the "Testament" published after his death—an amazing solution, based on the precedent of the two Roman Consuls, whereby two Presidents were to be elected, one by the

North and one by the South, with a veto on each other's acts. He probably did not expect that the wild proposal would be accepted. Indeed, he did not expect that anything that he loved would survive. With all his many errors on his head, there was this heroic thing about the man—that he was one of those who can despair of the Republic and yet not desert it. With an awful clearness he saw the future as it was to be, the division becoming ever wider, the contest more bitter, the sword drawn, and at the last—defeat. In the sad pride and defiance of his dying speech one catches continually an echo of the tragic avowal of Hector: "For in my heart and in my mind I know that Troy shall fall."

He delivered his soul, and went away to die. And the State to which he had given up everything showed its thought of him by carving above his bones, as sufficient epitaph, the single word: "CALHOUN."

Chapter 8

THE SLAVERY QUESTION

The Compromise of 1850, though welcomed on all sides as a final settlement, failed as completely as the Missouri Compromise had succeeded. It has already been said that the fault was not in any lack of skill in the actual framing of the plan. As a piece of political workmanship it was even superior to Clay's earlier masterpiece, as the rally to it at the moment of all but the extreme factions, North and South, sufficiently proves. That it did not stand the wear of a few years as well as the earlier settlement had stood the wear of twenty was due to a change in conditions, and to understand that change it is necessary to take up again the history of the Slavery Question where the founders of the Republic left it.

It can hardly be said that these great men were wrong in tolerating Slavery. Without such toleration at the time the Union could not have been achieved and the American Republic could not have come into being. But it can certainly be said that they were wrong in the calculation by means of which they largely justified such toleration not so much to their critics as to their own consciences. They certainly expected, when they permitted Slavery for a season, that Slavery would gradually weaken and disappear. But as a fact it strengthened itself, drove its roots deeper, gained a measure of moral prestige, and became every year harder to destroy.

Whence came their miscalculation? In part no doubt it was connected with that curious and recurrent illusion which postulates in human affairs—a thing called "Progress." This illusion, though both logically and practically the enemy of reform—for if things of themselves tend to grow better, why sweat and agonize to improve them?—is none the less characteristic, generally speaking, of reforming epochs, and it was not without its hold over the minds of the American Fathers. But there were also certain definite causes, some of which they could hardly have foreseen, some of which they might, which account for the fact that Slavery occupied a distinctly stronger position halfway through the nineteenth century than it had seemed to do at the end of the eighteenth.

The main cause was an observable fact of psychology, of which a thousand examples could be quoted, and which of itself disposes of the whole "Progressive" thesis—the ease with which the human conscience gets used to an evil. Time, so far from being a remedy—as the "Progressives" do vainly talk—is always, while no remedy is attempted, a factor in favour of the disease. We have seen this exemplified in the course of the present war. The mere delay in the punishment of certain gross outrages against the moral traditions of Europe has made those outrages seem just a little less horrible than they seemed at first, so that men can even bear to contemplate a peace by which their authors should escape punishment—a thing which would have been impossible while the anger of decent men retained its virginity. So it was with Slavery. Accepted at first as an unquestionable blot on American Democracy, but one which could not at the moment be removed, it came gradually to seem something normal. A single illustration will show the extent of this decline in moral sensitiveness. In the first days of the Republic Jefferson, a Southerner and a slave-owner, could declare, even while compromising with Slavery, that he trembled for his country when he remembered that God was just, could use of the peril of a slave insurrection this fine phrase: "The Almighty has no attribute that could be our ally in such a contest." Some sixty years later, Stephen Douglas, as sincere a democrat as Jefferson, and withal a Northerner with no personal interest in Slavery, could ask contemptuously whether if Americans were fit to rule themselves they were not fit to rule "a few niggers."

The next factor to be noticed was that to which Jefferson referred in the passage quoted above—the constant dread of a Negro rising. Such a rising actually took place in Virginia in the first quarter of the nineteenth century. It was a small affair, but the ghastly massacre of whites which accompanied it was suggestive of the horrors that might be in store for the South in the event of a more general movement among the slaves. The debates which this crisis produced in the Virginian legislature are of remarkable interest. They show how strong the feeling against Slavery as an institution still was in the greatest of Slave States. Speaker after speaker described it as a curse, as a permanent peril, as a "upas tree" which must be uprooted before the State could know peace and security. Nevertheless they did not uproot it. And from the moment of their refusal to uproot it or even to make a beginning of uprooting it they found themselves committed to the opposite policy which could only lead to its perpetuation. From the panic of that moment date the generality of the Slave Codes which so many of the Southern States adopted—codes deliberately framed to prevent any improvement in the condition of the slave population and to make impossible even their peaceful and voluntary emancipation.

There was yet another factor, the economic one, which to most modern writers, starting from the basis of historical materialism, has necessarily seemed the chief of all. It was really, I think, subsidiary, but it was present, and it certainly helped to intensify the evil. It consisted in the increased profitableness of Slavery, due, on the one hand, to the invention in America of Whitney's machine for extracting cotton, and, on the other, to the industrial revolution in England, and the consequent creation in Lancashire of a huge and expanding market for the products of American slave labour. This had a double effect. It not only strengthened Slavery, but also worsened its character. In place of the generally mild and paternal rule of the old gentlemen-planters came in many parts of the South a brutally commercial régime, which exploited and used up the Negro for mere profit. It was said that in this further degradation of Slavery the agents were often men from the commercial North; nor can this be pronounced a mere sectional slander in view of the testimony of two such remarkable witnesses as Abraham Lincoln and Mrs. Beecher Stowe.

All these things tended to establish the institution of Slavery in the Southern States. Another factor which, whatever its other effects, certainly consolidated Southern opinion in its defence, was to be found in the activities of the Northern Abolitionists.

In the early days of the Republic Abolition Societies had existed mainly, if not exclusively, in the South. This was only natural, for, Slavery having disappeared from the Northern States, there was no obvious motive for agitating or discussing its merits, while south of the Mason-Dixon line the question was still a practical one. The Southern Abolitionists do not appear to have been particularly unpopular with their fellow-citizens. They are perhaps regarded as something of cranks, but as well-meaning cranks whose object was almost everywhere admitted to be theoretically desirable. At any rate, there is not the suspicion of any attempt to suppress them; indeed, the very year before the first number of the Liberator was published in Boston, a great Conference of Anti-Slavery Societies, comprising delegates from every part of the South, met at Baltimore, the capital city of the Slave State of Maryland.

Northern Abolitionism was, however, quite a different thing. It owed its inception to William Lloyd Garrison, one of those enthusiasts who profoundly affect history solely by the tenacity with which they hold to and continually enforce a burning personal conviction. But for that tenacity and the unquestionable influence which his conviction exerted upon men, he would be a rather ridiculous figure, for he was almost every sort of crank—certainly a non-resister, and, I think, a vegetarian and teetotaller as well. But his burning conviction was the immorality of Slavery; and by this he meant something quite other than was meant by Jefferson or later by Lincoln. When these great men spoke of Slavery as a wrong, they regarded it as a social and political wrong, an evil and unjust system which the community as a community ought as soon as possible to abolish and replace by a better. But by Garrison slave-holding was accounted a personal sin like murder or adultery. The owner of slaves, unless he at once emancipated them at whatever cost to his own fortunes, was by that fact a wicked man, and if he professed a desire for ultimate extinction of the institution, that only made him a hypocrite as well. This, of course, was absurd; fully as absurd as the suggestion sometimes made in regard to wealthy Socialists, that if they were consistent they would give up all their property to the community. A man living under an economic system reposing on Slavery can no more help availing himself of its fruits than in a capitalist society he can help availing himself of capitalist organization. Obviously, unless he is a multi-millionaire, he cannot buy up all the slaves in the State and set them free, while, if he buys some and treats them with justice and humanity, he is clearly making things better for them than if he left them in the hands of masters possibly less scrupulous. But, absurd as the thesis was, Garrison pushed it to its wildest logical conclusions. No Christian Church ought, he maintained, to admit a slave-owner to communion. No honest man ought to count a slave-owner among his friends. No political connection with slave-owners was tolerable. The Union, since it involved such a connection, was "a Covenant with Death and an Agreement with Hell." Garrison publicly burnt the Constitution of the United States in the streets of Boston.

Abolitionist propaganda of this kind was naturally possible only in the North. Apart from all questions of self-interest, no Southerner, no reasonable person who knew anything about the South, though the knowledge might be as superficial and the indignation against Slavery as intense as was Mrs. Beecher Stowe's, could possibly believe the proposition that all Southern slave-owners were cruel and unjust men. But that was not all. Garrison's movement killed Southern Abolitionism. It may, perhaps, be owned that the Southern movement was not bearing much visible fruit. There was just a grain of truth, it may be, in Garrison's bitter and exaggerated taunt that the Southerners were ready enough to be Abolitionists if they were allowed "to assign the guilt of Slavery to a past generation, and the duty of emancipation to a future generation." Nevertheless, that movement was on the right lines. It was on Southern ground that the battle for the peaceful extinction of Slavery ought to have been fought. The intervention of the North would probably in any case have been resented; accompanied by a solemn accusation of specific personal immorality it was maddeningly provocative, for it could not but recall to the South the history of the issue as it stood between the sections.

For the North had been the original slave-traders. The African Slave Trade had been their particular industry. Boston itself, when the new ethical denunciation came, had risen to prosperity on the profits of that abominable traffic. Further, even in the act of clearing its own borders of Slavery, the North had dumped its negroes on the South. "What," asked the Southerners, "could exceed the effrontery of men who reproach us with grave personal sin in owning property which they themselves have sold us and the price of which is at this moment in their pockets?"

On a South thus angered and smarting under what is felt to be undeserved reproach, yet withal somewhat uneasy in its conscience, for its public opinion in the main still thought Slavery wrong, fell the powerful voice of a great Southerner proclaiming it "a positive good." Calhoun's defence of the institution on its merits probably did much to encourage the South to adopt a more defiant tone in place of the old apologies for delay in dealing with a difficult problem—apologies which sounded over-tame and almost humiliating in face of the bold invectives now hurled at the slave-owners by Northern writers and speakers. I cannot, indeed, find that Calhoun's specific arguments, forcible as they were—and they are certainly the most cogent that can be used in defence of such a thesis—were particularly popular, or, in fact, were ever used by any but himself. Perhaps there was a well-founded feeling that they proved too much. For Calhoun's case was as strong for white servitude as for black: it was a defence, not especially of Negro Slavery, but of what Mr. Belloc has called "the Servile State." More general, in the later Southern defences, was the appeal to religious sanctions, which in a nation Protestant and mainly Puritan in its traditions naturally became an appeal to Bible texts. St. Paul was claimed as a supporter of the Fugitive Slave Law on the strength of his dealings of Onesimus. But the favourite text was that which condemns Ham (assumed to be the ancestor of the Negro race) to be "a servant of servants." The Abolitionist text-slingers were not a whit more intelligent; indeed, I think it must be admitted that on the whole the pro-Slavery men had the best of this absurd form of controversy. Apart from isolated texts they had on their side the really unquestionable fact that both Old and New Testaments describe a civilization based on Slavery, and that in neither is there anything like a clear pronouncement that such a basis is immoral or displeasing to God. It is true that in the Gospels are to be found general principles or, at any rate, indications of general principles, which afterwards, in the hands of the Church, proved largely subversive of the servile organization of society; but that is a matter of historical, not of Biblical testimony, and would, if followed out, have led both Northern and Southern controversialists further than either of them wanted to go.

It would, however, be hasty, I think, to affirm that even to the very end of these processes a majority of Southerners thought with Calhoun that Slavery was "a positive good." The furthest, perhaps, that most of them went was the proposition that it represented the only relationship in which white and black races could safely live together in the same community—a proposition which was countenanced by Jefferson and, to a considerable extent at least, by Lincoln. To the last the full Jeffersonian view of the inherent moral and social evil of Slavery was held by many Southerners who were none the less wholeheartedly on the side of their own section in the sectional dispute. The chief soldier of the South in the war in which that dispute culminated both held that view and acted consistently upon it.

On the North the effect of the new propaganda was different, but there also it tended to increase the antagonism of the sections. The actual Abolitionists of the school of Garrison were neither numerous nor popular. Even in Boston, where they were strongest, they were often mobbed and their meetings broken up. In Illinois, a Northern State, one of them, Lovejoy, was murdered by the crowd. Such exhibitions of popular anger were not, of course, due to any love of Slavery. The Abolitionists were disliked in the North, not as enemies of Slavery but as enemies of the Union and the Constitution, which they avowedly were. But while the extreme doctrine of Garrison and his friends met with little acceptance, the renewed agitation of the question did bring into prominence the unquestionable fact that the great mass of sober Northern opinion thought Slavery a wrong, and in any controversy between master and slave was inclined to sympathize with the slave. This feeling was probably somewhat strengthened by the publication in 1852 and the subsequent huge international sale of Mrs. Stowe's "Uncle Tom's Cabin." The practical effect of this book on history is generally exaggerated, partially in consequence of the false view which would make of the Civil War a crusade against Slavery. But a certain effect it undoubtedly had. To such natural sympathy in the main, and not, as the South believed, to sectional jealousy and deliberate bad faith, must be attributed those "Personal Liberty Laws" by which in many Northern States the provision of the Constitution guaranteeing the return of fugitive slaves was virtually nullified. For some of the provisions of those laws an arguable constitutional case might be made, particularly for the provision which assured a jury trial to the escaped slave. The Negro, it was urged, was either a citizen or a piece of property. If he were a citizen, the Constitution expressly safeguarded him against imprisonment without such a trial. If, on the other hand, he were property, then he was property of the value of more than $50, and in cases where property of that value was concerned, a jury was also legally required. If two masters laid claim to the same Negro the dispute between them would have to be settled by a jury. Why should it not be so where a master claimed to own a Negro and the Negro claimed to own himself? Nevertheless, the effect, and to a great extent the intention, of these laws was to defeat the claim of bonâ fide owners to fugitive slaves, and as such they violated at least the spirit of the constitutional compact. They therefore afforded a justification for Clay's proposal to transfer the power of recovering fugitive slaves to the Federal authorities. But they also afforded an even stronger justification for Lincoln's doubt as to whether the American Commonwealth could exist permanently half slave and half free.

Finally, among the causes which made a sectional struggle the more inevitable must be counted one to which allusion has already been made in connection with the Presidential Election of 1848—the increasingly patent unreality of the existing party system. I have already said that a party system can endure only if it becomes unreal, and it may be well here to make clear how this is so.

Fundamental debates in a Commonwealth must be settled, or the Commonwealth dies. How, for instance, could England have endured if, throughout the eighteenth century, the Stuarts had alternately been restored and deposed every seven years? Or, again, suppose a dispute so fundamental as that between Collectivism and the philosophy of private property. How could a nation continue to exist if a Collectivist Government spent five years in attempting the concentration of all the means of production in the hands of the State and an Anti-Collectivist Government spent the next five years in dispersing them again, and so on for a generation? American history, being the history of a democracy, illustrates this truth with peculiar force. The controversy between Jefferson and Hamilton was about realities. The Jeffersonians won, and the Federalist Party disappeared. The controversy between Jackson and the Whigs was originally also real. Jackson won, and the Whigs would have shared the fate of the Federalists if they stood by their original principles and refused to accept the consequences of the Jacksonian Revolution. As a fact, however, they did accept these consequences and so the party system endured, but at the expense of its reality. There was no longer any fundamental difference of principle dividing Whigs from Democrats: they were divided arbitrarily on passing questions of policy, picked up at random and changing from year to year. Meanwhile a new reality was dividing the nation from top to bottom, but was dividing it in a dangerously sectional fashion, and for that reason patriotism as well as the requirements of professional politics induced men to veil it as much as might be. Yet its presence made the professional play-acting more and more unmeaning and intolerable.

It was this state of things which made possible the curious interlude of the "Know-Nothing" movement, which cannot be ignored, though it is a kind of digression from the main line of historical development. The United States had originally been formed by the union of certain seceding British colonies, but already, as a sort of neutral ground in the New World, their territory had become increasingly the meeting-place of streams of emigration from various European countries. As was natural, a certain amount of mutual jealousy and antagonism was making itself apparent as between the old colonial population and the newer elements. The years following 1847 showed an intensification of the problem due to a particular cause. That year saw the Black Famine in Ireland and its aggravation by the insane pedantry and folly of the British Government. Innumerable Irish families, driven from the land of their birth, found a refuge within the borders of the Republic. They brought with them their native genius for politics, which for the first time found free outlet in a democracy. They were accustomed to act together and they were soon a formidable force. This force was regarded by many as a menace, and the sense of menace was greatly increased by the fact that these immigrants professed a religious faith which the Puritan tradition of the States in which they generally settled held in peculiar abhorrence.

The "Know-Nothings" were a secret society and owed that name to the fact that members, when questioned, professed to know nothing of the ultimate objects of the organization to which they belonged. They proclaimed a general hostility to indiscriminate immigration, for which a fair enough case might be made, but they concentrated their hostility specially on the Irish Catholic element. I have never happened upon any explanation of the secrecy with which they deliberately surrounded their aims. It seems to me, however, that a possible explanation lies on the surface. If all they had wanted had been to restrict or regulate immigration, it was an object which could be avowed as openly as the advocacy of a tariff or of the restriction of Slavery in a territory. But if, as their practical operations and the general impression concerning their intentions seem to indicate, the real object of those who directed the movement was the exclusion from public trust of persons professing the Catholic religion, then, of course, it was an object which could not be avowed without bringing them into open conflict with the Constitution, which expressly forbade such differentiation on religious grounds.

Between the jealousy of new immigrants felt by the descendants of the original colonists and the religious antagonism of Puritan New England to the Catholic population growing up within its borders; intensified by the absence of any genuine issue of debate between the official candidates, the Know-Nothings secured at the Congressional Election of 1854 a quite startling measure of success. But such success had no promise of permanence. The movement lived long enough to deal a death-blow to the Whig Party, already practically annihilated by the Presidential Election of

1852, wherein the Democrats, benefiting by the division and confusion of their enemies, easily returned their candidate, Franklin Pierce.

It is now necessary to return to the Compromise of 1850, hailed at the time as a final settlement of the sectional quarrel and accepted as such in the platforms of both the regular political parties. That Compromise was made by one generation. It was to be administered by another. Henry Clay, as has already been noted, lived long enough to enjoy his triumph, not long enough to outlive it. Before a year was out the grave had closed over Webster. Calhoun had already passed away, bequeathing to posterity his last hopeless protest against the triumph of all that he most feared. Congress was full of new faces. In the Senate among the rising men was Seward of New York, a Northern Whig, whose speech in opposition to the Fugitive Slave clause in Clay's Compromise had given him the leadership of the growing Anti-Slavery opinion of the North. He was soon to be joined by Charles Sumner of Massachusetts, null in judgment, a pedant without clearness of thought or vision, but gifted with a copious command of all the rhetoric of sectional hate. The place of Calhoun in the leadership of the South had been more and more assumed by a soldier who had been forced to change his profession by reason of a crippling wound received at Monterey. Thenceforward he had achieved an increasing repute in politics, an excellent orator, with the sensitive face rather of a poet than of a man of affairs, vivid, sincere and careful of honour, though often uncertain in temper and judgment: Jefferson Davis of Mississippi. But for the moment none of these so dominated politics as did the Westerner whom Illinois had recently sent to the Senate—Stephen Douglas, surnamed "the Little Giant."

The physical impression which men seem to have received most forcibly concerning Douglas, and which was perhaps responsible for his nickname, was the contrast between his diminutive stature and the enormous power of his voice—trained no doubt in addressing the monster meetings of the West, where tens of thousands crowded everywhere to hear him speak. Along with this went the sense of an overwhelming vitality about the man; he seemed tingling with excess of life. His strong, square, handsome face bore a striking resemblance to that of Napoleon Bonaparte, and there was really something Napoleonic in his boldness, his instinctive sense of leadership, and his power of dominating weaker men. Withal he was a Westerner—perhaps the most typical and complete Westerner in American history, for half of Clay was of Washington, and Jackson and Lincoln were too great to be purely sectional. He had a Westerner's democratic feeling and a Westerner's enthusiasm for the national idea. But, especially, he had a peculiarly Western vision which is the key to a strangely misunderstood but at bottom very consistent political career.

This man, more than any other, fills American history during the decade that intervened between the death of Clay and the election of Lincoln. That decade is also full of the ever-increasing prominence of the Slavery Question. It is natural, therefore, to read Douglas's career in terms of that question, and historians, doing so, have been bewildered by its apparent inconsistency. Unable to trace any connecting principle in his changes of front, they have put them down to interested motives, and then equally unable to show that he himself had anything to gain from them, have been forced to attribute them to mere caprice. The fact is that Douglas cannot be understood along those lines at all. To understand him one must remember that he was indifferent on the Slavery Question, "did not care," as he said, "whether Slavery was voted up or voted down," but cared immensely for something else. That something else was the Westward expansion of the American nation till it should bridge the gulf between the two oceans. The thought of all those millions of acres of virgin land, the property of the American Commonwealth, crying out for the sower and the reaper, rode his imagination as the wrongs of the Negro slave rode the imagination of Garrison. There is a reality about the comparison which few will recognize, for this demagogue, whom men devoted to the Slavery issue thought cynical, had about him also something of the fanatic. He could forget all else in his one enthusiasm. It is the key to his career from the day when he entered Congress clamouring for Oregon or war with England to the day when he died appealing for soldiers to save the Union in the name of its common inheritance. And it is surely not surprising that, for the fulfilment of his vision, he was willing to conciliate the slave-owners, when one remembers that in earlier days he had been willing to conciliate the Mormons. Douglas stands out in history, as we now see it, as the man who by the Kansas and Nebraska Bill upset the tottering Compromise of 1850. Why did he so upset it? Not certainly because he wished to reopen the Slavery Question; nothing is less likely, for it was a question in which he avowedly felt no interest and the raising of which was bound to unsettle his plans. Not from personal ambition; for those who accuse him of having acted as he did for private advantage have to admit that in fact he lost by it. Why then did he so act? I think we shall get to the root of the matter if we assume that his motive in introducing his celebrated Bill was just the avowed motive of that Bill and no other. It was to set up territorial governments in Kansas and Nebraska. Douglas's mind was full of schemes for facilitating the march of American civilization westward, for piercing the prairies with roads and railways, for opening up communications with Oregon and the Pacific Slope. Kansas and Nebraska were then the outposts of such expansion. Naturally he was eager to develop them, to encourage squatters to settle within their borders, and for that purpose to give them an assured position and a form of stable government. If he could have effected this without touching the Slavery Question I think that he would gladly have done so. And, as a matter of fact, the Nebraska Bill as originally drafted by him was innocent of the clause which afterwards caused so much controversy. That clause was forced on him by circumstances.

The greater part of the territory which Douglas proposed to develop lay within the limits of the Louisiana Purchase and north of latitude 36° 30'. It was therefore free soil by virtue of the Missouri Compromise. But the Southerners now disputed the validity of that Congressional enactment, and affirmed their right under the Constitution as they interpreted it to take and hold their "property" in any territories belonging to the United States. Douglas had some reason to fear Southern opposition to his plans on other grounds, for the South would naturally have preferred that the main road to the Pacific Slope should run from Tennessee through Arizona and New Mexico to California. If Kansas and Nebraska were declared closed against slave property their opposition would be given a rallying cry and would certainly harden. Douglas therefore proposed a solution which would at any rate get rid of the Slavery debate so far as Congress was concerned, and which had also a democratic ring about it acceptable to his Western instincts and, as he hoped, to his Western following. The new doctrine, called by him that of "Popular Sovereignty" and by his critics that of "Squatter Sovereignty," amounted to this: that the existing settlers in the territories concerned should, in the act of forming their territorial governments, decide whether they would admit or exclude Slavery.

It was a plausible doctrine; but one can only vindicate Douglas's motives, as I have endeavoured to do, at the expense of his judgment, for his policy had all the consequences which he most desired to avoid. It produced two effects which between them brought the sectional quarrel to the point of heat at which Civil War became possible and perhaps inevitable. It threw the new territories down as stakes to be scrambled for by the rival sections, and it created by reaction a new party, necessarily sectional, having for its object the maintenance and reinforcement of the Missouri Compromise. It will be well to take the two points separately.

Up to the passing of Kansas and Nebraska Law, these territories had been populated exactly as such frontier communities had theretofore been populated, by immigrants from all the States and from Europe who mingled freely, felt no ill-will to each other, and were early consolidated by the fact of proximity into a homogeneous community. But from the moment of its passage the whole situation was altered. It became a political object to both sections to get a majority in Kansas. Societies were formed in Boston and other Northern cities to finance emigrants who proposed to settle there. The South was equally active, and, to set off against the disadvantage of a less fluid population, had the advantage of the immediate proximity of the Slave State of Missouri. Such a contest, even if peaceably conducted, was not calculated to promote either the reconciliation of the sections or the solidarity and stability of the new community. But in a frontier community without a settled government, and with a population necessarily armed for self-defence, it was not likely to be peaceably conducted. Nor was it. For years Kansas was the scene of what can only be described as spasmodic civil war. The Free Soil settlement of Lawrence was, after some bloodshed, seized and burnt by "border ruffians," as they were called, from Missouri. The North cried out loudly against "Southern outrages," but it is fair to say that the outrages were not all on one side. In fact, the most amazing crime in the record of Kansas was committed by a Northerner, the notorious John Brown. This man presents rather a pathological than a historical problem. He had considerable military talents, and a curious power of persuading men. But he was certainly mad. A New England Puritan by extraction, he was inflamed on the subject of Slavery by a fanaticism somewhat similar to that of Garrison. But while Garrison blended his Abolitionism with the Quaker dogma of Non-Resistance, Brown blended his with the ethics of a seventeenth-century Covenanter who thought himself divinely commanded to hew the Amalakites in pieces before the Lord. In obedience to his peculiar code of morals he not only murdered Southern immigrants without provocation, but savagely mutilated their bodies. If his act did not prove him insane his apology would. In defence of his conduct he explained that "disguised as a surveyor" he had interviewed his victims and discovered that every one of them had "committed murder in his heart."

The other effect of the Kansas-Nebraska policy was the rise of a new party formed for the single purpose of opposing it. Anti-Slavery parties had already come into being from time to time in the North, and had at different times exerted a certain influence on elections, but they made little headway because they were composed mainly of extremists, and their aim appeared to moderate men inconsistent with the Constitution. The attack on the time-honoured Missouri Compromise rallied such men to the opposition, for it appeared to them clearly that theirs was now the legal, constitutional, and even conservative side, and that the Slave Power was now making itself responsible for a revolutionary change to its own advantage.

Nor was the change on the whole unjust. The programme to which the South committed itself after the direction of its policy fell from the hands of Calhoun was one which the North could not fail to resent. It involved the tearing up of all the compromises so elaborately devised and so nicely balanced, and it aimed at making Slavery legal certainly in all the new territories and possibly even in the Free States. It was, indeed, argued that this did not involve any aggravating of the evil of Slavery, if it were an evil. The argument will be found very ingeniously stated in the book which Jefferson Davis subsequently wrote—professedly a history of the Southern Confederacy, really rather an Apologia pro Vita Sua. Davis argues that since the African Slave Trade was prohibited, there could be no increase in the number of slaves save by the ordinary process of propagation. The opening of Kansas to Slavery would not therefore mean that there would be more slaves. It would merely mean that men already and in any case slaves would be living in Kansas instead of in Tennessee; and, it is further suggested, that the taking of a Negro slave from Tennessee, where Slavery was rooted and normal, to Kansas, where it was new and exceptional, would be a positive advantage to him as giving him a much better chance of emancipation. The argument reads plausibly enough, but it is, like so much of Davis's book, out of touch with realities. Plainly it would make all the difference in the world whether the practice of, say, the Catholic religion were permitted only in Lancashire or were lawful throughout England, and that even though there were no conversions, and the same Catholics who had previously lived in Lancashire lived wherever they chose. The former provision would imply that the British Government disapproved of the Catholic religion, and would tolerate it only where it was obliged to do so. The latter would indicate an attitude of indifference towards it. Those who disapproved of Slavery naturally wished it to remain a sectional thing and objected to its being made national. But the primary feeling was that it was the South that had broken the truce. The Northerners had much justification in saying that their opponents, if not the aggressors in the Civil War, were at least the aggressors in the controversy of which the Civil War was the ultimate outcome.

Under the impulse of such feelings a party was formed which, adopting—without, it must be owned, any particular appropriateness—the old Jeffersonian name of "Republican," took the field at the Presidential Election of 1856. Its real leader was Seward of New York, but it was thought that electioneering exigencies would be better served by the selection of Captain Frémont of California, who, as a wandering discoverer and soldier of fortune, could be made a picturesque figure in the public eye. Later, when Frémont was entrusted with high military command he was discovered to be neither capable nor honest, but in 1856 he made as effective a figure as any candidate could have done, and the results were on the whole encouraging to the new party. Buchanan, the Democratic candidate, was elected, but the Republicans showed greater strength in the Northern States than had been anticipated. The Whig Party was at this election finally annihilated.

The Republicans might have done even better had the decision of the Supreme Court on an issue which made clear the full scope of the new Southern claim been known just before instead of just after the election. This decision was the judgment of Roger Taney, whom we have seen at an earlier date as Jackson's Attorney-General and Secretary to the Treasury, in the famous Dred Scott case. Dred Scott was a Negro slave owned by a doctor of Missouri. His master had taken him for a time into the free territory of Minnesota, afterwards bringing him back to his original State. Dred Scott was presumably not in a position to resent either operation, nor is it likely that he desired to do so. Later, however, he was induced to bring an action in the Federal Courts against his master on the ground that by being taken into free territory he had ipso facto ceased to be a slave. Whether he was put up to this by the Anti-Slavery party, or whether—for his voluntary manumission after the case was settled seems to suggest that possibility—the whole case was planned by the Southerners to get a decision of the territorial question in their favour, might be an interesting subject for inquiry. I can express no opinion upon it. The main fact is that Taney, supported by a bare majority of the judges, not only decided for the master, but laid down two important principles. One was that no Negro could be an American citizen or sue in the American courts; the other and more important that the Constitution guaranteed the right of the slave-holder to his slaves in all United States territories, and that Congress had no power to annul this right. The Missouri Compromise was therefore declared invalid.

Much of the Northern outcry against Taney seems to me unjust. He was professedly a judge pronouncing on the law, and in giving his ruling he used language which seems to imply that his ethical judgment, if he had been called upon to give it, would have been quite different. But, though he was a great lawyer as well as a sincere patriot, and though his opinion is therefore entitled to respect, especially from a foreigner ignorant of American law, it is impossible to feel that his decision was not open to criticism on purely legal grounds. It rested upon the assertion that property in slaves was "explicitly recognized" by the Constitution. If this were so it would seem to follow that since under the Constitution a man's property could not be taken from him "without due process of law" he could not without such process lose his slaves. But was it so? It is difficult, for a layman at any rate, to find in the Constitution any such "explicit recognition." The slave is there called a "person" and defined as a "person bound to service or labour" while his master is spoken of as one "to whom such service or labour may be due." This language seems to suggest the relation of creditor and debtor rather than that of owner and owned. At any rate, the Republicans refused to accept the judgment except so far as it determined the individual case of Dred Scott, taking up in regard to Taney's decision the position which, in accordance with Taney's own counsel, Jackson had taken up in regard to the decision which affirmed the constitutionality of a bank.

Douglas impetuously accepted the decision and, forgetting the precedent of his own hero Jackson, denounced all who challenged it as wicked impugners of lawful authority. Yet, in fact, the decision was as fatal to his own policy as to that of the Republicans. It really made "Popular Sovereignty" a farce, for what was the good of leaving the question of Slavery to be settled by the territories when the Supreme Court declared that they could only lawfully settle it one way? This obvious point was not lost upon the acute intelligence of one man, a citizen of Douglas's own State and one of the "moderates" who had joined the Republican Party on the Nebraska issue.

Abraham Lincoln was by birth a Southerner and a native of Kentucky, a fact which he never forgot and of which he was exceedingly proud. After the wandering boyhood of a pioneer and a period of manual labour as a "rail-splitter" he had settled in Illinois, where he had picked up his own education and become a successful lawyer. He had sat in the House of Representatives as a Whig from 1846 to 1848, the period of the Mexican

War, during which he had acted with the main body of his party, neither defending the whole of the policy which led to the war nor opposing it to the extent of refusing supplies for its prosecution. He had voted, as he said, for the Wilmot Proviso "as good as fifty times," and had made a moderate proposition in relation to Slavery in the District of Columbia, for which Garrison's Liberator had pilloried him as "the Slave-Hound of Illinois." He had not offered himself for re-election in 1848. Though an opponent of Slavery on principle, he had accepted the Compromise of 1850, including its Fugitive Slave Clauses, as a satisfactory all- round settlement, and was, by his own account, losing interest in politics when the action of Douglas and its consequences called into activity a genius which few, if any, had suspected.

A man like Lincoln cannot be adequately described in the short space available in such a book as this. His externals are well appreciated, his tall figure, his powerful ugliness, his awkward strength, his racy humour, his fits of temperamental melancholy; well appreciated also his firmness, wisdom and patriotism. But if we wish to grasp the peculiar quality which makes him almost unique among great men of action, we shall perhaps find the key in the fact that his favourite private recreation was working out for himself the propositions of Euclid. He had a mind not only peculiarly just but singularly logical, one might really say singularly mathematical. His reasoning is always so good as to make his speeches in contrast to the finest rhetorical oratory a constant delight to those who have something of the same type of mind. In this he had a certain affinity with Jefferson. But while in Jefferson's case the tendency has been to class him, in spite of his great practical achievements, as a mere theorizer, in Lincoln it has been rather to acclaim him as a strong, rough, practical man, and to ignore the lucidity of thought which was the most marked quality of his mind. He was eminently practical; and he was not less but more practical for realizing the supreme practical importance of first principles. According to his first principles Slavery was wrong. It was wrong because it was inconsistent with the doctrines enunciated in the Declaration of Independence in which he firmly believed. Really good thinking like Lincoln's is necessarily outside time, and therefore he was not at all affected by the mere use and wont which had tended to reconcile so many to Slavery. Yet he was far from being a fanatical Abolitionist. Because Slavery was wrong it did not follow that it should be immediately uprooted. But it did follow that whatever treatment it received should be based on the assumption of its wrongness. An excellent illustration of his attitude of mind will be found in the exact point at which he drew the line. For the merely sentimental opponent of Slavery, the Fugitive Slave Law made a much more moving appeal to the imagination than the extension of Slavery in the territories. Yet Lincoln accepted the Fugitive Slave Law. He supported it because, as he put it, it was "so nominated in the bond." It was part of the terms which the Fathers of the Republic, disapproving of Slavery, had yet made with Slavery. He also, disapproving of Slavery, could honour those terms. But it was otherwise in regard to the territorial controversy. Douglas openly treated Slavery not as an evil difficult to cure, but as a thing merely indifferent. Southern statesmen were beginning to echo Calhoun's definition of it as "a positive good." On the top of this came Taney's decision making the right to own slaves a fundamental part of the birthright of an American citizen. This was much more important than the most drastic Fugitive Slave Law, for it indicated a change in first principles.

This is the true meaning of his famous use of the text "a house divided against itself cannot stand," and his deduction that the Union could not "permanently exist half slave and half free." That it had so existed for eighty years he admitted, but it had so existed, he considered, because the Government had acted on the first principle that Slavery was an evil to be tolerated but curbed, and the public mind had "rested in the belief that it was in process of ultimate extinction." It was now, as it seemed, proposed to abandon that principle and assume it to be good or at least indifferent. If that principle were accepted there was nothing to prevent the institution being introduced not only into the free territories but into the Free States. And indeed the reasoning of Taney's judgment, though not the judgment itself, really seemed to point to such a conclusion. Lincoln soon became the leader of the Illinois Republicans, and made ready to match himself against Douglas when the "Little Giant" should next seek re-election.

Meanwhile a new development of the Kansas affair had split the Democratic Party and ranged Senator Douglas and President Buchanan on opposite sides in an open quarrel. The majority of the population now settled in Kansas was of Northern origin, for the conditions of life in the North were much more favourable to emigration into new lands than those of the slave-owning States. Had a free ballot been taken of the genuine settlers there would certainly have been a large majority against Slavery. But in the scarcely disguised civil war into which the competition for Kansas had developed, the Slave-State party had the support of bands of "border ruffians" from the neighbouring State, who could appear as citizens of Kansas one day and return to their homes in Missouri the next. With such aid that party succeeded in silencing the voices of the Free State men while they held a bogus Convention at Lecompton, consisting largely of men who were not really inhabitants of Kansas at all, adopted a Slave Constitution, and under it applied for admission to the Union. Buchanan, who, though a Northerner, was strongly biased in favour of the Slavery party, readily accepted this as a bonâ fide application, and recommended Congress to accede to it. Douglas was much better informed as to how things were actually going in Kansas, and he felt that if the Lecompton Constitution were acknowledged his favourite doctrine of Popular Sovereignty would be justly covered with odium and contempt. He therefore set himself against the President, and his personal followers combined with the Republicans to defeat the Lecompton proposition.

The struggle in Illinois thus became for Douglas a struggle for political life or death. At war with the President and with a large section of his party, if he could not keep a grip on his own State his political career was over. Nor did he underrate his Republican opponent; indeed, he seems to have had a keener perception of the great qualities which were hidden under Lincoln's rough and awkward exterior than anyone else at that time exhibited. When he heard of his candidature he looked grave. "He is the strongest man of his party," he said, "and thoroughly honest. It will take us all our time to beat him."

It did. Douglas was victorious, but only narrowly and after a hard-fought contest. The most striking feature of that contest was the series of

Lincoln-Douglas debates in which, by an interesting innovation in electioneering, the two candidates for the Senatorship contended face to face in the principal political centres of the State. In reading these debates one is impressed not only with the ability of both combatants, but with their remarkable candour, good temper and even magnanimity. It is very seldom, if ever, that either displays malice or fails in dignity and courtesy to his opponent. When one remembers the white heat of political and sectional rivalry at that time—when one recalls some of Sumner's speeches in the Senate, not to mention the public beating which they brought on him—it must be confessed that the fairness with which the two great Illinois champions fought each other was highly to the honour of both.

Where the controversy turned on practical or legal matters the combatants were not ill-matched, and both scored many telling points. When the general philosophy of government came into the question Lincoln's great superiority in seriousness and clarity of thought was at once apparent. A good example of this will be found in their dispute as to the true meaning of the Declaration of Independence. Douglas denied that the expression "all men" could be meant to include Negroes. It only referred to "British subjects in this continent being equal to British subjects born and residing in Great Britain." Lincoln instantly knocked out his adversary by reading the amended version of the Declaration: "We hold these truths to be self-evident, that all British subjects who were on this Continent eighty-one years ago were created equal to all British subjects born and then residing in Great Britain." This was more than a clever debating point. It was a really crushing exposure of intellectual error. The mere use of the words "truths" and "self-evident" and their patently ridiculous effect in the Douglas version proves conclusively which interpreter was nearest to the mind of Thomas Jefferson. And the sense of his superiority is increased when, seizing his opportunity, he proceeds to offer a commentary on the Declaration in its bearing on the Negro Question so incomparably lucid and rational that Jefferson himself might have penned it.

In the following year an incident occurred which is of some historical importance, not because, as is sometimes vaguely suggested, it did anything whatever towards the emancipation of the slaves, but because it certainly increased, not unnaturally, the anger and alarm of the South. Old John Brown had suspended for a time his programme of murder and mutilation in Kansas and returned to New England, where he approached a number of wealthy men of known Abolitionist sympathies whom he persuaded to provide him with money for the purpose of raising a slave insurrection. That he should have been able to induce men of sanity and repute to support him in so frantic and criminal an enterprise says much for the personal magnetism which by all accounts was characteristic of this extraordinary man. Having obtained his supplies, he collected a band of nineteen men, including his own sons, with which he proposed to make an attack on the Government arsenal at Harper's Ferry in Virginia, which, when captured, he intended to convert into a place of refuge and armament for fugitive slaves and a nucleus for the general Negro rising which he expected his presence to produce. The plan was as mad as its author, yet it is characteristic of a peculiar quality of his madness that he conducted the actual operations not only with amazing audacity but with remarkable skill, and the first part of his programme was successfully carried out. The arsenal was surprised, and its sleeping and insufficient garrison overpowered. Here, however, his success ended. No fugitives joined him, and there was not the faintest sign of a slave rising. In fact, as Lincoln afterwards said, the Negroes, ignorant as they were, seem to have had the sense to see that the thing would come to nothing. As soon as Virginia woke up to what had happened troops were sent to recapture the arsenal. Brown and his men fought bravely, but the issue could not be in doubt. Several of Brown's followers and all his sons were killed. He himself was wounded, captured, brought to trial and very properly hanged—unless we take the view that he should rather have been confined in an asylum. He died with the heroism of a fanatic. Emerson and Longfellow talked some amazing nonsense about him which is frequently quoted. Lincoln talked some excellent sense which is hardly ever quoted. And the Republican

Party was careful to insert in its platform a vigorous denunciation of his Harper's Ferry exploit.

Both sides now began to prepare for the Presidential Election of 1860. The selection of a Republican candidate was debated at a large and stormy Convention held in Chicago. Seward was the most prominent Republican politician, but he had enemies, and for many reasons it was thought that his adoption would mean the loss of available votes. Chase was the favourite of the Radical wing of the party, but it was feared that the selection of a man who was thought to lean to Abolitionism would alienate the moderates. To secure the West was an important element in the electoral problem, and this, together with the zealous backing of his own State, within whose borders the Convention met, and the fact that he was recognized as a "moderate," probably determined the choice of Lincoln. It does not appear that any of those who chose him knew that they were choosing a great man. Some acute observers had doubtless noted the ability he displayed in his debates with Douglas, but in the main he seems to have been recommended to the Chicago Convention, as afterwards to the country, mainly on the strength of his humble origin, his skill as a rail-splitter, and his alleged ability to bend a poker between his fingers.

While the Republicans were thus choosing their champion, much fiercer quarrels were rending the opposite party, whose Convention met at Charleston. The great majority of the Northern delegates were for choosing Douglas as candidate, and fighting on a programme of "Popular Sovereignty." But the Southerners would not hear of either candidate or programme. His attitude on the Lecompton business was no longer the only count against Douglas. The excellent controversial strategy of Lincoln had forced from him during the Illinois debates an interpretation of "Popular Sovereignty" equally offensive to the South. Lincoln had asked him how a territory whose inhabitants desired to exclude Slavery could, if the Dred Scott decision were to be accepted, lawfully exclude it. Douglas had answered that it could for practical purposes exclude it by withholding legislation in its support and adopting "unfriendly legislation" towards it. Lincoln at once pointed out that Douglas was virtually advising a territorial government to nullify a judgment of the Supreme Court. The cry was caught up in the South and was fatal to Douglas's hopes of support from that section.

The Charleston Convention, split into two hostile sections, broke up without a decision. The Douglas men, who were the majority, met at Baltimore, acclaimed him as Democratic candidate and adopted his programme. The dissentients held another Convention at Charleston and adopted Breckinridge with a programme based upon the widest interpretation of the Dred Scott judgment. To add to the multiplicity of voices the rump of the old Whig Party, calling themselves the party of "the Union, the Constitution and the Laws," nominated Everett and Bell.

The split in the Democratic Party helped the Republicans in another than the obvious fashion of giving them the chance of slipping in over the heads of divided opponents. It helped their moral position in the North. It deprived the Democrats of their most effective appeal to Union-loving men—the assertion that their party was national while the Republicans were sectional. For Douglas was now practically as sectional as Lincoln. As little as Lincoln could he command any considerable support south of the Potomac. Moreover, the repudiation of Douglas seemed to many Northerners to prove that the South was arrogant and unreasonable beyond possibility of parley or compromise. The wildest of her protagonists could not pretend that Douglas was a "Black Abolitionist," or that he meditated any assault upon the domestic institutions of the Southern States. If the Southerners could not work with him, with what Northerner, not utterly and unconditionally subservient to them, could they work? It seemed to many that the choice lay between a vigorous protest now and the acceptance of the numerically superior North of a permanently inferior position in the Confederation.

In his last electoral campaign the "Little Giant" put up a plucky fight against his enemies North and South. But he had met his Waterloo. In the whole Union he carried but one State and half of another. The South was almost solid for Breckinridge. The North and West, from New England to California, was as solid for Lincoln. A few border States gave their votes for Everett. But, owing to the now overwhelming numerical superiority of the Free States, the Republicans had in the Electoral College a decided majority over all other parties.

Thus was Abraham Lincoln elected President of the United States. But many who voted for him had hardly recorded their votes before they became a little afraid of the thing they had done. Through the whole continent ran the ominous whisper: "What will the South do?"

And men held their breath, waiting for what was to follow.

Chapter 9

SECESSION AND CIVIL WAR

It is a significant fact that the news of Lincoln's election which caused so much dismay and searching of heart throughout the Southern and Border States was received with defiant cheers in Charleston, the chief port of South Carolina. Those cheers meant that there was one Southern State that was ready to answer on the instant the whispered question which was troubling the North, and to answer it by no means in a whisper.

South Carolina occupied a position not exactly parallel to that of any other State. Her peculiarity was not merely that her citizens held the dogma of State Sovereignty. All the States from Virginia southward, at any rate, held that dogma in one form or another. But South Carolina held it in an extreme form, and habitually acted on it in an extreme fashion. It is not historically true to say that she learnt her political creed from Calhoun. It would be truer to say that he learnt it from her. But it may be that the leadership of a man of genius, who could codify and expound her thought, and whose bold intellect shrank from no conclusion to which his principles led, helped to give a peculiar simplicity and completeness to her interpretation of the dogma in question. The peculiarity of her attitude must be expressed by saying that most Americans had two loyalties, while the South Carolinian had only one. Whether in the last resort a citizen should prefer loyalty to his State or loyalty to the Union was a question concerning which man differed from man and State from State. There were men, and indeed whole States, for whom the conflict was a torturing, personal tragedy, and a tearing of the heart in two. But practically all Americans believed that some measure of loyalty was due to both connections. The South Carolinan did not. All his loyalty was to his State. He scarcely pretended to anything like national feeling. The Union was at best a useful treaty of alliance with foreigners to be preserved only so far as the interests of the Palmetto State were advantaged thereby. His representatives in House and Senate, the men he sent to take part as electors in the choosing of a President, had rather the air of ambassadors than of legislators. They were in Congress to fight the battles of their State, and avowed quite frankly that if it should ever appear that "the Treaty called the Constitution of the United States" (as South Carolina afterwards designated it in her Declaration of Independence) were working to its disadvantage, they would denounce it with as little scruple or heart-burning as the Washington Government might denounce a commercial treaty with England or Spain.

South Carolina had been talking freely of secession for thirty years. As I have said, she regarded the Union simply as a diplomatic arrangement to be maintained while it was advantageous, and again and again doubts had been expressed as to whether in fact it was advantageous. The fiscal question which had been the ostensible cause of the Nullification movement in the 'thirties was still considered a matter of grievance. As an independent nation, it was pointed out, South Carolina would be free to meet England on the basis of reciprocal Free Trade, to market her cotton in Lancashire to the best advantage, and to receive in return a cheap and plentiful supply of British manufactures. At any moment since 1832 a good opportunity might have led her to attempt to break away. The election of Lincoln was to her not so much a grievance as a signal—and not altogether an unwelcome one. No time was lost in discussion, for the State was unanimous. The legislature had been in session choosing Presidential electors—for in South Carolina these were chosen by the legislature and not by the people. When the results of the voting in Pennsylvania and Indiana made it probable that the Republicans would have a majority, the Governor intimated that it should continue to sit in order to consider the probable necessity of taking action to save the State. The news of Lincoln's election reached Charleston on the 7th of November. On the 10th of November the legislature unanimously voted for the holding of a specific Convention to consider the relations of South Carolina with the United States. The Convention met early in December, and before the month was out South Carolina had in her own view taken her place in the world as an independent nation. The Stars and Stripes was hauled down, and the new "Palmetto Flag"—a palm-tree and a single star—raised over the public buildings throughout the State.

Many Southerners, including not a few who were inclined to Secession as the only course in the face of the Republican victory, considered the precipitancy of South Carolina unwise and unjustifiable. She should, they thought, rather have awaited a conference with the other Southern States and the determination of a common policy. But in fact there can be little doubt that the audacity of her action was a distinct spur to the Secessionist movement. It gave it a focus, a point round which to rally. The idea of a Southern Confederacy was undoubtedly already in the air. But it might have remained long and perhaps permanently in the air if no State had been ready at once to take the first definite and material step. It was now no longer a mere abstract conception or inspiration. The nucleus of the thing actually existed in the Republic of South Carolina, which every believer in State Sovereignty was bound to recognize as a present independent State. It acted, so to speak, as a magnet to draw other alarmed and discontented States out of the Union. The energy of the South Carolinian Secessionists might have produced less effect had anything like a corresponding energy been displayed by the Government of the United States. But when men impatiently looked to Washington for counsel and decision they found neither. The conduct of President Buchanan moved men at the time to contemptuous impatience, and history has echoed the contemporary verdict. Just one fact may perhaps be urged in extenuation: if he was a weak man he was also in a weak position. A real and very practical defect, as it seems to me, in the Constitution of the United States is the four months' interval between the election of a President and his installation. The origin of the practice is obvious enough: it is a relic of the fiction of the Electoral College, which is supposed to be spending those months in searching America for the fittest man to be chief magistrate. But now that everyone knows on the morrow of the election of the College who is to be President, the effect may easily be to leave the immense power and responsibility of the American Executive during a critical period in the hands of a man who has no longer the moral authority of a popular mandate—whose policy the people have perhaps just rejected. So it was in this case. Buchanan was called upon to face a crisis produced by the defeat of his own party, followed by the threatened rebellion of the men to whom he largely owed his election, and with it what moral authority he might be supposed to possess. Had Lincoln been able to take command in November he might, by a combination of firmness and conciliation, have checked the Secessionist movement. Buchanan, perhaps, could do little; but that little he did not do.

When all fair allowance has been made for the real difficulties of his position it must be owned that the President cut a pitiable figure. What was wanted was a strong lead for the Union sentiment of all the States to rally to. What Buchanan gave was the most self-confessedly futile manifesto that any American President has ever penned. His message to the Congress began by lecturing the North for having voted Republican. It went on to lecture the people of South Carolina for seceding, and to develop in a lawyer-like manner the thesis that they had no constitutional right to do so. This was not likely to produce much effect in any case, but any effect that it might have produced was nullified by the conclusion which appeared to be intended to show, in the same legal fashion, that, though South Carolina had no constitutional right to secede, no one had any constitutional right to prevent her from seceding. The whole wound up with a tearful demonstration of the President's own innocence of any responsibility for the troubles with which he was surrounded.

It was not surprising if throughout the nation there stirred a name and memory, and too many thousands of lips sprang instinctively and simultaneously a single sentence: "Oh for one hour of Jackson!"

General Scott, who was in supreme command of the armed forces of the Union, had, as a young man, received Jackson's instructions for "the

Secession and Civil War 159

execution of the laws" in South Carolina. He sent a detailed specification of them to Buchanan; but it was of no avail. The great engine of democratic personal power which Jackson had created and bequeathed to his successors was in trembling and incapable hands. With a divided Cabinet—for his Secretary of State, Cass, was for vigorous action against the rebellious State, while his Secretary for War, Floyd, was an almost avowed sympathizer with secession—and with a President apparently unable to make up his own mind, or to keep to one policy from hour to hour, it was clear that South Carolina was not to be dealt with in Jackson's fashion. Clay's alternative method remained to be tried.

It was a disciple of Clay's, Senator Crittenden, who made the attempt, a Whig and a Kentuckian like his master. He proposed a compromise very much in Clay's manner, made up for the most part of carefully balanced concessions to either section. But its essence lay in its proposed settlement of the territorial problem, which consisted of a Constitutional Amendment whereby territories lying south of latitude 36° 30' should be open to Slavery, and those north of that line closed against it. This was virtually the extension of the Missouri Compromise line to the Pacific, save that California, already accepted as a Free State, was not affected. Crittenden, though strenuously supported by Douglas, did not meet with Clay's measure of success. The Senate appointed a committee to consider the relations of the two sections, and to that committee, on which he had a seat, he submitted his plan. But its most important clause was negatived by a combination of extremes, Davis and the other Southerners from the Cotton States combining with the Republicans to reject it. There is, however, some reason to believe that the Southerners would have accepted the plan if the Republicans had done so. The extreme Republicans, whose representative on the committee was Wade of Ohio, would certainly have refused it in any case, but the moderates on that side might probably have accepted and carried it had not Lincoln, who had been privately consulted, pronounced decidedly against it. This fixes upon Lincoln a considerable responsibility before history, for it seems probable that if the Crittenden Compromise had been carried the Cotton States would not have seceded, and South Carolina would have stood alone. The refusal, however, is very characteristic of his mind. No-one, as his whole public conduct showed, was more moderate in counsel and more ready to compromise on practical matters than he. Nor does it seem that he would have objected strongly to the Crittenden plan—though he certainly feared that it would lead to filibustering in Mexico and Cuba for the purpose of obtaining more slave territory—if it could have been carried out by Congressional action alone. But the Dred Scott judgment made it necessary to give it the form of a Constitutional Amendment, and a Constitutional Amendment on the lines proposed would do what the Fathers of the Republic had so carefully refrained from doing—make Slavery specifically and in so many words part of the American system. This was a price which his intellectual temper, so elastic in regard to details, but so firm in its insistence on sound first principles, was not prepared to pay.

The rejection of the Crittenden Compromise gave the signal for the new and much more formidable secession which marked the New Year. Before January was spent Alabama, Florida, and Mississippi were, in their own view, out of the Union. Louisiana and Texas soon followed their example. In Georgia the Unionists put up a much stronger fight, led by Alexander Stephens, afterwards Vice-President of the Confederacy. But even there they were defeated, and the Cotton States now formed a solid phalanx openly defying the Government at Washington.

The motives of this first considerable secession—for I have pointed out that the case of South Carolina was unique—are of great importance, for they involve our whole view of the character of the war which was to follow. In England there is still a pretty general impression that the States rose in defence of Slavery. I find a writer so able and generally reliable as Mr. Alex. M. Thompson of the Clarion giving, in a recent article, as an example of a just war, "the war waged by the Northern States to extinguish Slavery." This view is, of course, patently false. The Northern States waged no war to extinguish Slavery; and, had they done so, it would not have been a just but a flagrantly unjust war. No-one could deny for a moment that under the terms of Union the Southern States had a right to keep their slaves as long as they chose. If anyone thought such a bargain too immoral to be kept, his proper place was with Garrison, and his proper programme the repudiation of the bargain and the consequent disruption of the Union. But the North had clearly no shadow of right to coerce the Southerners into remaining in the Union and at the same time to deny them the rights expressly reserved to them under the Treaty of Union. And of such a grossly immoral attempt every fair-minded historian must entirely acquit the victorious section. The Northerners did not go to war to abolish Slavery. The original basis of the Republican Party, its platform of 1860, the resolutions passed by Congress, and the explicit declarations of Lincoln, both before and after election, all recognize specifically and without reserve the immunity of Slavery in the Slave States from all interference by the Federal Government.

American writers are, of course, well acquainted with such elementary facts, and, if they would attempt to make Slavery the cause of the rebellion, they are compelled to use a different but, I think, equally misleading phrase. I find, for instance, Professor Rhodes saying that the South went to war for "the extension of Slavery." This sounds more plausible, because the extension of the geographical area over which Slavery should be lawful had been a Southern policy, and because the victory of the party organized to oppose this policy was in fact the signal for secession. But neither will this statement bear examination, for it must surely be obvious that the act of secession put a final end to any hope of the extension of Slavery. How could Georgia and Alabama, outside the Union, effect anything to legalize Slavery in the Union territories of Kansas and New Mexico?

A true statement of the case would, I think, be this: The South felt itself threatened with a certain peril. Against that peril the extension of the slave area had been one attempted method of protection. Secession was an alternative method.

The peril was to be found in the increasing numerical superiority of the North, which must, it was feared, reduce the South to a position of impotence in the Union if once the rival section were politically united. Lowell spoke much of the truth when he said that the Southern grievance was the census of 1860; but not the whole truth. It was the census of 1860 plus the Presidential Election of 1860, and the moral to be drawn from the two combined. The census showed that the North was already greatly superior in numbers, and that the disproportion was an increasing one. The election showed the North combined in support of a party necessarily and almost avowedly sectional, and returning its candidate triumphantly, although he had hardly a vote south of the Mason-Dixon line. To the South this seemed to mean that in future, if it was to remain in the Union at all, it must be on sufferance. A Northerner would always be President, a Northern majority would always be supreme in both Houses of Congress, for the admission of California, already accomplished, and the now certain admission of Kansas as a Free State had disturbed the balance in the Senate as well as in the House. The South would henceforward be unable to influence in any way the policy of the Federal Government. It would be enslaved.

It is true that the South had no immediate grievance. The only action of the North of which she had any sort of right to complain was the infringement of the spirit of the Constitutional compact by the Personal Liberty Laws. But these laws there was now a decided disposition to amend or repeal—a disposition strongly supported by the man whom the North had elected as President. It is also true, that this man would never have lent himself to any unfair depression of the Southern part of the Union. This last fact, however, the South may be pardoned for not knowing. Even those Northerners who had elected Lincoln knew little about him except that he was the Republican nominee and had been a "rail-splitter." In the South, so far as one can judge, all that was heard about him was that he was a "Black Abolitionist," which was false, and that in appearance he resembled a gorilla, which was, at least by comparison, true.

But, even if Lincoln's fairness of mind and his conciliatory disposition towards the South had been fully appreciated, it is not clear that the logic of the Secessionist case would have been greatly weakened. The essential point was that the North, by virtue of its numerical superiority, had elected a purely Northern candidate on a purely Northern programme. Though both candidate and programme were in fact moderate, there was no longer any security save the will of the North that such moderation would continue. If the conditions remained unaltered, there was nothing to prevent the North at a subsequent election from making Charles Sumner

President with a programme conceived in the spirit of John Brown's raid. It must be admitted that the policy adopted by the dominant North after the Civil War might well appear to afford a measure of posthumous justification for these fears.

In the North at first all seemed panic and confusion of voices. To many—and among them were some of those who had been keenest in prosecuting the sectional quarrel of which Secession was the outcome—it appeared the wisest course to accept the situation and acquiesce in the peaceable withdrawal of the seceding States. This was the position adopted almost unanimously by the Abolitionists, and it must be owned that they at least were strictly consistent in taking it. "When I called the Union 'a League with Death and an Agreement with Hell,'" said Garrison, "I did not expect to see Death and Hell secede from the Union." Garrison's disciple, Wendell Phillips, pronounced the matter one for the Gulf States themselves to decide, and declared that you could not raise troops in Boston to coerce South Carolina or Florida. The same line was taken by men who carried greater weight than did the Abolitionists. No writer had rendered more vigorous service to the Republican cause in 1860 than Horace Greeley of the New York Tribune. His pronouncement in that journal on the Southern secessions was embodied in the phrase: "Let our erring sisters go."

But while some of the strongest opponents of the South and of Slavery were disposed to accept the dismemberment of the Union almost complacently, there were men of a very different type to whom it seemed an outrage to be consummated only over their dead bodies. During the wretched months of Buchanan's incurable hesitancy the name of Jackson had been in every mouth. And at the mere sound of that name there was a rally to the Union of all who had served under the old warrior in the days when he had laid his hand of steel upon the Nullifiers. Some of them, moved by that sound and by the memory of the dead, broke through the political ties of a quarter of a century. Among those in whom that memory overrode every other passion were Holt, a Southerner and of late the close ally of Davis; Cass, whom Lowell had pilloried as the typical weak-kneed Northerner who suffered himself to be made the lackey of the South; and Taney, who had denied that, in the contemplation of the American

Constitution, the Negro was a man. It was Black, an old Jacksonian, who in the moment of peril held the nerveless hands of the President firm to the tiller. It was Dix, another such, who sent to New Orleans the very Jacksonian order: "If any man attempts to haul down the American flag, shoot him at sight."

War is always the result of a conflict of wills.

The conflict of wills which produced the American Civil War had nothing directly to do with Slavery. It was the conflict between the will of certain Southern States to secede rather than accept the position of a permanent minority and the will expressed in Jackson's celebrated toast: "Our Union, it must be preserved." It is the Unionist position which clearly stands in need of special defence, since it proposed the coercion of a recalcitrant population. Can such a defence be framed in view of the acceptance by most of us of the general principle which has of late been called "the self-determination of peoples"?

I think it can. One may at once dismiss the common illusion—for it is often in such cases a genuine illusion, though sometimes a piece of hypocrisy—which undoubtedly had possession of many Northern minds at the time, that the Southern people did not really want to secede, but were in some mysterious fashion "intimidated" by a disloyal minority. How, in the absence of any special means of coercion, one man can "intimidate" two was never explained any more than it is explained when the same absurd hypothesis is brought forward in relation to Irish agrarian and English labour troubles. At any rate in this case there is not, and never has been, the slightest justification for doubting that Secessionism was from the first a genuine popular movement, that it was enthusiastically embraced by hundreds of thousands who no more expected ever to own a slave than an English labourer expects to own a carriage and pair; that in this matter the political leaders of the States, and Davis in particular, rather lagged behind than outran the general movement of opinion; that the Secessionists were in the Cotton States a great majority from the first; that they became later as decided a majority in Virginia, North Carolina, and Tennessee; and that by the time the sword was drawn there was behind the Confederate Government a unanimity very rare in the history of revolutions—certainly much greater than existed in the colonies at the time of the Declaration of Independence. To oppose so formidable a mass of local opinion and to enforce opposition by the sword was for a democracy a grave responsibility.

Yet it was a responsibility which had to be accepted if America was to justify her claim to be a nation. To understand this certain further propositions must be grasped.

First, the resistance of the South, though so nearly universal, was not strictly national. You cannot compare the case with that of Ireland or Poland. The Confederacy was never a nation, though, had the war had a different conclusion, it might perhaps have become one. It is important to remember that the extreme Southern view did not profess to regard the South as a nationality. It professed to regard South Carolina as one nationality, Florida as another, Virginia as another. But this view, though it had a strong hold on very noble minds, was at bottom a legalism out of touch with reality. It may be doubted whether any man felt it in his bones as men feel a genuine national sentiment.

On the other hand American national sentiment was a reality. It had been baptized in blood. It was a reality for Southerners as well as for Northerners, for Secessionists as well as for Union men. There was probably no American, outside South Carolina, who did not feel it as a reality, though it might be temporarily obscured and overborne by local loyalties, angers, and fears. The President of the Confederacy had himself fought under the Stars and Stripes, and loved it so well that he could not bear to part with it and wished to retain it as the flag of the South. Had one generation of excited men, without any cognate and definable grievance, moved only by anger at a political reverse and the dread of unrealized and dubious evils, the right to undo the mighty work of consolidation now so nearly accomplished, to throw away at once the inheritance of their fathers and the birthright of their children? Nor would they and their children be the only losers: it was the great principles on which the American Commonwealth was built that seemed too many to be on trial for their life. If the Union were broken up, what could men say but that Democracy had failed? The ghost of Hamilton might grin from his grave; though his rival had won the laurel, it was he who would seem to have proved his case. For the first successful secession would not necessarily have been the last. The thesis of State Sovereignty established by victory in arms—which always does in practice establish any thesis for good or evil—meant the break-up of the free and proud American nation into smaller and smaller fragments as new disputes arose, until the whole fabric planned by the Fathers of the Republic had disappeared. It is impossible to put this argument better than in the words of Lincoln himself. "Must a government, of necessity, be too strong for the liberties of its own people, or too weak to maintain its own existence?" That was the issue as he saw it, an issue which he was determined should be decided in the negative, even at the cost of a long and bloody Civil War.

I have endeavoured to state fairly the nature of the conflict of wills which was to produce Civil War, and to explain how each side justified morally its appeal to arms. Further than that I do not think it necessary to go. But I will add just this one historical fact which, I think, supplies some degree of further justification for the attitude of the North—that concerning this matter of the Union, which was the real question in debate, though not in regard to other subsidiary matters which will demand our attention in the next chapter, the South was ultimately not only conquered but persuaded. There are among the millions of Southerners alive to-day few who will admit that their fathers fought in an unjust cause, but there are probably still fewer, if any at all, who would still wish to secede if they had the power. Jefferson Davis himself could, at the last, close his record of his own defeat and of the triumph of the Union with the words Esto Perpetua.

Lincoln took the oath as President on March 4, 1861. His inaugural address breathes the essential spirit of his policy—firmness in things fundamental, conciliation in things dispensable. He reiterated his declaration that he had neither right nor inclination to interfere with Slavery in the Slave States. He quoted the plank in the Republican platform which affirmed the right of each State to control its own affairs, and vigorously condemned John Brown's insane escapade. He declared for an effective Fugitive Slave Law, and pledged himself to its faithful execution. He expressed his approval of the amendment to the Constitution which Congress had just resolved to recommend, forbidding the Federal Government ever to interfere with the domestic institutions of the several States, "including that of persons held to service." But on the question of Secession he took firm ground. "I hold that, in contemplation of universal law and of the Constitution, the union of these States is perpetual.... It follows from these views that no State upon its own mere motion can lawfully get out of the Union; that resolves and ordinances to that effect are legally void; and that acts of violence within any State or States, against the authority of the United States, are insurrectionary or revolutionary, according to circumstances." He accepted the obligation which the Constitution expressly enjoined on him, to see "that the laws of the Union be faithfully executed in all the States." He would use his power "to hold, occupy, and possess the property and places belonging to the Government and to collect the duties and imposts," but beyond that there would be no interference or coercion. There could be no conflict or bloodshed unless the Secessionists were themselves the aggressors. "In your hands, my dissatisfied fellow-countrymen, and not in mine is the momentous issue of Civil War.... You have no oath registered in heaven to destroy the Government, while I have the most solemn one to 'preserve, protect and defend it.'"

He ended with the one piece of rhetoric in the whole address—rhetoric deliberately framed to stir those emotions of loyalty to the national past and future which he knew to endure, howsoever overshadowed by anger and misunderstanding, even in Southern breasts. "We are not enemies, but friends. We must not be enemies. Though passion may have strained it must not break our bonds of affection. The mystic chords of memory, stretching from every battlefield and patriot grave to every living heart and hearthstone all over this broad land, will yet swell the chorus of Union, when again touched, as surely they will be, by the better angels of our nature."

But there was not much evidence of the active operation of such "better angels" at the moment. Half the Southern States had not only seceded, but had already formed themselves into a hostile Confederacy. They framed a Constitution modelled in essentials on that of the United

States, but with the important difference that "We the deputies of the Sovereign and Independent States" was substituted for "We the people of the United States," and with certain minor amendments, some of which were generally thought even in the North to be improvements.

They elected Jefferson Davis as President, and as Vice-President Alexander Stephens of Georgia, who had been a Unionist, but had accepted the contrary verdict of his State.

The choice was, perhaps, as good as could have been made. Davis was in some ways well fitted to represent the new Commonwealth before the world. He had a strong sense of what befitted his own dignity and that of his office. He had a keen eye for what would attract the respect and sympathy of foreign nations. It is notable, for instance, that in his inaugural address, in setting forth the grounds on which secession was to be justified, he made no allusion to the institution of Slavery. There he may be contrasted favourably with Stephens, whose unfortunate speech declaring Slavery to be the stone which the builders of the old Constitution rejected, and which was to become the corner-stone of the new Confederacy, was naturally seized upon by Northern sympathizers at the time, and has been as continually brought forward since by historians and writers who wish to emphasize the connection between Slavery and the Southern cause. Davis had other qualifications which might seem to render him eminently fit to direct the policy of a Confederation which must necessarily begin its existence by fighting and winning a great and hazardous war. He had been a soldier and served with distinction. Later he had been, by common consent, one of the best War Secretaries that the United States had possessed. It was under his administration that both Lee and McClellan, later to be arrayed against each other, were sent to the Crimea to study modern war at first hand.

But Davis had faults of temper which often endangered and perhaps at last ruined the cause he served. They can be best appreciated by reading his own book. There is throughout a note of querulousness which weakens one's sympathy for the hero of a lost cause. He is always explaining how things ought to have happened, how the people of Kentucky ought to have been angry with Lincoln instead of siding with him, and so on. One understands at once how he was bested in democratic diplomacy by his rival's lucid realism and unfailing instinct for dealing with men as men. One understands also his continual quarrels with his generals, though in that department he was from the first much better served than was the Government at Washington. A sort of nervous irritability, perhaps a part of what is called "the artistic temperament," is everywhere perceptible. Nowhere does one find a touch of that spirit which made Lincoln say, after an almost insolent rebuff to his personal and official dignity from McClellan: "Well, I will hold his horse for him if he will give us a victory."

The prize for which both parties were contending in the period of diplomatic skirmishing which marks the opening months of Lincoln's administration was the adherence of those Slave States which had not yet seceded. So far disruptional doctrines had triumphed only in the Cotton States. In Virginia Secession had been rejected by a very decided majority, and the rejection had been confirmed by the result of the subsequent elections for the State legislature. The Secessionists had also seen their programme defeated in Tennessee, Arkansas, and North Carolina, while Kentucky, Missouri and Maryland had as yet refused to make any motion towards it. In Texas the general feeling was on the whole Secessionist, but the Governor was a Unionist, and succeeded for a time in preventing definite action. To keep these States loyal, while keeping at the same time his pledge to "execute the laws," was Lincoln's principal problem in the first days of his Presidency.

His policy turned mainly on two principles. First, the South must see that the administration of the laws was really impartial, and that the President executed them because he had taken an oath to do so; not because the North wanted to trample on the South. This consideration explains the extreme rigour with which he enforced the Fugitive Slave Law. Here was a law involving a Constitutional obligation, which he, with his known views on Slavery, could not possibly like executing, which the North certainly did not want him to execute, which he could be executing only from a sense of obligation under the Constitution. Such an example would make it easier for moderate Southern opinion to accept the application of a similar strictness to the seceding States. The second principle was the strict confinement of his intervention within the limits presented by his Inaugural. This was calculated to bear a double effect. On the one hand, it avoided an immediate practical challenge to the doctrine of State Sovereignty, strongly held by many in the Middle States who were nevertheless opposed to Secession. On the other, it tended, if prolonged, to render the Southern assumption of the rôle of "a people risen against tyrants" a trifle ridiculous. A freeman defying the edicts of the oppressor is a dignified spectacle: not so that of a man desperately anxious to defy edicts which the oppressor obstinately refuses to issue. It was possible for Lincoln to put the rebels in this position because under the American Constitution nine-tenths of the laws which practically affected the citizen were State and not Federal laws. When people began to talk of protesting against tyranny by refusing to allow the tyrant to deliver their mails to them, it was obvious how near the comic the sublime defiance of the Confederates was treading. There were men in the South who fully realized the disconcerting effect of the President's moderation. "Unless you baptize the Confederacy in blood," said a leading Secessionist of Alabama to Jefferson Davis, "Alabama will be back in the Union within a month." Unfortunately Lincoln's attitude of masterly inactivity could not be kept up for so long, for a problem, bequeathed him by his predecessor, pressed upon him, demanding action, just where action might, as he well knew, mean a match dropped in the heart of a powder-magazine. On an island in the very harbour of Charleston itself stood Fort Sumter, an arsenal held by the Federal Government. South Carolina, regarding herself as now an independent State, had sent an embassy to Washington to negotiate among other things for its surrender and transfer to the State authorities. Buchanan had met these emissaries and temporized without definitely committing himself. He had been on the point of ordering Major Anderson, who was in command of the garrison, to evacuate the fort, when under pressure from Black, his Secretary of State, he changed his mind and sent a United States packet, called Star of the West, with reinforcements for Anderson. The State authorities at Charleston fired on the ship, which, being unarmed, turned tail and returned to Washington without fulfilling its mission. The problem was now passed on to Lincoln, with this aggravation: that Anderson's troops had almost consumed their stores, could get no more from Charleston, and, if not supplied, must soon succumb to starvation. Lincoln determined to avoid the provocation of sending soldiers and arms, but to despatch a ship with food and other necessaries for the garrison. This resolution was duly notified to the authorities at Charleston.

Their anger was intense. They had counted on the evacuation of the fort, and seem to have considered that they held a pledge from Seward, who was now Secretary of State, and whose conduct in the matter seems certainly to have been somewhat devious, to that effect. The Stars and Stripes waving in their own harbour in defiance of their Edict of Secession seemed to them and to all their people a daily affront. Now that the President had intimated in the clearest possible fashion that he intended it to be permanent, they and all the inhabitants of Charleston, and indeed of South Carolina, clamoured loudly for the reduction of the fortress. In an evil hour Jefferson Davis, though warned by his ablest advisers that he was putting his side in the wrong, yielded to their pressure. Anderson was offered the choice between immediate surrender or the forcible reduction of the fortress. True to his military duty, though his own sympathies were largely Southern, he refused to surrender, and the guns of three other forts, which the Confederates had occupied, began the bombardment of Sumter.

It lasted all day, the little fortress replying with great spirit, though with insufficient and continually diminishing means. It is an astonishing fact that in this, the first engagement of the Civil War, though much of the fort was wrecked, no life was lost on either side. At length Anderson's ammunition was exhausted, and he surrendered at discretion. The Stars and Stripes were pulled down and the new flag of the Confederacy, called the Stars and Bars, waved in its place.

The effect of the news in the North was electric. Never before and never after was it so united. One cry of anger went up from twenty million throats. Whitman, in the best of his "Drum Taps," has described the spirit in which New York received the tidings; how that great metropolitan city, which had in the past been Democrat in its votes and half Southern in its political connections—"at dead of night, at news from the South, incensed, struck with clenched fist the pavement."

It is important to the true comprehension of the motive power behind the war to remember what this "news from the South" was. It was not the news of the death of Uncle Tom or of the hanging of John Brown. It had not the remotest connection with Slavery. It was an insult offered to the flag. In the view of every Northern man and woman there was but one appropriate answer—the sentence which Barrère had passed upon the city of Lyons: "South Carolina has fired upon Old Glory: South Carolina is no more."

Lincoln, feeling the tide of the popular will below him as a good boatman feels a strong and deep current, issued an appeal for 75,000 militia from the still loyal States to defend the flag and the Union which it symbolized. The North responded with unbounded enthusiasm, and the number of volunteers easily exceeded that for which the President had asked and Congress provided. In the North-West Lincoln found a powerful ally in his old antagonist Stephen Douglas. In the dark and perplexing months which intervened between the Presidential Election and the outbreak of the Civil War, no public man had shown so pure and selfless a patriotism. Even during the election, when Southern votes were important to him and when the threat that the election of the Republican nominee would lead to secession was almost the strongest card in his hand, he had gone out of his way to declare that no possible choice of a President could justify the dismemberment of the Republic. When Lincoln was elected, he had spoken in several Southern States, urging acquiescence in the verdict and loyalty to the Union. He had taken care to be present on the platform at his rival's inauguration, and, after the affair of Sumter, the two had had a long and confidential conversation. Returning to his native West, he commenced the last of his campaigns—a campaign for no personal object but for the raising of soldiers to keep the old flag afloat. In that campaign the "Little Giant" spent the last of his unquenchable vitality; and in the midst of it he died.

For the North and West the firing on the Stars and Stripes was the decisive issue. For Virginia and to a great extent for the other Southern

States which had not yet seceded it was rather the President's demands for State troops to coerce a sister State. The doctrine of State Sovereignty was in these States generally held to be a fundamental principle of the Constitution and the essential condition of their liberties. They had no desire to leave the Union so long as it were understood that it was a union of Sovereign States. But the proposal to use force against a recalcitrant State seemed to them to upset the whole nature of the compact and reduce them to a position of vassalage. This attitude explains the second Secession, which took Virginia, Tennessee, North Carolina, and Arkansas out of the Union. It explains also why the moment the sword was drawn the opinion of these States, strongly divided up to that very moment, became very nearly unanimous. Not all their citizens, even after the virtual declaration of war against South Carolina, wanted their States to secede, but all, or nearly all, claimed that they had the right to secede if they wanted to, and therefore all, or nearly all, accepted the decision of their States even if it were contrary to their own judgment and preference.

It is important to understand this attitude, not only because it was very general, but because it was the attitude of one of the noblest sons the Republic ever bore, who yet felt compelled, regretfully but with full certitude that he did right, to draw the sword against her.

Robert Lee was already recognized as one of the most capable captains in the service of the United States. When it became obvious that General Scott, also a Virginian, but a strong Unionist, was too old to undertake the personal direction of the approaching campaign, Lee was sounded as to his readiness to take his place. He refused, not desiring to take part in the coercion of a State, and subsequently, when his own State became involved in the quarrel, resigned his commission. Later he accepted the chief command of the Virginian forces and became the most formidable of the rebel commanders. Yet with the institution, zeal for which is still so largely thought to have been the real motive of the South, he had no sympathy. Four years before the Republican triumph, he had, in his correspondence, declared Slavery to be "a moral and political evil." Nor was he a Secessionist. He deeply regretted and so far as he could, without meddling in politics—to which, in the fashion of good soldiers, he was strongly averse—opposed the action which his State eventually took. But he thought that she had the right to take it if she chose, and, the fatal choice having been made, he had no option in his own view but to throw in his lot with her and accept his portion of whatever fate might be in store for her armies and her people.

Virginia now passed an Ordinance of Secession, and formed a military alliance with the Southern Confederacy. Later she was admitted to membership of that Confederacy, and the importance attached to her accession may be judged by the fact that the new Government at once transferred its seat to her capital, the city of Richmond. The example of Virginia was followed by the other Southern States already enumerated.

There remained four Southern States in which the issue was undecided. One of them, Delaware, caused no appreciable anxiety. She was the smallest State in the Union in population, almost the smallest in area, and though technically a Slave State, the proportion of negroes within her borders was small. It was otherwise with the three formidable States which still hung in the balance, Missouri, Kentucky, and Maryland. That these were saved to the Union was due almost wholly to the far-sighted prudence and consummate diplomacy of Abraham Lincoln.

Missouri was the easiest to hold. Geographically she was not really a Southern State at all, and, though she was a Slave State by virtue of Clay's Compromise, the institution had not there struck such deep roots as in the true South. The mass of her people were recruited from all the older States, North and South, with a considerable contingent fresh from Europe. Union feeling was strong among them and State feeling comparatively weak. Her Governor, indeed, was an ardent Southern sympathizer and returned a haughty and defiant reply to Lincoln's request for soldiers. But Francis Blair, a prominent and popular citizen, and Captain Lyon, who had raised and commanded a Union force within her borders, between them carried the State against him. He was deposed, a Unionist Governor substituted, and Missouri ranged herself definitely with the North.

The case of Maryland was much more critical, for it appeared to involve the fate of the Capital. Washington lay between Maryland and Virginia, and if Maryland joined Virginia in rebellion it could hardly be held. Yet its abandonment might entail the most serious political consequences, certainly an enormous encouragement to the seceding Confederacy, quite probably its immediate recognition by foreign Powers. At first the omens looked ugly. The populace of Baltimore, the capital of the State, were at this time pronouncedly Southern in their sentiments, and the first Massachusetts regiment sent to the relief of Washington was hustled and stoned in its streets. The soldiers fired on the mob and there were casualties on both sides. Immediately afterwards the legislature of Maryland protested against the violation of its territory. Lincoln acted with admirable sense and caution. He pointed out that the Federal armies could not fly, and that therefore to reach Washington they must pass over the soil of Maryland; but he made no point of their going through Baltimore, and he wisely provided that further contingents should, for a time, proceed by water to Annapolis. Meanwhile he strained every nerve to reassure and conciliate Maryland with complete success. Within a month or two Federal troops could be brought to Baltimore without the smallest friction or disturbance. Later the loyalty of Maryland was, as we shall see, put to a much more critical test and passed it triumphantly.

The President naturally felt a special interest in the attitude of his native state, Kentucky. That attitude would have perplexed and embarrassed a less discerning statesman. Taking her stand on the dogma of State Sovereignty Kentucky declared herself "neutral" in the impending war between the United and Confederate States, and forbade the troops of either party to cross her territory. Lincoln could not, of course, recognize the validity of such a declaration, but he was careful to avoid any act in open violation of it. Sometimes openly and sometimes secretly he worked hard to foster, consolidate, and encourage the Union party in Kentucky. With his approval and probably at his suggestion loyalist levies were voluntarily recruited on her soil, drilled and prepared for action. But no Northern troops were sent across her frontier. He was undoubtedly working for a violation of Kentuckian "neutrality" by the other side. Circumstances and geographical conditions helped him. The frontier between Kentucky and Tennessee was a mere degree of latitude corresponding to no militarily defensible line, nor did any such line exist to the south of it capable of covering the capital of Tennessee. On the other hand, an excellent possible line of defence existed in Southern Kentucky. The Confederate commanders were eager to seize it, but the neutrality of Kentucky forbade them. When, however, they saw the hold which Lincoln seemed to be acquiring over the counsels of the "neutrals," they felt they dared not risk further delay. Justifying their act by the presence in Kentucky of armed bodies of local Unionists, they advanced and occupied the critical points of Columbus and Bowling Green, stretching their line between them on Kentuckian soil. The act at once determined the course of the hesitating State. Torn hitherto between loyalty to the Union and loyalty to State Rights, she now found the two sentiments synchronize. In the name of her violated neutrality she declared war on the Confederacy and took her place under the Stars and Stripes.

The line between the two warring confederations of States was now definitely fixed, and it only remained to try the issue between them by the arbitrament of the sword.

At first the odds might seem very heavy against the Confederacy, for its total white population was only about five and a half million, while the States arrayed against it mustered well over twenty million. But there were certain considerations which tended to some extent to equalize the contest.

First there is the point which must always be taken into consideration when estimating the chances of war—the political objective aimed at. The objective of the North was the conquest of the South. But the objective of the South was not the conquest of the North. It was the demonstration that such conquest as the North desired was impracticable, or at least so expensive as not to be worth pursuing. That the Union, if the States that composed it remained united and determined and no other factor were introduced, could eventually defeat the Confederacy was from the first almost mathematically certain; and between complete defeat and conquest there is no such distinction as some have imagined, for a military force which has destroyed all military forces opposed to it can always impose its will unconditionally on the conquered. But that these States would remain united and determined was not certain at all. If the South put up a sufficiently energetic fight, there might arise in the dominant section a considerable body of opinion which felt that too high a price was being paid for the enterprise. Moreover, there was always the possibility and often the probability of another factor—the intervention of some foreign Power in favour of the South, as France had intervened in favour of the Americans in 1781. Such were the not unlikely chances upon which the South was gambling.

Another factor in favour of the South was preparation. South Carolina had begun raising and drilling soldiers for a probable war as soon as Lincoln was elected. The other Southern States had at various intervals followed her example. On the Northern side there had been no preparation whatever under the Buchanan régime, and Lincoln had not much chance of attempting such preparation before the war was upon him.

Further, it was probably true that, even untrained, the mass of Southerners were better fitted for war than the mass of Northerners. They were, as a community, agrarian, accustomed to an open-air life, proud of their skill in riding and shooting. The first levies of the North were drawn mostly from the urban population, and consisted largely of clerks, artisans, and men of the professional class, in whose previous modes of life there was nothing calculated to prepare them in any way for the duties of a soldier. To this general rule there was, however, an important reservation, of which the fighting at Fort Donelson and Shiloh afforded an early illustration. In dash and hardihood, and what may be called the raw materials of soldiership the South, whatever it may have had to teach the North, had little to teach the West.

In the matter of armament the South, though not exactly advantageously placed, was at the beginning not so badly off as it might well have been. Floyd, at one time Buchanan's Secretary for War, was accused, and indeed, after he had joined the Secessionists, virtually admitted having deliberately distributed the arms of the Federal Government to the advantage of the Confederacy. Certainly the outbreak of war found some well-stocked arsenals within the grasp of the rebellion. It was not until its later phases that the great advantage of the industrial North in facilities for the manufacture of armaments made itself apparent.

But the great advantage which the South possessed, and which accounts for the great measure of military success which it enjoyed, must be regarded as an accidental one. It consisted in the much greater capacity of the commanders whom the opening of the war found in control of its forces. The North had to search for competent generals by a process of trial and error, almost every trial being marked by a disaster; nor till the very end of the war did she discover the two or three men who were equal to their job. The South, on the other hand, had from the beginning the good luck to possess in its higher command more than one captain whose talents were on the highest possible level.

The Confederate Congress was summoned to meet at Richmond on July 20th. A cry went up from the North that this event should be prevented by the capture before that date of the Confederate capital. The cry was based on an insufficient appreciation of the military resources of the enemy, but it was so vehement and universal that the Government was compelled to yield to it. A considerable army had by this time been collected in Washington, and under the command of General McDowell it now advanced into Virginia, its immediate objective being Manassas Junction. The opposing force was under the Southern commander Beauregard, a Louisianian of French extraction. The other gate of Eastern Virginia, the Shenandoah Valley, was held by Joseph Johnstone, who was to be kept engaged by an aged Union general named Patterson. Johnstone, however, broke contact and got away from Patterson, joining Beauregard behind the line of a small river called Bull Run, to which the latter had retired. Here McDowell attacked, and the first real battle of the Civil War followed. For a time it wavered between the two sides, but the arrival in flank of the forces of Johnstone's rearguard, which had arrived too late for the opening of the battle, threw the Union right wing into confusion. Panic spread to the whole army, which, with the exception of a small body of regular troops, flung away its arms and fled in panic back to Washington.

Thus unauspiciously opened the campaign against the Confederacy. The impression produced on both sides was great. The North set its teeth and determined to wipe out the disgrace at the first possible moment. The South was wild with joy. The too-prevalent impression that the "Yankees" were cowards who could not and would not fight seemed confirmed by the first practical experiment. The whole subsequent course of the war showed how false was this impression. It has been admitted that the Southerners were at first, on the whole, both better fitted and better prepared for war than their opponents. But all military history shows that what enables soldiers to face defeat and abstain from panic in the face of apparent disaster is not natural courage, but discipline. Had the fight gone the other way the Southern recruits would probably have acted exactly as did the fugitive Northerners. Indeed, as it was, at an earlier stage of the battle a panic among the Southerners was only averted by the personal exertions of Beauregard, whose horse was shot under him, and by the good conduct of the Virginian contingent and its leader. "Look at Jackson and his Virginians," cried out the Southern commander in rallying his men, "standing like a stone wall." The great captain thus acclaimed bore ever after, through his brief but splendid military career, the name of "Stonewall" Jackson.

Bull Run was fought and won in July. The only other important operations of the year consisted in the successful clearing, by the Northern commander, McClellan, of Western Virginia, where a Unionist population had seceded from the Secession. Lincoln, with bold statesmanship, recognized it as a separate State, and thus further consolidated the Unionism of the Border. In recognition of this service McClellan was appointed, in succession to McDowell, to the command of the army of the Potomac, as the force entrusted with the invasion of Eastern Virginia was called.

At the first outbreak of the war English sympathies, except perhaps for a part of the travelled and more or less cosmopolitan aristocracy which found the Southern gentleman a more socially acceptable type than the Yankee, seem to have been decidedly with the North. Public opinion in this country was strong against Slavery, and therefore tended to support the Free States in the contest of which Slavery was generally believed to be the cause. Later this feeling became a little confused. Our people did not understand the peculiar historical conditions which bound the Northern side, and were puzzled and their enthusiasm damped by the President's declaration that he had no intention of interfering with Slavery, and still more by the resolution whereby Congress specifically limited the objective of the war and the preservation of the Union, expressly guaranteeing the permanence of Slavery as a domestic institution. These things made it easy for the advocates of the South to maintain that Slavery had nothing to do with the issue—as, indeed, directly, it had not. Then came Bull Run—the sort of Jack-the-Giant-Killer incident which always and in a very human fashion excites the admiration of sportsmanlike foreigners. One may add to this the fact that the intelligent governing class at that time generally regarded the Americans, as the Americans regarded us, as rivals and potential enemies, and would not have been sorry to see one strong power in the New World replaced by two weak ones. On the other hand, the British Government's very proper proclamation of neutrality as between the United States and the Confederacy had been somewhat unreasonably criticized in America.

Yet the general sympathy with the Free as against the Slave States might have had a better chance of surviving but for the occurrence in November, 1861, of what is called the "Trent" dispute. The Confederacy was naturally anxious to secure recognition from the Powers of Western Europe, and with this object despatched two representatives, Mason of Virginia and Slidell of South Carolina, the one accredited to the Court of St. James's and the other to the Tuileries. They took passage to Europe in a British ship called the Trent. The United States cruiser San Jacinto, commanded by Captain Wilkes of the American Navy, overhauled this vessel, searched it and seized and carried off the two Confederate envoys.

The act was certainly a breach of international law; but that was almost the smallest part of its irritant effect. In every detail it was calculated to outrage British sentiment. It was an affront offered to us on our own traditional element—the sea. It was also a blow offered to our traditional pride as impartial protectors of political exiles of all kind. The Times —in those days a responsible and influential organ of opinion—said quite truly that the indignation felt here had nothing to do with approval of the rebellion; that it would have been just as strong if, instead of Mason and Slidell, the victims had been two of their own Negro slaves. Indeed, for us there were no longer Northern and Southern sympathizers: there were only Englishmen indignant at an insult openly offered to the Union Jack. Northerners might have understood us better, and been less angry at our attitude, if they had remembered how they themselves had felt when the guns opened on Sumter.

The evil was aggravated by the triumphant rejoicings with which the North celebrated the capture and by the complicity of responsible and even official persons in the honours showered on Captain Wilkes. Seward, who had a wild idea that a foreign quarrel would help to heal domestic dissensions, was somewhat disposed to defend the capture. But the eminently just mind of Lincoln quickly saw that it could not be defended, while his prudence perceived the folly of playing the Southern game by forcing England to recognize the Confederacy. Mason and Slidell were returned, and the incident as a diplomatic incident was closed. But it had its part in breeding in these islands a certain antagonism to the Government at Washington, and thus encouraging the growing tendency to sympathize with the South.

With the opening of the new year the North was cheered by a signal and very important success. In the course of February Fort Henry and Fort Donelson, essential strategic points on the front which the Confederate invaders had stretched across Southern Kentucky, were captured by General Ulysses Grant, in command of a Western army. The Confederate forces were compelled to a general retirement, sacrificing the defensive line for the sake of which they had turned the "neutral" border State into an enemy, uncovering the whole of Western Tennessee, including the capital of Nashville, and also yielding the Upper Mississippi. The importance of the latter gain—for the Mississippi, once mastered, would cut the Confederacy in two—was clearly apparent to Beauregard, who at once marched northward and attacked Grant at Shiloh. The battle was indecisive, but in its military effect it was a success for the North. Grant was compelled to abandon the ground upon which his army stood, but he kept all the fruits of his recent campaign.

Another incident, not only picturesque in itself but of great importance in the history of naval war, marks the opening months of 1862. After the failure of the first attempt to take Richmond by a coup de main the war became in its essence a siege of the Confederacy. To give it this character, however, one thing was essential—the control of the sea by the Union forces. The regular United States Navy—unlike the regular army, which was divided—was fully under the control of the Federal Government, and was able to blockade the Southern ports. Davis had attempted to meet this menace by issuing letters of marque to privateers; but this could be little more than an irritant to the dominant power. It so happened, however, that a discovery had recently been made which was destined to revolutionize the whole character of naval war. Experiments in the steel-plating of ships had already been made in England and in France, but the first war vessel so fitted for practical use was produced by the Southern Confederacy—the celebrated Merrimac. One fine day she steamed into Hampton Roads under the guns of the United States fleet and proceeded to sink ship after ship, the heavy round shot leaping off her like peas. It was a perilous moment, but the Union Government had only been a day behind in perfecting the same experiment. Next day the Monitor arrived on the scene, and the famous duel between the first two ironclads ever constructed commenced. Each proved invulnerable to the other, for neither side had yet constructed pieces capable of piercing protection, but the victory was so far with the North that the hope that the Confederacy might obtain, by one bold and inventive stroke, the mastery of the sea was for the moment at an end.

Meanwhile all eyes were fixed on McClellan, who was busy turning the mob that had fled from Bull Run into an army. His work of organization and discipline was by common consent admirable; yet when the time came when he might be expected to take the field, that defect in his quality as a commander showed itself which was to pursue him throughout his campaigns. He was extravagantly over-cautious. His unwillingness to fight, combined with the energy he put into bringing the army into an efficient state and gaining influence over its officers and men, gave rise to the wildest rumours and charges. It was suggested that he intended to use the force he was forming, not against Richmond but against Washington; to seize supreme power by military force and reconcile the warring States under the shadow of his sword. It is certain that there was no kind of foundation for such suspicions. He was a perfectly patriotic and loyal soldier who studied his profession diligently. Perhaps he had studied it too diligently. He seems to have resolved never to risk an engagement unless under conditions which according to the text-books should assure victory. Ideal conditions of this sort were not likely to occur often in real war, especially when waged against such an antagonist as Robert Lee.

McClellan remained in front of the Confederate positions throughout the winter and early spring. In reply to urgent appeals from Washington he declared the position of the enemy to be impregnable, and grossly exaggerated his numbers. When at last, at the beginning of March, he was induced to move forward, he found that the enemy had slipped away, leaving behind, as if in mockery, a large number of dummy wooden guns which had helped to impress McClellan with the hopelessness of assailing his adversaries.

The wooden guns, however little damage they could do to the Federal army, did a good deal of damage to the reputation of the Federal commander. Lincoln, though pressed to replace him, refused to do so, having no one obviously better to put in his room, and knowing that the outcry against him was partly political—for McClellan was a Democrat. The general now undertook the execution of a plan of his own for the reduction of Richmond. Leaving McDowell on the Potomac, he transported the greater part of his force by water and effected a landing on the peninsula of Yorktown, where some eighty years before Cornwallis had surrendered to Washington and Rochambeau.

The plan was not a bad one, but the general showed the same lack of enterprise which had made possible the escape of Johnstone. It is probable that if he had struck at once at the force opposed to him, he could have destroyed it and marched to Richmond almost unopposed.

Instead of striking at a vulnerable point he sat down in a methodical fashion to besiege Yorktown. While he was waiting for the reinforcements he had demanded, the garrison got away as Johnstone had done from before Manassas, and an attempt to push forward resulted in the defeat of his lieutenant, Hooker, at Williamsburg.

McDowell, who was at Fredericksburg, was ordered to join and reinforce McClellan, but the junction was never made, for at the moment Jackson took the field and effected one of the most brilliant exploits of the war. The Union troops in the Shenandoah Valley were much more numerous than the force which Jackson had at his disposal, but they were scattered at various points, and by a series of incalculably rapid movements the Southern captain attacked and overwhelmed each in turn. The alarm at Washington was great, and McDowell hastened to cut him off, only to discover that Jackson had slipped past him and was back in his own country. Meanwhile McClellan, left without the reinforcements he had expected, was attacked by Lee and beaten back in seven days' consecutive fighting right to Harrison's Landing, where he could only entrench himself and stand on the defensive. Richmond was as far off as ever.

One piece of good news, however, reached Washington at about this time, and once again it came from the West. Towards the end of April Farragut, the American admiral, captured the city of New Orleans. The event was justly thought to be of great importance, for Grant already dominated the Upper Mississippi, and if he could join hands with a Union force operating from the mouth of the great river, the Confederacy would be cut in two.

Perhaps the contrast between the good fortune which had attended the Federal arms in the West and the failure of the campaign in Eastern Virginia was responsible for the appointment of a general taken from the Western theatre of war to command the army of the Potomac. Lincoln, having supported McClellan as long as he could, was now obliged to abandon his cause, and General Pope was appointed to supreme command of the campaign in Eastern Virginia.

The change brought no better fortune; indeed, it was the prelude to a disaster worse than any that McClellan had suffered. Pope advanced by the route of the original invasion, and reached exactly the point where McDowell's army had been routed. Here he paused and waited. While he lay there Jackson made another of his daring raids, got between him and Washington and cut his communications, while Lee fell upon him and utterly destroyed his army in the second battle of Bull Run.

Lee's victory left him in full possession of the initiative, with no effective force immediately before him and with a choice of objectives. It was believed by many that he would use his opportunity to attack Washington. But he wisely refrained from such an attempt. Washington was guarded by a strong garrison, and its defences had been carefully prepared. To take it would involve at least something like a siege, and while he was reducing it the North would have the breathing space it needed to rally its still unexhausted powers. He proposed to himself an alternative, which, if he had been right in his estimate of the political factors, would have given him Washington and much more, and probably decided the war in favour of the Confederacy. He crossed the Potomac and led his army into Maryland.

The stroke was as much political as military in its character. Maryland was a Southern State. There was a sort of traditional sisterhood between her and Virginia. Though she had not seceded, it was thought that her sympathies must be with the South. The attack on the Union troops in Baltimore at the beginning of the war had seemed strong confirmation of this belief. The general impression in the South, which the Southern general probably shared, was that Maryland was at heart Secessionist, and that a true expression of her will was prevented only by force. The natural inference was that when a victorious Southern commander appeared within her borders, the people would rally to him as one man, Washington would be cut off from the North, the President captured, the Confederacy recognized by the European Powers, and the North would hardly continue the hopeless struggle. This idea was embodied in a fierce war-song which had recently become popular throughout the Confederate States and was caught up by Lee's soldiers on their historic march. It began—

"The despot's heel is on thy shore, Maryland! My Maryland!" And it ended—

"She is not dead, nor deaf, nor dumb! Hurrah! She spurns the Yankee scum! She breathes! She lives! She'll come! she'll come! Maryland! My Maryland!"

But Maryland did not come. The whole political conception which underlay Lee's move was false. It may seem curious that those who, when everything seemed to be in favour of the North, had stoned Union soldiers in the streets of the State capital, should not have moved a finger when a great Southern soldier came among them with the glamour of victory around him and proclaimed himself their liberator. Yet so it proved. The probable explanation is that, Maryland lying under the shadow of the capital, which was built for the most part on her territory, Lincoln could deal with her people directly. And wherever he could get men face to face and show the manner of man he was, he could persuade. Maryland was familiar with "the despot" and did not find his "heel" at all intolerable. The image of the horrible hairy Abolitionist gloating constantly over the thought of a massacre of Southerners by Negroes, which did duty for a portrait of Lincoln in the South, was not convincing to Marylanders, who knew the man himself and found him a kindly, shrewd, and humorous man of the world, with much in his person and character that recalled his Southern origin, who enforced the law with strict impartiality wherever his power extended, and who, above all, punctiliously returned any fugitive slaves that might seek refuge in the District of Columbia.

Lee issued a dignified and persuasive proclamation in which he declared that he came among the people of Maryland as a friend and liberator. But Maryland showed no desire to be liberated. He and his soldiers were everywhere coldly received. Hardly a volunteer joined them. In many towns Union flags were flaunted in their faces—a fact upon which is based the fictitious story of Barbara Fritchie.

The political failure of the move led to considerable military embarrassments. Lee met with no defeat in arms, but his difficulties increased day by day.

Believing that he would be operating among a friendly population he had given less thought than he would otherwise have done to the problem of supplies, supposing that he could obtain all he needed from the country. That problem now became acute, for the Marylanders refused to accept the Confederate paper, which was all he had to tender in payment, and the fact that he professed to be their liberator actually made his position more difficult, for he could not without sacrificing a moral asset treat them avowedly as an enemy people. He found himself compelled to send Jackson back to hold Harper's Ferry lest his communications might be endangered. Later he learnt that McClellan, who had been restored to the chief command after Pope's defeat, was moving to cut off his retreat. He hastened back towards his base, and the two armies met by Antietam Creek.

Antietam was not really a Union victory. It was followed by the retirement of Lee into Virginia, but it is certain that such retirement had been intended by him from the beginning—was indeed his objective. The objective of McClellan was, or should have been, the destruction of the Confederate army, and this was not achieved. Yet, as marking the end of the Southern commander's undoubted failure in Maryland, it offered enough of the appearance of a victory to justify in Lincoln's judgment an executive act upon which he had determined some months earlier, but which he thought would have a better effect coming after a military success than in time of military weakness and peril.

We have seen that both the President and Congress had been careful to insist that the war was not undertaken on behalf of the Negroes. Yet the events of the war had forced the problem of the Negro into prominence. Fugitive slaves from the rebel States took refuge with the Union armies, and the question of what should be done with them was forced on the Government. Lincoln knew that in this matter he must move with the utmost caution. When in the early days of the war, Frémont, who had been appointed to military commander in Missouri, where he showed an utter unfitness, both intellectual and moral, for his place, proclaimed on his own responsibility the emancipation of the slaves of "disloyal" owners, his headstrong vanity would probably have thrown both Missouri and Kentucky into the arms of the Confederacy if the President had not promptly disavowed him. Later he disavowed a similar proclamation by General Hunter. When a deputation of ministers of religion from Chicago urged on him the desirability of immediate action against Slavery, he met them with a reply the opening passage of which is one of the world's masterpieces of irony. When Horace Greeley backed the same appeal with his "Prayer of Twenty Millions," Lincoln in a brief letter summarized his policy with his usual lucidity and force.

"My paramount object in this struggle is to save the Union, and is not either to save or to destroy Slavery. If I could save the Union without freeing any slaves, I would do it; and if I could save it by freeing some and leaving others alone, I would also do that. What I do about Slavery and the coloured race, I do because I believe it helps to save the Union; and what I forbear, I forbear because I do not believe it would help to save the Union."

At the time he wrote these words Lincoln had already decided on a policy of military emancipation in the rebel States. He doubtless wrote them with an eye of the possible effects of that policy. He wished the Northern Democrats and the Unionists of Border States to understand that his action was based upon considerations of military expediency and in no way upon his personal disapproval of Slavery, of which at the same time he made no recantation. On the military ground he had a strong case. If, as the South maintained, the slave was simply a piece of property, then the slave of a rebel was a piece of enemy property—and enemy property used or usable for purposes of war. To confiscate enemy property which may be of military use was a practice as old as war itself. The same principle which justified the North in destroying a Southern cotton crop or tearing up the Southern railways justified the emancipation of Negroes within the bounds of the Southern Confederacy. In consonance with this principle Lincoln issued on September 22nd a proclamation declaring slaves free as from January 1, 1863, in such districts as the President should on that date specify as being in rebellion against the Federal Government. Thus a chance was deliberately left open for any State, or part of a State, to save its slaves by submission. At the same time Lincoln renewed the strenuous efforts which he had already made more than once to induce the Slave States which remained in the Union to consent voluntarily to some scheme of gradual and compensated emancipation.

One effect of the Emancipation Proclamation upon which Lincoln had calculated was the approval of the civilized world and especially of England. This was at that moment of the more importance because the growing tendency of Englishmen to sympathize with the South, which was largely the product of Jackson's daring and picturesque exploits, had already produced a series of incidents which nearly involved the two nations in war. The chief of these was the matter of the Alabama. This cruiser was built and fitted up in the dockyards of Liverpool by the British firm of Laird. She was intended, as the contractors of course knew, for the service of the Confederacy, and, when completed, she took to the sea under pretext of a trial trip, in spite of the protests of the representative of the American Republic. The order to detain her arrived too late, and she reached a Southern port, whence she issued to become a terror to the commerce of the United States. That the fitting up of such a vessel, if carried out with the complicity of the Government, was a gross breach of neutrality is unquestionable. That the Government of Lord Russell connived at the escape of the Alabama, well knowing her purpose and character, though generally believed in America at the time, is most unlikely. That the truth was known to the authorities at Liverpool, where Southern sympathies were especially strong, is on the other hand almost certain, and these authorities must be held mainly responsible for misleading the Government and so preventing compliance with the quite proper demands of Adams, the American Ambassador. Finally, an International Court found that Great Britain had not shown "reasonable care" in fulfilling her obligations, and in this verdict a fair-minded student of the facts will acquiesce. At a later date we paid to the United States a heavy sum as compensation for the depredations of the Alabama. Meanwhile, neither Antietam nor the Proclamation appeared to bring any luck to the Union armies in the field. McClellan showed his customary over-caution in allowing Lee to escape unhammered; once more he was superseded, and once more his supersession only replaced inaction by disaster. Hooker, attempting an invasion of Virginia, got caught in the tangled forest area called "the Wilderness." Jackson rode round him, cutting his communications and so forcing him to fight, and Lee beat him soundly at Chancellorsville. The battle was, however, won at a heavy cost to the Confederacy, for towards the end of the day the mistake of a picket caused the death by a Southern bullet of the most brilliant, if not the greatest, of Southern captains. As to what that loss meant we have the testimony of his chief and comrade-in-arms. "If I had had Jackson with me," said Lee after Gettysburg, "I should have won a complete victory." This, however, belongs to a later period. Burnside, succeeding Hooker, met at Lee's hands with an even more crushing defeat at Fredericksburg.

And now, as a result of these Southern successes, began to become dangerous that factor on which the South had counted from the first—the increasing weariness and division of the North. I have tried in these pages to put fairly the case for the defeated side in the Civil War. But one can have a reasonable understanding of and even sympathy with the South without having any sympathy to waste on those who in the North were called "Copperheads." A Northerner might, indeed, honestly think the Southern cause just and coercion of the seceding States immoral. But if so he should have been opposed to such coercion from the first. The Confederate case was in no way morally stronger in 1863 than it had been in 1861. If, therefore, a man had been in favour of coercion in 1861—as practically all Northerners were—his weakening two years later could not point to an unwillingness to do injustice, but only to the operation of fear or fatigue as deterrents from action believed to be just. Moreover, the ordinary "Copperhead" position was so plainly in contradiction of known facts that it must be pronounced either imbecile or dishonest. If these men had urged the acceptance of disunion as an accomplished fact, a case might be made out for them. But they generally professed the strongest desire to restore the Union, accompanied by vehement professions of the belief that this could in some fashion be achieved by "negotiation." The folly of such a supposition was patent. The Confederacy was in arms for the one specific purpose of separating itself from the Union, and so far its appeal to arms had been on the whole successful. That it would give up the single object for which it was fighting for any other reason than military defeat was, on the face of it, quite insanely unlikely; and, as might have been expected, the explicit declarations of Davis and all the other Confederate leaders were at this time uniformly to the effect that peace could be had by the recognition of Southern independence and in no other fashion. The "Copperheads," however, seem to have suffered from that amazing illusion which we have learnt in recent times to associate with the Russian Bolsheviks and their admirers in other countries—the illusion that if one side leaves off fighting the other side will immediately do the same, though all the objects for which it ever wanted to fight are unachieved. They persisted in maintaining that in some mysterious fashion the President's "ambition" was standing between the country and a peace based on reunion. The same folly was put forward by Greeley, perhaps the most consistently wrong-headed of American public men: in him it was the more absurd since on the one issue, other than that of union or separation, which offered any possible material for a compromise, that of Slavery, he was professedly against all compromise, and blamed the President for attempting any.

Little as can be said for the "Copperhead" temper, its spread in the Northern States during the second year of the war was a serious menace to the Union cause. It showed itself in the Congressional elections, when the Government's majority was saved only by the loyalty of the Border Slave States, whose support Lincoln had been at pains to conciliate in the face of so much difficulty and misunderstanding. It showed itself in the increased activity of pacifist agitators, of whom the notorious Vallandingham may be taken as a type.

Lincoln met the danger in two fashions. He met the arguments and appeals of the "Copperheads" with unanswerable logic and with that lucidity of thought and expression of which he was a master. One pronouncement of his is worth quoting, and one wishes that it could have been reproduced everywhere at the time of the ridiculous Stockholm project. "Suppose refugees from the South and peace men of the North get together and frame and proclaim a compromise embracing a restoration of the Union: in what way can that compromise be used to keep Lee's army out of Pennsylvania? Meade's army can keep Lee's out of Pennsylvania, and, I think, can ultimately drive it out of existence. But no paper compromise, to which the controllers of Lee's army are not agreed, can at all affect that army." Reasoning could not be more conclusive; but Lincoln did not stop at reasoning. Now was to be shown how powerful an instrument of authority the Jacksonian Revolution had created in the popular elective Presidency. Perhaps no single man ever exercised so much direct personal power as did Abraham Lincoln during those four years of Civil War. The Habeas Corpus Act was suspended by executive decree, and those whose action was thought a hindrance to military success were arrested in shoals by the orders of Stanton, the new energetic War Secretary, a Jacksonian Democrat whom Lincoln had put in the place of an incompetent Republican, though he had served under Buchanan and supported Breckinridge. The constitutional justification of these acts was widely challenged, but the people in the main supported the Executive.

Lincoln, like Jackson, understood the populace and knew just how to appeal to them. "Must I shoot a simple-minded boy for deserting, and spare the wily agitator whose words induce him to desert?" Vallandingham himself met a measure of justice characteristic of the President's humour and almost recalling the jurisprudence of Sir W. S. Gilbert's Mikado. Originally condemned to detention in a fortress, his sentence was commuted by Lincoln to banishment, and he was conducted by the President's orders across the army lines and dumped on the Confederacy! He did not stay there long. The Southerners had doubtless some reason to be grateful to him; but they cannot possibly have liked him. With their own Vallandinghams they had an even shorter way.

The same sort of war-weariness was perhaps a contributory cause of an even more serious episode—the Draft Riots of New York City. Here, however, a special and much more legitimate ground of protest was involved. The Confederacy had long before imposed Conscription upon the youth of the South. It was imperative that the North should do the same, and, though the constitutional power of the Federal Government to make such a call was questioned, its moral right to do so seems to me unquestionable, for if the common Government has not the right in the last resort to call upon all citizens to defend its own existence, it is difficult to see what rights it can possess. Unfortunately, Congress associated with this just claim a provision for which there was plenty of historical precedent but no justification in that democratic theory upon which the American Commonwealth was built. It provided that a man whose name had been drawn could, if he chose, pay a substitute to serve in his stead. This was obviously a privilege accorded to mere wealth, odious to the morals of the Republic and especially odious to the very democratic populace of New York. The drawing of the names was there interrupted by violence, and for some days the city was virtually in the hands of the insurgents. The popular anger was complicated by a long-standing racial feud between the Irish and the Negroes, and a good many lynchings took place. At last order was restored by the police, who used to restore it a violence as savage as that of the crowd they were suppressing.

We must now turn back to the military operations. Lee had once more broken through, and was able to choose the point where a sortie might most effectually be made. He resolved this time to strike directly at the North itself, and crossing a strip of Maryland he invaded Pennsylvania, his ultimate objective being probably the great bridge over the Susquehanna at Harrisburg, the destruction of which would seriously hamper communication between North and West. At first he met with no opposition, but a Federal army under Meade started in pursuit of him and caught him up at Gettysburg. In the battle which followed, as at Valmy, each side had its back to its own territory. The invader, though inferior in numbers, was obliged by the conditions of the struggle to take the offensive. The main feature of the fighting was the charge and repulse of Pickett's Brigade. Both sides stood appalling losses with magnificent steadiness. The Union troops maintained their ground in spite of all that Southern valour could do to dislodge them. It is generally thought that if Meade had followed up his success by a vigorous offensive Lee's army might have been destroyed. As things were, having failed in its purpose of breaking the ring that held the Confederacy, it got back into Virginia unbroken and almost unpunished.

Gettysburg is generally considered as the turning-point of the war, though perhaps from a purely military point of view more significance ought to be attached to another success which almost exactly synchronized with it. The same 4th of July whereon the North learnt of Lee's failure brought news of the capture of Vicksburg by Grant. This meant that the whole course of the Mississippi was now in Federal hands, and made possible an invasion of the Confederacy from the West such as ultimately effected its overthrow.

Lincoln, whose judgment in such matters was exceptionally keen for a civilian, had long had his eye on Grant. He had noted his successes and his failures, and he had noted especially in him the quality which he could not find in McClellan or in Meade—a boldness of plan, a readiness to take risks, and above all a disposition to press a success vigorously home even at a heavy sacrifice. "I can't spare that man; he fights," he had said when some clamoured for Grant's recall after Shiloh. For those who warned him that Grant was given to heavy drinking he had an even more characteristic reply: "I wish I knew what whisky he drinks: I would send a cask to some of the other generals."

Meade's hesitation after Gettysburg and Grant's achievement at Vicksburg between them decided him. Grant was now appointed to supreme command of all the armies of the Union.

Ulysses S. Grant stands out in history as one of those men to whom a uniform seems to be salvation. As a young man he had fought with credit in the Mexican War; later he had left the army, and seemingly gone to the dogs. He took to drink. He lost all his employments. He became to all appearances an incorrigible waster, a rolling stone, a man whom his old friends crossed the road to avoid because a meeting with him always meant an attempt to borrow money.

Then came the war, and Grant grasped—as such broken men often do—at the chance of a new start. Not without hesitation, he was entrusted with a subordinate command in the West, and almost at once he justified those who had been ready to give him a trial by his brilliant share in the capture of Fort Donelson. From that moment he was a new man, repeatedly displaying not only the soldierly qualities of iron courage and a thorough grasp of the practice of fighting, but moral qualities of a high order, a splendid tenacity in disaster and hope deferred, and in victory a noble magnanimity towards the conquered. One wishes that the story could end there. But it must, unfortunately, be added that when at last he laid aside his sword he seemed to lay aside all that was best in him with it, while the weaknesses of character which were so conspicuous in Mr. Ulysses Grant, and which seemed so completely bled out of General Grant, made many a startling and disastrous reappearance in President Grant.

Grant arrived at Washington and saw the President for the first time. The Western campaign he left in the hands of two of his ablest lieutenants—Sherman, perhaps in truth the greatest soldier that appeared on the Northern side, and Thomas, a Virginian Unionist who had left his State at the call of his country. There was much work for them to do, for while the capture of Vicksburg and its consequences gave them the Mississippi, the first attempt to invade from that side under Rosecrans had suffered defeat in the bloody battle of the Chickamauga. Sherman and Thomas resolved to reverse this unfavourable decision and attacked at the same crucial point. An action lasting four days and full of picturesque episodes gave them the victory which was the starting-point of all that followed. To that action belongs the strange fight of Look-Out Mountain fought "above the clouds" by men who could not see the wide terrain for the mastery of which they were contending, and the marvellous charge of the Westerners up Missionary Ridge, one of those cases where soldiers, raised above themselves and acting without orders, have achieved a feat which their commander had dismissed as impossible. To the whole action is given the name of the Battle of Chattanooga, and its effect was to give Sherman the base he needed from which to strike at the heart of the Confederacy.

Grant in Virginia was less successful. An examination of his campaign will leave the impression that, however superior he was to previous Northern commanders in energy, as a strategist he was no match for Lee. The Southern general, with inferior forces, captured the initiative and did what he chose with him, caught him in the Wilderness as he had previously caught Hooker, and kept him there on ground which gave every advantage to the Confederate forces, who knew every inch of it, where Grant's superiority in numbers could not be brought fully into play, and where his even greater superiority in artillery was completely neutralized. At the end of a week's hard fighting, Grant had gained no advantage, while the Northern losses were appalling—as great as the total original numbers of the enemy that inflicted them. At Spottsylvania, where Grant attempted a flanking movement, the same tactics were pursued with the same success, while a final attempt of the Northern general at a frontal assault ended in a costly defeat.

In the darkest hour of this campaign Grant had told the Government at Washington that he would "fight it out on that line if it took all the summer." It was, however, on another line that the issue was being fought out and decided against the Confederacy. From Chattanooga Sherman moved on Atlanta, the capital of Georgia. Joseph Johnstone disputed every step of the advance, making it as costly as possible, but wisely refused to risk his numerically inferior army in a general engagement. He fell back slowly, making a stand here and there, till the Northern general stood before Atlanta.

It was at this moment that the leaders of the Confederacy would have acted wisely in proposing terms of peace. Their armies were still in being, and could even boast conspicuous and recent successes. If the war went on it would probably be many months before the end came, while the North was bitterly weary of the slaughter and would not tolerate the refusal of reasonable settlement. Yet, if the war went on, the end could no longer be in doubt. Had that golden moment been seized, the seceding States might have re-entered the Union almost on their own terms. Certainly they could have avoided the abasement and humiliation which was to come upon them as the consequence of continuing their resistance till surrender had to be unconditional. It might seem at first that Emancipation Proclamation had introduced an additional obstacle to accommodation. But this was largely neutralized by the fact that everyone, including Jefferson Davis himself, recognized that Slavery had been effectively destroyed by the war and could never be revived, even were the South victorious. The acceptance by the Confederacy of a policy suggested by Lee, whereby Negroes were to be enlisted as soldiers and freed on enlistment, clinched this finally. On the other hand, Lincoln let it be clearly understood that if the Union could be restored by consent he was prepared to advocate the compensation of Southern owners for the loss of their slaves. The blame for the failure to take advantage of this moment must rest mainly on Davis. It was he who refused to listen to any terms save the recognition of

Southern independence; and this attitude doomed the tentative negotiations entered into at Hampton Roads to failure.

Meanwhile, in the North, Lincoln was chosen President for a second term. At one time his chances had looked gloomy enough. The Democratic Party had astutely chosen General McClellan as its candidate. His personal popularity with the troops, and the suggestion that he was an honest soldier ill-used by civilian politicians, might well gain him much support in the armies, for whose voting special provision had been made, while among the civil population he might expect the support of all who, for one reason or another, were discontented with the Government. At the same time the extreme Anti-Slavery wing of the Republican Party, alienated by the diplomacy of the President in dealing with the Border States, and by the moderation of his views concerning the Negro and his future, put forward another displaced general, Frémont. But in the end circumstances and the confidence which his statesmanship had created combined to give Lincoln something like a walk-over. The Democratic Party got into the hands of the "Copperheads" at the very moment when facts were giving the lie to the "Copperhead" thesis. Its platform described the course of the war as "four years of failure," and its issue as hopeless, while before the voting began even a layman could see that the Confederacy was, from the military point of view, on its last legs. The War Democrats joined hands with the Republicans, and the alliance was sealed by the selection of Andrew Johnson, a Jacksonian Democrat from Tennessee, as candidate for the Vice-Presidency. The Radical Republicans began to discover how strong a hold Lincoln had gained on the public mind in the North, and to see that by pressing their candidate they would only expose the weakness of their faction. Frémont was withdrawn and McClellan easily defeated. A curious error has been constantly repeated in print in this country to the effect that Lincoln was saved only by the votes of the army. There is no shadow of foundation for this statement. The proportion of his supporters among the soldiers was not much greater than among the civil population. But in both it was overwhelming.

Meanwhile Atlanta had fallen, and Davis had unwisely relieved Johnstone of his command. It was now that Sherman determined on the bold scheme which mainly secured the ultimate victory of the North. Cutting himself loose from his base and abandoning all means of communication with the North, he advanced into the country of the enemy, living on it and laying it waste as he passed. For a month his Government had no news of him. Ultimately he reached the sea at Savannah, and was able to tell his supporters that he had made a desert in the rear of the main Confederate armies. Thence he turned again, traversed South Carolina, and appeared, so to speak, on the flank of the main Confederate forces which were holding Grant.

The ethics of Sherman's famous March to the Sea have been much debated. He was certainly justified by the laws of war in destroying the military resources of the Confederacy, and it does not seem that more than this was anywhere done by his orders. There was a good deal of promiscuous looting by his troops, and still more by camp followers and by the Negroes who, somewhat to his annoyance, attached themselves to his columns. The march through South Carolina was the episode marked by the harshest conduct, for officers and men had not forgotten Sumter, and regarded the devastation of that State as a just measure of patriotic vengeance on the only begetter of the rebellion; but the burning of Columbus seems to have been an accident, for which at least Sherman himself was not responsible. It is fair to him to add that in the very few cases—less than half a dozen in all—where a charge of rape or murder can be brought home, the offender was punished with death.

As a military stroke the March to the Sea was decisive. One sees its consequences at once in the events of the Virginian campaign. Lee had suffered no military defeat; indeed, the balance of military success, so far as concerned the army directly opposed to him, was in his favour. Sheridan's campaign in the Shenandoah Valley had delighted the North as much as Jackson's earlier exploits in the same region had delighted the South; but its direct military effect was not great. From the moment, however, of Sherman's successful completion of his march, the problem of the Southern general becomes wholly different. It is no longer whether he can defeat the enemy, but whether he can save his army. He determined to abandon Richmond, and effect, if possible, a union with Johnstone, who was again watching and checking Sherman.

Did space permit, it would be a noble task to chronicle the last wonderful fight of the Lion of the South; how, with an exhausted and continually diminishing army, he still proved how much he was to be feared; how he turned on Sheridan and beat him, checked Grant and broke away again only to find his path barred by another Union army.

At Appomattox Court House the end came. The lion was trapped and caught at last. There was nothing for it but to make the best terms he could for his men. The two generals met. Both rose to the nobility of the occasion. Lee had never been anything but great, and Grant was never so great again. The terms accorded to the vanquished were generous and honourable to the utmost limit of the victor's authority. "This will have the happiest effect on my people," said Lee, in shaking hands with his conqueror. They talked a little of old times at West Point, where they had studied together, and parted. Lee rode away to his men and addressed them: "We have fought through this war together. I did my best for you." With these few words, worth the whole two volumes of Jefferson Davis's rather tiresome apologetics, one of the purest, bravest, and most chivalrous figures among those who have followed the noble profession of arms rides out of history.

Chapter 10

"THE BLACK TERROR"

The surrender of Lee and his army was not actually the end of the war. The army of General Johnstone and some smaller Confederate forces were still in being; but their suppression seemed clearly only a matter of time, and all men's eyes were already turned to the problem of reconstruction, and on no man did the urgency of that problem press more ominously than on the President.

Slavery was dead. This was already admitted in the South as well as in the North. Had the Confederacy, by some miracle, achieved its independence during the last year of the war, it is extremely unlikely that Slavery would have endured within its borders. This was the publicly expressed opinion of Jefferson Davis even before the adoption of Lee's policy of recruiting slaves and liberating them on enlistment had completed the work which the Emancipation Proclamation of Lincoln had begun. Before the war was over, Missouri, where the Slavery problem was a comparatively small affair, and Maryland, which had always had a good record for humanity and justice in the treatment of its slave population, had declared themselves Free States. The new Governments organized under Lincoln's superintendence in the conquered parts of the Confederacy had followed suit. It was a comparatively easy matter to carry the celebrated Thirteenth Amendment to the Constitution declaring Slavery illegal throughout the Union.

But, as no one knew better than the President, the abolition of Slavery was a very different thing from the solution of the Negro problem. Six years before his election he had used of the problem of Slavery in the South these remarkable words: "I surely will not blame them (the Southerners) for not doing what I should not know how to do myself. If all earthly power was given I should not know what to do as to the existing institution." The words now came back upon him with an awful weight which he fully appreciated. All earthly power was given—direct personal power to a degree perhaps unparalleled in history—and he had to find out what to do.

His own belief appears always to have been that the only permanent solution of the problem was Jefferson's. He did not believe that black and white races would permanently live side by side on a footing of equality, and he loathed with all the loathing of a Kentuckian the thought of racial amalgamation. In his proposal to the Border States he had suggested repatriation in Africa, and he now began to develop a similar project on a larger scale.

But the urgent problem of the reconstruction of the Union could not wait for the completion of so immense a task. The seceding States must be got into their proper relation with the Federal Government as quickly as possible, and Lincoln had clear ideas as to how this should be done. The reconstructed Government of Louisiana which he organized was a working model of what he proposed to do throughout the South. All citizens of the State who were prepared to take the oath of allegiance to the Federal Government were to be invited to elect a convention and frame a constitution. They were required to annul the ordinances of Secession, to ratify the Thirteenth Amendment, and to repudiate the Confederate Debt. The Executive would then recognize the State as already restored to its proper place within the Union, with the full rights of internal self-government which the Constitution guaranteed. The freedmen were of course not citizens, and could, as such, take no part in these proceedings; but Lincoln recommended, without attempting to dictate, that the franchise should be extended to "the very intelligent and those who have fought for us during the war."

Such was Lincoln's policy of reconstruction. He was anxious to get as much as possible of that policy in working order before Congress should meet. His foresight was justified, for as soon as Congress met the policy was challenged by the Radical wing of the Republican Party, whose spokesman was Senator Sumner of Massachusetts.

Charles Sumner has already been mentioned in these pages. The time has come when something like a portrait of him must be attempted. He was of a type which exists in all countries, but for which America has found the exact and irreplaceable name. He was a "high-brow." The phrase hardly needs explanation; it corresponds somewhat to what the French mean by intellectuel, but with an additional touch of moral priggishness which exactly suits Sumner. It does not, of course, imply that a man can think. Sumner was conspicuous even among politicians for his ineptitude in this respect. But it implies a pose of superiority both as regards culture and as regards what a man of that kind calls "idealism" which makes such an one peculiarly offensive to his fellow-men. "The Senator so conducts himself," said Fessenden, a Republican, and to a great extent an ally, "that he has no friends." He had a peculiar command of the language of insult and vituperation that was all the more infuriating because obviously the product not of sudden temper, but of careful and scholarly preparation. In all matters requiring practical action he was handicapped by an incapacity for understanding men; in matters requiring mental lucidity by an incapacity for following a line of consecutive thought.

The thesis of which Sumner appeared as the champion was about as silly as ever a thesis could be. It was that the United States were bound by the doctrine set out in the Declaration of Independence to extend the Franchise indiscriminately to the Negroes.

Had Sumner had any sense it might have occurred to him that the author of the Declaration of Independence might be presumed to have some knowledge of its meaning and content. Did Thomas Jefferson think that his doctrines involved Negro Suffrage? So far from desiring that Negroes should vote with white men, he did not believe that they could even live in the same free community. Yet since Sumner's absurd fallacy has a certain historical importance through the influence it exerted on Northern opinion, it may be well to point out where it lay.

The Declaration of Independence lays down three general principles fundamental to Democracy. One is that all men are equal in respect of their natural rights. The second is that the safeguarding of men's natural rights is the object of government. The third that the basis of government is contractual—its "just powers" being derived from the consent of the governed to an implied contract.

The application of the first of these principles to the Negro is plain enough. Whatever else he was, the Negro was a man, and, as such, had an equal title with other men to life, liberty, and the pursuit of happiness. But neither Jefferson nor any other sane thinker ever included the electoral suffrage among the natural rights of men. Voting is part of the machinery of government in particular States. It is, in such communities, an acquired right depending according to the philosophy of the Declaration of Independence on an implied contract.

Now if such a contract did really underlie American, as all human society, nothing can be more certain than that the Negro had neither part nor lot in it. When Douglas pretended that the black race was not included in the expression "all men" he was talking sophistry, but when he said that the American Republic had been made "by white men for white men" he was stating, as Lincoln readily acknowledged, an indisputable historical fact. The Negro was a man and had the natural rights of a man; but he could have no claim to the special privileges of an American citizen because he was not and never had been an American citizen. He had not come to America as a citizen; no one would ever have dreamed of bringing him or even admitting him if it had been supposed that he was to be a citizen. He was brought and admitted as a slave. The fact that the servile relationship was condemned by the democratic creed could not make the actual relationship of the two races something wholly other than what it plainly was. A parallel might be found in the case of a man who, having entered into an intrigue with a woman, wholly animal and mercenary in its character, comes under the influence of a philosophy which condemns such a connection as sinful. He is bound to put an end to the connection.

He is bound to act justly and humanely towards the woman. But no sane moralist would maintain that he was bound to marry the woman—that is, to treat the illicit relationship as if it were a wholly different lawful relationship such as it was never intended to be and never could have been.

Such was the plain sense and logic of the situation. To drive such sense into Sumner's lofty but wooden head would have been an impossible enterprise, but the mass of Northerners could almost certainly have been persuaded to a rational policy if a sudden and tragic catastrophe had not altered at a critical moment the whole complexion of public affairs.

Lincoln made his last public speech on April 11, 1865, mainly in defence of his Reconstruction policy as exemplified in the test case of Louisiana. On the following Good Friday he summoned his last Cabinet, at which his ideas on the subject were still further developed. That Cabinet meeting has an additional interest as presenting us with one of the best authenticated of those curious happenings which we may attribute to coincidence or to something deeper, according to our predilections. It is authenticated by the amplest testimony that Lincoln told his Cabinet that he expected that that day would bring some important piece of public news—he thought it might be the surrender of Johnstone and the last of the Confederate armies—and that he gave as a reason the fact that he had had a certain dream, which had come to him on the night before Gettysburg and on the eve of almost every other decisive event in the history of the war. Certain it is that Johnstone did not surrender that day, but before midnight an event of far graver and more fatal purport had changed the destiny of the nation. Abraham Lincoln was dead.

A conspiracy against his life and that of the Northern leaders had been formed by a group of exasperated and fanatical Southerners who met at the house of a Mrs. Suratt in the neighbourhood of Washington. One of the conspirators was to kill Seward, who was confined to his bed by illness, but on whom an unsuccessful attempt was made. Another, it is believed, was instructed to remove Grant, but the general unexpectedly left Washington, and no direct threat was offered to him. The task of making away with the President was assigned to John Wilkes Booth, a dissolute and crack-brained actor. Lincoln and his wife were present that night at a gala performance of a popular English comedy called "Our American Cousin." Booth obtained access to the Presidential box and shot his victim behind the ear, causing instant loss of consciousness, which was followed within a few hours by death. The assassin leapt from the box on to the stage shouting: "Sic semper Tyrannis!" and, though he broke his leg in the process, succeeded, presumably by the aid of a confederate among the theatre officials, in getting away. He was later hunted down, took refuge in a bar, which was set on fire, and was shot in attempting to escape.

The murder of Lincoln was the work of a handful of crazy fools. Already the South, in spite of its natural prejudices, was beginning to understand that he was its best friend. Yet on the South the retribution was to fall. It is curious to recall the words which Lincoln himself had used in repudiating on behalf of the Republican Party the folly of old John Brown, words which are curiously apposite to his own fate and its consequences.

"That affair, in its philosophy," he had said, "corresponds to the many attempts related in history at the assassination of kings and emperors. An enthusiast broods over the oppression of a people till he fancies himself commissioned by Heaven to liberate them. He ventures the attempt, which ends in little else than his own execution. Orsini's attempt on Louis Napoleon and John Brown's attempt at Harper's Ferry were, in their philosophy, precisely the same. The eagerness to cast blame on Old England in the one case and on New England in the other does not disprove the sameness of the two things." It may be added that the "philosophy" of Booth was also "precisely the same" as that of Orsini and Brown, and that the "eagerness to cast blame" on the conquered South was equally unjustifiable and equally inevitable.

The anger of the North was terrible, and was intensified by the recollection of the late President's pleas for lenity and a forgetfulness of the past. "This is their reply to magnanimity!" was the almost universal cry. The wild idea that the responsible heads of the Confederacy were privy to the deed found a wide credence which would have been impossible in cooler blood. The justifiable but unrestrained indignation which Booth's crime provoked must be counted as the first of the factors which made possible the tragic blunders of the Reconstruction.

Another factor was the personality of the new President. Andrew Johnson occupied a position in some ways analogous to that of Tyler a generation earlier. He had been chosen Vice-President as a concession to the War Democrats and to the Unionists of the Border States whose support had been thought necessary to defeat McClellan. With the Northern Republicans who now composed the great majority of Congress he had no political affinity whatever. Yet at the beginning of his term of office he was more popular with the Radicals than Lincoln had ever been. He seemed to share to the full the violence of the popular mood. His declaration that as murder was a crime, so treason was a crime, and "must be made odious," was welcomed with enthusiasm by the very men who afterwards impeached him. Nor, when we blame these men for trafficking with perjurers and digging up tainted and worthless evidence for the purpose of sustaining against him the preposterous charge of complicity in the murder of his predecessor, must we forget that he himself, without any evidence at all, had under his own hand and seal brought the same monstrous accusation against Jefferson Davis. Davis, when apprehended, met the affront with a cutting reply. "There is one man at least who knows this accusation to be false—the man who makes it. Whatever else Andrew Johnson knows, he knows that I preferred Mr. Lincoln to him."

It was true. Between Johnson and the chiefs of the Confederacy there was a bitterness greater than could be found in the heart of any Northerner. To him they were the seducers who had caught his beloved South in a net of disloyalty and disaster. To them he was a traitor who had sold himself to the Yankee oppressor. A social quarrel intensified the political one. Johnson, who had been a tailor by trade, was the one political representative of the "poor whites" of the South. He knew that the great slave-owning squires despised him, and he hated them in return. It was only when the issues cut deeper that it became apparent that, while he would gladly have hanged Jeff Davis and all his Cabinet on a sufficient number of sour apple trees (and perhaps he was the one man in the United States who really wanted to do so), he was none the less a Southerner to the backbone; it was only when the Negro question was raised that the Northern men began to realize, what any Southerner or man acquainted with the South could have told them, that the attitude of the "poor white" towards the Negro was a thousand times more hostile than that of the slave-owner.

Unfortunately, by the same token, the new President had not, as Lincoln would have had, the ear of the North.

Had Lincoln lived he would have approached the task of persuading the North to support his policy with many advantages which his successor necessarily lacked. He would have had the full prestige of the undoubted Elect of the People—so important to an American President, especially in a conflict with Congress. He would have had the added prestige of the ruler under whose administration the Rebellion had been crushed and the Union successfully restored. But he would also have had an instinctive understanding of the temper of the Northern masses and a thorough knowledge of the gradations of opinion and temper among the Northern politicians.

Johnson had none of these qualifications, while his faults of temper were a serious hindrance to the success of his policy. He was perhaps the purest lover of his country among all the survivors of Lincoln: the fact that told so heavily against his success, that he had no party, that he broke with one political connection in opposing Secession and with another in opposing Congressional Reconstruction, is itself a sign of the integrity and consistency of his patriotism. Also he was on the right side. History, seeing how cruelly he was maligned and how abominably he was treated, owes him these acknowledgments. But he was not a prudent or a tactful man. Too much importance need not be attached to the charge of intemperate drinking, which is probably true but not particularly serious. If Johnson had got drunk every night of his life he would only have done what some of the greatest and most successful statesmen in history had done before him. But there was an intemperance of character about the man which was more disastrous in its consequences than a few superfluous whiskies could have been. He was easily drawn into acrimonious personal disputes, and when under their influence would push a quarrel to all lengths with men with whom it was most important in the public interest that he should work harmoniously.

For the extremists, of whom Sumner was a type, were still a minority even among the Republican politicians; nor was Northern opinion, even after the murder of Lincoln, yet prepared to support their policy. There did, however, exist in the minds of quite fair-minded Northerners, in and out of Congress, certain not entirely unreasonable doubts, which it should have been the President's task—as it would certainly have been Lincoln's—to remove by reason and persuasion. He seems to have failed to see that he had to do this; and certainly he altogether failed to do it.

The fears of such men were twofold. They feared that the "rebel" States, if restored immediately to freedom of action and to the full enjoyment of their old privileges, would use these advantages for the purpose of preparing a new secession at some more favourable opportunity. And they feared that the emancipated Negro would not be safe under a Government which his old masters controlled.

It may safely be said that both fears were groundless, though they were both fears which a reasonable man quite intelligibly entertains. Naturally, the South was sore; no community likes having to admit defeat. Also, no doubt, the majority of Southerners would have refused to admit that they were in the wrong in the contest which was now closed; indeed, it was by pressing this peculiarly tactless question that Sumner and his friends procured most of their evidence of the persistence of "disloyalty" in the South. On the other hand, two facts already enforced in these pages have to be remembered. The first is that the Confederacy was not in the full sense a nation. Its defenders felt their defeat as men feel the downfall of a political cause to which they are attached, not quite as men feel the conquest of their country by foreigners. The second is that from the first there had been many who, while admitting the right of secession—and therefore, by implication, the justice of the Southern cause—had yet doubted its expediency. It is surely not unnatural to suppose that the disastrous issue of the experiment had brought a great many round to this point of view. No doubt there was still a residue—perhaps a large residue—of quite impenitent "rebels" who were prepared to renew the battle if they saw a good chance, but the conditions under which the new Southern Governments had come into existence offered sufficient security against such men controlling them. Irreconcilables of that type would not have taken the oath of allegiance, would not have repealed the Ordinances of Secession or repudiated the Confederate Debt, and, if they had no great objection to abolishing Slavery, would probably have made it a point of honour not to do it at Northern dictation. What those who were now asking for re-admission to their ancient rights in the Union had already done or were prepared to do was sufficient evidence that moderation and an accessible temper were predominant in their counsels. The other fear was even more groundless. There might in the South be a certain bitterness against the Northerner; there was none at all against the Negro. Why should there be? During the late troubles the Negro had deserved very well of the South. At a time when practically every active male of the white population was in the fighting line, when a slave insurrection might have brought ruin and disaster on every Southern home, not a slave had risen. The great majority of the race had gone on working faithfully, though the ordinary means of coercion were almost necessarily in abeyance. Even when the Northern armies came among them, proclaiming their emancipation, many of them continued to perform their ordinary duties and to protect the property and secrets of their masters. Years afterwards the late Dr. Booker Washington could boast that there was no known case of one of his race betraying a trust. All this was publicly acknowledged by leading Southerners and one-time supporters of Slavery like Alexander Stephens, who pressed the claims of the Negro to fair and even generous treatment at the hands of the Southern whites. It is certain that these in the main meant well of the black race. It is equally certain that, difficult as the problem was, they were more capable of dealing with it than were alien theorizers from the North, who had hardly seen a Negro save, perhaps, as a waiter at a hotel.

It is a notable fact that the soldiers who conquered the South were at this time practically unanimous in support of a policy of reconciliation and confidence. Sherman, to whom Johnstone surrendered a few days after Lincoln's death, wished to offer terms for the surrender of all the Southern forces which would have guaranteed to the seceding States the full restoration of internal self-government. Grant sent to the President a reassuring report as to the temper of the South which Sumner compared to the "whitewashing message of Franklin Pierce" in regard to Kansas.

Yet it would be absurd to deny that the cleavage between North and South, inevitable after a prolonged Civil War, required time to heal. One event might indeed have ended it almost at once, and that event almost occurred. A foreign menace threatening something valued by both sections would have done more than a dozen Acts of Congress or Amendments to the Constitution. There were many to whom this had always appeared the most hopeful remedy for the sectionable trouble. Among them was Seward, who, having been Lincoln's Secretary of State, now held the same post under Johnson. While secession was still little more than a threat he had proposed to Lincoln the deliberate fomentation of a dispute with some foreign power—he did not appear to mind which. It is thought by some that, after the war, he took up and pressed the Alabama claims with the same notion. That quarrel, however, would hardly have met the case. The ex-Confederates could not be expected to throw themselves with enthusiasm into a war with England to punish her for providing them with a navy. It was otherwise with the trouble which had been brewing in Mexico.

Napoleon III had taken advantage of the Civil War to violate in a very specific fashion the essential principle of the Monroe Doctrine. He had interfered in one of the innumerable Mexican revolutions and taken advantage of it to place on the throne an emperor of his own choice, Maximilian, a cadet of the Hapsburg family, and to support his nominee by French bayonets. Here was a challenge which the South was even more interested in taking up than the North, and, if it had been persisted in, it is quite thinkable that an army under the joint leadership of Grant and Lee and made up of those who had learnt to respect each other on a hundred fields from Bull Run to Spottsylvania might have erased all bitter memories by a common campaign on behalf of the liberties of the continent. But Louis Napoleon was no fool; and in this matter he acted perhaps with more regard to prudence than to honour. He withdrew the French troops, leaving Maximilian to his fate, which he promptly met at the hands of his own subjects.

The sectional quarrel remained unappeased, and the quarrel between the President and Congress began. Congress was not yet Radical, but it was already decidedly, though still respectfully, opposed to Johnson's policy. While only a few of its members had yet made up their minds as to what ought to be done about Reconstruction, the great majority had a strong professional bias which made them feel that the doing or not doing of it should be in their hands and not in those of the Executive. It was by taking advantage of this prevailing sentiment that the Radicals, though still a minority, contrived to get the leadership more and more into their own hands.

Of the Radicals Sumner was the spokesman most conspicuous in the public eye. But not from him came either the driving force or the direction which ultimately gave them the control of national policy.

Left to himself, Sumner could never have imposed the iron oppression from which it took the South a life-and-death wrestle of ten years to shake itself free. At the worst he would have been capable of imposing a few paper pedantries, such as his foolish Civil Rights Bill, which would have been torn up before their ink was dry. The will and intelligence which dictated the Reconstruction belonged to a very different man, a man entitled to a place not with puzzle-headed pedants or coat-turning professionals but with the great tyrants of history.

Thaddeus Stevens of Pennsylvania was in almost every respect the opposite of his ally, Charles Sumner of Massachusetts. Sumner, empty of most things, was especially empty of humour. Stevens had abundance of humour of a somewhat fierce but very real kind. Some of his caustic strokes are as good as anything recorded of Talleyrand: notably his reply to an apologist of Johnson who urged in the President's defence that he was "a selfmade man." "I am delighted to hear it," said Stevens grimly; "it relieves the Creator of a terrible responsibility." With this rather savage wit went courage which could face the most enormous of tests; like Rabelais, like Danton, he could jest with death when death was touching him on the shoulder. In public life he was not so much careless of what he considered conventions as defiantly happy in challenging them. It gave him keen delight to outrage at once the racial sentiments of the South and the

Puritanism of the North by compelling the politicians whom he dominated and despised to pay public court to his mulatto mistress.

The inspiring motive of this man was hatred of the South. It seems probable that this sentiment had its origin in a genuine and honourable detestation of Slavery.

As a practising lawyer in Pennsylvania he had at an earlier period taken a prominent part in defending fugitive slaves. But by the time that he stood forward as the chief opponent of the Presidential policy of conciliation, Slavery had ceased to exist; yet his passion against the former slave-owners seemed rather to increase than to diminish. I think it certain, though I cannot produce here all the evidence that appears to me to support such a conclusion, that it was the negative rather than the positive aspect of his policy that attracted him most. Sumner might dream of the wondrous future in store for the Negro race—of whose qualities and needs he knew literally nothing—under Bostonian tutelage. But I am sure that for Stevens the vision dearest to his heart was rather that of the proud Southern aristocracy compelled to plead for mercy on its knees at the tribunal of its hereditary bondsmen.

Stevens was a great party leader. Not such a leader as Jefferson or Jackson had been: a man who sums up and expresses the will of masses of men. Nor yet such a leader as later times have accustomed us to; a man who by bribery or intrigue induces his fellow-professionals to support him. He was one of those who rule by personal dominance. His courage has already been remarked; and he knew how much fearlessness can achieve in a profession where most men are peculiarly cowardly. It was he who forced the issue between the President and Congress and obtained at a stroke a sort of captaincy in the struggle by moving in the House of Representatives that the consideration of Reconstruction by Congress would precede any consideration of the President's message asking for the admission of the representatives of the reorganized States.

By a combination of forceful bullying and skilful strategy Stevens compelled the House of Representatives to accept his leadership in this matter, but the action of Congress on other questions during these early months of the contest shows how far it still was from accepting his policy.

The plan of Reconstruction which the majority now favoured is to be found outlined in the Fourteenth Constitutional Amendment which, at about this time, it recommended for adoption by the States.

The provisions of this amendment were threefold. One, for which a precedent had been afforded by the President's own action, declared that the public debt incurred by the Federal Government should never be repudiated, and also that no State should pay or accept responsibility for any debt incurred for the purpose of waging war against the Federation. Another, probably unwise from the point of view of far-sighted statesmanship but more or less in line with the President's policy, provided for the exclusion from office of all who, having sworn allegiance to the Constitution of the United States, had given aid to a rebellion against its Government. The third, which was really the crucial one, provided a settlement of the franchise question which cannot be regarded as extreme or unreasonable. It will be remembered that the original Constitutional Compromise had provided for the inclusion, in calculating the representation of a State, of all "free persons" and of three-fifths of the "other persons"—that is, of the slaves. By freeing the slaves the representation to which the South was entitled was automatically increased by the odd two-fifths of their number, and this seemed to Northerners unreasonable, unless the freedmen were at the same time enfranchised. Congress decided to recommend that the representation of the South should be greater or less according to the extent to which the Negro population were admitted to the franchise or excluded from it. This clause was re-cast more than once in order to satisfy a fantastic scruple of Sumner's concerning the indecency of mentioning the fact that some people were black and others white, a scruple which he continued to enforce with his customary appeals to the Declaration of Independence, until even his ally Stevens lost all patience with him. But in itself it was not, perhaps, a bad solution of the difficulty. Had it been allowed to stand and work without further interference it is quite likely that many Southern States would have been induced by the prospect of larger representation to admit in course of time such Negroes as seemed capable of understanding the meaning of citizenship in the European sense. Such, at any rate, was the opinion of General Lee, as expressed in his evidence before the Reconstruction Committee.

The South was hostile to the proposed settlement mainly on account of the second provision. It resented the proposed exclusion of its leaders. The sentiment was an honourable and chivalrous one, and was well expressed by Georgia in her protest against the detention of Jefferson Davis: "If he is guilty so are we." But the rejection of the Amendment by the Southern States had a bad effect in the North. It may be convenient here to remark that Davis was never tried. He was brought up and admitted to bail (which the incalculable Greeley found for him), and the case against him was not further pressed. In comparison with almost every other Government that has crushed an insurrection, the Government of the United States deserves high credit for its magnanimity in dealing with the leaders of the Secession. Yet the course actually pursued, more in ignorance than in malice so far as the majority were concerned, probably caused more suffering and bitterness among the vanquished than a hundred executions.

For the Radicals were more and more gaining control of Congress, now openly at war with the Executive. The President had been using his veto freely, and, as many even of his own supporters thought, imprudently. The Republicans were eager to obtain the two-thirds majority in both Houses necessary to carry measures over his veto, and to get it even the meticulous Sumner was ready to stoop to some pretty discreditable manœuvres. The President had taken the field against Congress and made some rather violent stump speeches, which were generally thought unworthy of the dignity of the Chief Magistracy. Meanwhile alleged "Southern outrages" against Negroes were vigorously exploited by the Radicals, whose propaganda was helped by a racial riot in New Orleans, the responsibility for which it is not easy to determine, but the victims of which were mostly persons of colour. The net result was that the new Congress, elected in 1866, not only gave the necessary two-thirds majority, but was more Radical in its complexion and more strictly controlled by the Republican machine than the old had been.

The effect was soon apparent. A Reconstruction Bill was passed by the House and sent up to the Senate. It provided for the military government of the conquered States until they should be reorganized, but was silent in regard to the conditions of their re-admission. The Republican caucus met to consider amendments, and Sumner moved that in the new Constitutions there should be no exclusion from voting on account of colour. This was carried against the strong protest of John Sherman, the brother of the general and a distinguished Republican Senator. But when the Senate met, even he submitted to the decision of the caucus, and the Amendment Bill was carried by the normal Republican majority. Johnson vetoed it, and it was carried by both Houses over his veto. The Radicals had now achieved their main object. Congress was committed to indiscriminate Negro Suffrage, and the President against it; the controversy was narrowed down to that issue. From that moment they had the game in their hands.

The impeachment of Johnson may be regarded as an interlude. The main mover in the matter was Stevens. The main instrument Ben Butler—a man disgraced alike in war and peace, the vilest figure in the politics of that time. It was he who, when in command at New Orleans (after braver men had captured it), issued the infamous order which virtually threatened Southern women who showed disrespect for the Federal uniform with rape—an order which, to the honour of the Northern soldiers, was never carried out. He was recalled from his command, but his great political "influence" saved him from the public disgrace which should have been his portion. Perhaps no man, however high his character, can mix long in the business of politics and keep his hands quite clean. The leniency with which Butler was treated on this occasion must always remain an almost solitary stain upon the memory of Abraham Lincoln. On the memory of Benjamin Butler stains hardly show. At a later stage of the war Butler showed such abject cowardice that Grant begged that if his political importance required that he should have some military command he should be placed somewhere where there was no fighting. This time Butler saved himself by blackmailing his commanding officer. At the conclusion of peace the man went back to politics, a trade for which his temperament was better fitted; and it was he who was chosen as the chief impugner of the conduct and honour of Andrew Johnson!

The immediate cause of the impeachment was the dismissal of Stanton, which Congress considered, wrongly as it would appear, a violation of an Act which, after the quarrel became an open one, they had framed for the express purpose of limiting his prerogative in this direction. In his quarrel with Stanton the President seems to have had a good case, but he was probably unwise to pursue it, and certainly unwise to allow it to involve him in a public quarrel with Grant, the one man whose prestige in the North might have saved the President's policy. The quarrel threw Grant, who was already ambitious of the Presidency, into the hands of the Republicans, and from that moment he ceased to count as a factor making for peace and conciliation.

Johnson was acquitted, two or three honest Republican Senators declaring in his favour, and so depriving the prosecution of the two-thirds majority. Each Senator gave a separate opinion in writing. These documents are of great historical interest; Sumner's especially—which is of inordinate length and intensely characteristic—should be studied by anyone who thinks that in these pages I have given an unfair idea of his character.

In the meantime far more important work was being done in the establishment of Negro rule in the South. State after State was "reconstructed" under the terms of the Act which had been passed over the President's veto. In every case as many white men as possible were disfranchised on one pretext or another as "disloyal." In every case the whole Negro population was enfranchised. Throughout practically the whole area of what had been the Confederate States the position of the races was reversed.

So far, in discussing the Slavery Question and all the issues which arose out of it, I have left one factor out of account—the attitude of the slaves themselves. I have done so deliberately because up to the point which we have now reached that attitude had no effect on history. The slaves had no share in the Abolition movement or in the formation of the Republican Party. Even from John Brown's Raid they held aloof. The President's proclamation which freed them, the Acts of Congress which now gave them supreme power throughout the South, were not of their making or inspiration. In politics the negro was still an unknown factor.

There can be little doubt that under Slavery the relations of the two races were for the most part kindly and free from rancour, that the master was generally humane and the slave faithful. Had it not been so, indeed, the effect of the transfer of power to the freedmen must have been much more horrible than it actually was. On the other hand, it is certain that when some Southern apologists said that the slaves did not want their freedom they were wrong. Dr. Booker Washington, himself a slave till his sixth or seventh year, has given us a picture of the vague but very real longing which was at the back of their minds which bears the stamp of truth. It is confirmed by their strange and picturesque hymnology, in which the passionate desire to be "free," though generally apparently invoked in connection with a future life, is none the less indicative of their temper, and in their preoccupation with those parts of the Old Testament—the history of the Exodus, for instance—which appeared applicable to their own condition. Yet it is clear that they had but the vaguest idea of what "freedom" implied. Of what "citizenship" implied they had, of course, no idea at all.

It is very far from my purpose to write contemptuously of the Negroes. There is something very beautiful about a love of freedom wholly independent of experience and deriving solely from the just instinct of the human soul as to what is its due. And if, as some Southerners said, the Negro understood by freedom mainly that he need not work, there was a truth behind his idea, for the right to be idle if and when you choose without reason given or permission sought is really what makes the essential difference between freedom and slavery. But it is quite another thing when we come to a complex national and historical product like American citizenship. Of all that great European past, without the memory of which the word "Republic" has no meaning, the Negro knew nothing: with it he had no link. A barbaric version of the more barbaric parts of the Bible supplied him with his only record of human society.

Yet Negro Suffrage, though a monstrous anomaly, might have done comparatively little practical mischief if the Negro and his white neighbour had been left alone to find their respective levels. The Negro might have found a certain picturesque novelty in the amusement of voting; the white American might have continued to control the practical operation of Government. But it was no part of the policy of those now in power at Washington to leave either black or white alone. "Loyal" Governments were to be formed in the South; and to this end political adventurers from the North—"carpet-baggers," as they were called—went down into the conquered South to organize the Negro vote. A certain number of disreputable Southerners, known as "scallywags," eagerly took a hand in the game for the sake of the spoils. So of course did the smarter and more ambitious of the freedmen. And under the control of this ill-omened trinity of Carpet-Bagger, Scallywag, and Negro adventurer grew up a series of Governments the like of which the sun has hardly looked upon before or since.

The Negro is hardly to be blamed for his share in the ghastly business. The whole machinery of politics was new to him, new and delightful as a toy, new and even more delightful as a means of personal enrichment. That it had or was intended to have any other purpose probably hardly crossed his mind. His point of view—a very natural one, after all—was well expressed by the aged freedman who was found chuckling over a pile of dollar bills, the reward of some corrupt vote, and, when questioned, observed: "Wal, it's de fifth time I's been bo't and sold, but, 'fo de Lord, it's de fust I eber got de money!" Under administrations conducted in this spirit the whole South was given up to plunder. The looting went on persistently and on a scale almost unthinkable. The public debts reached amazing figures, while Negro legislators voted each other wads of public money as a kind of parlour game, amid peals of hearty African laughter.

Meanwhile the Governments presided over by Negroes, or white courtiers of the Negro and defended by the bayonets of an armed black militia, gave no protection to the persons or property of the whites.

Daily insults were offered to what was now the subject race. The streets of the proud city of Charleston, where ten years before on that fatal November morning the Palmetto flag had been raised as the signal of Secession, were paraded by mobs of dusky freedmen singing: "De bottom rail's on top now, and we's g'wine to keep it dar!" It says much for the essential kindliness of the African race that in the lawless condition of affairs there were no massacres and deliberate cruelties were rare. On the other hand, the animal nature of the Negro was strong, and outrages on white women became appallingly frequent and were perpetrated with complete impunity. Every white family had to live in something like a constant state of siege.

It was not to be expected that ordinary men of European origin would long bear such government. And those on whom it was imposed were no ordinary men. They were men whose manhood had been tried by four awful years of the supreme test, men such as had charged with Pickett up the bloody ridge at Gettysburg, and disputed with the soldiers of Grant every inch of tangled quagmire in the Wilderness. They found a remedy.

Suddenly, as at a word, there appeared in every part of the downtrodden country bands of mysterious horsemen. They rode by night, wearing long white garments with hoods that hid their faces, and to the terror-stricken Negroes who encountered them they declared themselves— not without symbolic truth—the ghosts of the great armies that had died in defence of the Confederacy. But superstitious terrors were not the only ones that they employed.

The mighty secret society called the Ku-Klux-Klan was justified by the only thing that can justify secret societies—gross tyranny and the denial of plain human rights. The method they employed was the method so often employed by oppressed peoples and rarely without success—the method by which the Irish peasantry recovered their land. It was to put fear into the heart of the oppressor. Prominent men, both black and white, who were identified with the evils which afflicted the State, were warned generally by a message signed "K.K.K." to make themselves scarce. If they neglected the warning they generally met a sudden and bloody end. At the same time the Klan unofficially tried and executed those criminals whom the official Government refused to suppress. These executions had under the circumstances a clear moral justification. Unfortunately it had the effect of familiarizing the people with the irregular execution of Negroes, and so paved the way for those "lynchings" for which, since the proper authorities are obviously able and willing to deal adequately with such crimes, no such defence can be set up.

Both sides appealed to Grant, who had been elected President on the expiration of Johnson's term in 1868.

Had he been still the Grant of Appomattox and of the healing message to which reference has already been made, no man would have been better fitted to mediate between the sections and to cover with his protection those who had surrendered to his sword. But Grant was now a mere tool in the hands of the Republican politicians, and those politicians were determined that the atrocious system should be maintained. They had not even the excuse of fanaticism. Stevens was dead; he had lived just long enough to see his policy established, not long enough to see it imperilled. Sumner still lived, but he had quarrelled with Grant and lost much of his influence. The men who surrounded the President cared little enough for the Negro. Their resolution to support African rule in the South depended merely upon the calculation that so long as it endured the reign of the Republican Party and consequently their own professional interests were safe. A special Act of Congress was passed to put down the Ku-Klux-Klan, and the victorious army of the Union was again sent South to carry it into execution. But this time it found an enemy more invulnerable than Lee had been—invulnerable because invisible. The whole white population was in the conspiracy and kept its secrets. The army met with no overt resistance with which it could deal, but the silent terrorism went on. The trade of "Carpet-bagger" became too dangerous. The ambitious Negro was made to feel that the price to be paid for his privileges was a high one. Silently State after State was wrested from Negro rule.

Later the Ku-Klux-Klan—for such is ever the peril of Secret Societies and the great argument against them when not demanded by imperative necessity—began to abuse its power. Reputable people dropped out of it, and traitors were found in its ranks. About 1872 it disappeared. But its work was done. In the great majority of the Southern States the voting power of the Negro was practically eliminated. Negroid Governments survived in three only—South Carolina, Florida, and Louisiana. For these the end came four years later.

The professional politicians of the North, whose motive for supporting the indefensible régime established by the Reconstruction Act has already been noted, used, of course, the "atrocities" of the Ku-Klux-Klan as electioneering material in the North. "Waving the bloody shirt," it was called. But the North was getting tired of it, and was beginning to see that the condition of things in the conquered States was a national disgrace. A Democratic House of Representatives had been chosen, and it looked as if the Democrats would carry the next Presidential election. In fact they did carry it. But fraudulent returns were sent in by the three remaining Negro Governments, and these gave the Republicans a majority of one in the Electoral College. A Commission of Enquiry was demanded and appointed, but it was packed by the Republicans and showed itself as little scrupulous as the scoundrels who administered the "reconstructed" States. Affecting a sudden zeal for State Rights, it declared itself incompetent to inquire into the circumstances under which the returns were made. It accepted them on the word of the State authorities and declared Hayes, the Republican candidate, elected.

It was a gross scandal, but it put an end to a grosser one. Some believe that there was a bargain whereby the election of Hayes should be acquiesced in peaceably on condition that the Negro Governments were not further supported. It is equally possible that Hayes felt his moral position too weak to continue a policy of oppression in the South. At any rate, that policy was not continued. Federal support was withdrawn from the remaining Negro Governments, and they fell without a blow. The second rebellion of the South had succeeded where the first had failed. Eleven years after Lee had surrendered to Grant at Appomattox, Grant's successor in the Presidency surrendered to the ghost of Lee.

Negro rule was at an end. But the Negro remained, and the problem which his existence presented was, and is, to-day, further from solution that when Lincoln signed the Emancipation Proclamation. The signs of the Black Terror are still visible everywhere in the South. They are visible in the political solidarity of those Southern States—and only of those States—which underwent the hideous ordeal, what American politicians call "the solid South." All white men, whatever their opinions, must vote together, lest by their division the Negro should again creep in and regain his supremacy. They are visible in those strict laws of segregation which show how much wider is the gulf between the races than it was under Slavery—when the children of the white slave-owner, in Lincoln's words, "romped freely with the little negroes." They are visible above all in acts of unnatural cruelty committed from time to time against members of the dreaded race. These things are inexplicable to those who do not know the story of the ordeal which the South endured, and cannot guess at the secret panic with which white men contemplate the thought of its return.

Well might Jefferson tremble for his country. The bill which the first slave-traders ran up is not yet paid. Their dreadful legacy remains and may remain for generations to come a baffling and tormenting problem to every American who has a better head than Sumner's and a better heart than Legree's.

Chapter 11

THE NEW PROBLEMS

Most of us were familiar in our youth with a sort of game or problem which consisted in taking a number, effecting a series of additions, multiplications, subtractions, etc., and finally "taking away the number you first thought of." Some such process might be taken as representing the later history of the Republican Party.

That party was originally founded to resist the further extension of Slavery. That was at first its sole policy and objective. And when Slavery disappeared and the Anti-Slavery Societies dissolved themselves it might seem that the Republican Party should logically have done the same. But no political party can long exist, certainly none can long hold power, while reposing solely upon devotion to a single idea. For one thing, the mere requirements of what Lincoln called "national housekeeping" involves an accretion of policies apparently unconnected with its original doctrine. Thus the Republican Party, relying at first wholly upon the votes of the industrial North, which was generally in favour of a high tariff, took over from the old Whig Party a Protectionist tradition, though obviously there is no logical connection between Free Trade and Slavery. Also, in any organized party, especially where politics are necessarily a profession, there is an even more powerful factor working against the original purity of its creed in the immense mass of vested interests which it creates, especially when it is in power—men holding positions under it, men hoping for a "career" through its triumphs, and the like. It may be taken as certain that no political body so constituted will ever voluntarily consent to dissolve itself, as a merely propagandist body may naturally do when its object is achieved.

For some time, as has been seen, the Republicans continued to retain a certain link with their origin by appearing mainly as a pro-Negro and anti-Southern party, with "Southern outrages" as its electoral stock-in-trade and the maintenance of the odious non-American State Governments as its programme. The surrender of 1876 put an end even to this link. The "bloody shirt" disappeared, and with it the last rag of the old Republican garment. A formal protest against the use of "intimidation" in the "Solid South" continued to figure piously for some decades in the quadrennial platform of the party. At last even this was dropped, and its place was taken by the much more defensible demand that Southern representatives should be so reduced as to correspond to the numbers actually suffered to vote. It is interesting to note that if the Republicans had not insisted on supplementing the Fourteenth Amendment by the Fifteenth, forbidding disqualification on grounds of race or colour, and consequently compelling the South to concede in theory the franchise of the blacks and then prevent its exercise, instead of formally denying it them, this grievance would automatically have been met.

What, then, remained to the Republican Party when the "number it first thought of" had been thus taken away? The principal thing that remained was a connection already established by its leading politicians with the industrial interests of the North-Eastern States and with the groups of wealthy men who, in the main, controlled and dealt in those interests. It became the party of industrial Capitalism as it was rapidly developing in the more capitalist and mercantile sections of the Union.

The first effect of this was an appalling increase of political corruption. During Grant's second Presidency an amazing number of very flagrant scandals were brought to light, of which the most notorious were the Erie Railway scandal, in which the rising Republican Congressional leader, Blaine, was implicated, and the Missouri Whisky Ring, by which the President himself was not unbesmirched. The cry for clean government became general, and had much to do with the election of a Democratic House of Representatives in 1874 and the return by a true majority vote—thought defeated by a trick—of a Democratic President in 1876. Though the issue was somewhat overshadowed in 1880, when Garfield was returned mainly on the tariff issue—to be assassinated later by a disappointed place-hunter named Guiteau and succeeded by Arthur—it revived in full force in 1884 when the Republican candidate was James G. Blaine.

Blaine was personally typical of the degeneration of the Republican Party after the close of the Civil War. He had plenty of brains, was a clever speaker and a cleverer intriguer. Principles he had none. Of course he had in his youth "waved the bloody shirt" vigorously enough, was even one of the last to wave it, but at the same time he had throughout his political life stood in with the great capitalist and financial interests of the North-East—and that not a little to his personal profit. The exposure of one politico-financial transaction of his—the Erie Railway affair—had cost him the Republican nomination in 1876, in spite of Ingersoll's amazing piece of rhetoric delivered on his behalf, wherein the celebrated Secularist orator declared that "like an armed warrior, like a plumed knight, James G. Blaine strode down the floor of Congress and flung his shining lance, full and fair"—at those miscreants who objected to politicians using their public status for private profit. By 1884 it was hoped that the scandal had blown over and was forgotten.

Fortunately, however, the traditions of the country were democratic. Democracy is no preservative against incidental corruption; you will have that wherever politics are a profession. But it is a very real preservative against the secrecy in which, in oligarchical countries like our own, such scandals can generally be buried. The Erie scandal met Blaine on every side. One of the most damning features of the business was a very compromising letter of his own which ended with the fatal words: "Please burn this letter." As a result of its publication, crowds of Democratic voters paraded the streets of several great American cities chanting monotonously

"Burn, burn, burn this letter! James G. Blaine. Please, please! Burn this letter! James G. Blaine. Oh! Do! Burn this letter! James G. Blaine."

The result was the complete success of the clean government ticket, and the triumphant return of Grover Cleveland, the first Democrat to take the oath since the Civil War, and perhaps the strongest and best President since Lincoln.

Meanwhile, the Republic had found itself threatened with another racial problem, which became acute at about the time when excitement on both sides regarding the Negro was subsiding. Scarcely had the expansion of the United States touched the Pacific, when its territories encountered a wave of immigration from the thickly populated countries on the other side of that ocean. The population which now poured into California and Oregon was as alien in race and ideals as the Negro, and it was, perhaps, the more dangerous because, while the Negro, so far as he had not absorbed European culture, was a mere barbarian, these people had a very old and elaborate civilization of their own, a civilization picturesque and full of attraction when seen afar off, but exhibiting, at nearer view, many characteristics odious to the traditions, instincts and morals of Europe and white America. There was also the economic evil—really, of course, only an aspect of the conflict of types of civilization—arising from the fact that these immigrants, being used to a lower standard of life, undercut and cheapened the labour of the white man.

Various Acts were passed by Congress from time to time for the restriction and exclusion of Chinese and other Oriental immigrants, and the trouble, though not even yet completely disposed of, was got under a measure of control. Sumner lived long enough to oppose the earlier of these very sensible laws, and, needless to say, trotted out the Declaration of Independence, though in this case the application was even more absurd than in that of the Negro. The Negro, at any rate, was already resident in America, and had been brought there in the first instance without his own consent; and this fact, though it did not make him a citizen, did create a moral responsibility towards him on the part of the American Commonwealth. Towards the Chinaman it had no responsibility whatever.

Doubtless he had, as a man, his natural rights to "life, liberty, and the pursuit of happiness"—in China. But whoever said anything so absurd as that it was one of the natural rights of man to live in America? It was, however, less to the increased absurdity of his argument than to the less favourable bias of his audience that Sumner owed his failure to change the course of legislation in this instance. An argument only one degree less absurd had done well enough as a reason for the enslavement and profanation of the South a year or two before. But there was no great party hoping to perpetuate its power by the aid of the Chinese, nor was there a defeated and unpopular section to be punished for its "treason" by being made over to Mongolian masters. Indeed, Congress, while rejecting Sumner's argument, made a concession to his monomania on the subject of Negroes, and a clause was inserted in the Act whereby no person "of African descent" should be excluded—with the curious result that to this day, while a yellow face is a bar to the prospective immigrant, a black face is, theoretically at any rate, actually a passport.

The exclusion of the Chinese does but mark the beginning of a very important change in the attitude of the Republic towards immigration. Up to this time, in spite of the apparent exception of the Know-Nothing movement, of which the motive seems to have been predominantly sectarian, it had been at once the interest and the pride of America to encourage immigration on the largest possible scale without troubling about its source or character: her interest because her undeveloped resources were immense and apparently inexhaustible, and what was mainly needed was human labour to exploit them; her pride, because she boasted, and with great justice, that her democratic creed was a force strong enough to turn any man who accepted citizenship, whatever his origin, into an American. But in connection with the general claim, which experience has, on the whole, justified, there are two important reservations. One is that such a conversion is only possible if the American idea—that is, the doctrine set forth by Jefferson—when once propounded awakens an adequate response from the man whom it is hoped to assimilate. This can generally be predicted of Europeans, since the idea is present in the root of their own civilization: it derives from Rome. But it can hardly be expected of peoples of a wholly alien tradition from which the Roman Law and the Gospel of Rousseau are alike remote. This consideration lies at the root of the exception of the Negro, the exception of the Mongol, and may one day produce the exception of the Jew.

The other reservation is this: that if the immigration of diverse peoples proceeds at too rapid a rate, it may be impossible for absorption to keep pace with it. Nay, absorption may be grievously hindered by it. This has been shown with great force and clearness by Mr. Zangwill under his excellent image of the "Melting Pot." Anyone even casually visiting New York, for instance, can see on every side the great masses of unmelted foreign material and their continual reinforcement from overseas, probably delaying continually the process of fusion—and New York is only typical in this of other great American cities.

A new tendency to limit immigration and to seek some test of its quality has been a marked feature of the last quarter of a century. The principle is almost certainly sound; the right to act on it, to anyone who accepts the doctrine of national self-government, unquestionable. Whether the test ultimately imposed by a recent Act passed by Congress over President Wilson's veto, that of literacy, is a wise one, is another question. Its tendency may well be to exclude great masses of the peasantry of the Old World, men admirably fitted to develop by their industry the resources of America, whose children at least could easily be taught to read and write the American language and would probably become excellent American citizens. On the other hand, it does not exclude the criminal, or at any rate the most dangerous type of criminal. It does not exclude the submerged population of great European cities, the exploitation of whose cheap labour is a menace to the American workman's standard of life. And it does not, generally speaking, exclude the Jew.

The problem of the Jew exists in America as elsewhere—perhaps more formidably than elsewhere. This, of course, is not because Jews, as such, are worse than other people: only idiots are Anti-Semites in that sense. It arises from the fact that America, more than any other nation, lives by its power of absorption, and the Jew has, ever since the Roman Empire, been found a singularly unabsorbable person. He has an intense nationalism of his own that transcends and indeed ignores frontiers, but to the nationalism of European peoples he is often consciously and almost always subconsciously hostile. In various ways he tends to act as a solvent of such nationalism. Cosmopolitan finance is one example of such a tendency. Another, more morally sympathetic but not much less dangerous to nationalism in such a country as America, is cosmopolitan revolutionary idealism. The Socialist and Anarchist movements of America, divided of course in philosophy, but much more akin in temper than in European countries, are almost wholly Jewish, both in origin and leadership. For this reason, since America's entrance into the Great War, these parties, in contrast to most of the European Socialist parties, have shown themselves violently anti-national and what we now call "Bolshevist."

But organized Socialism is, in America, almost a negligible force; not so organized labour. In no country has the Trade Union movement exercised more power, and in no country has it fought with bolder weapons. In the early struggles between the organized workers and the great capitalists, violence and even murder was freely resorted to on both sides, for if the word must be applied to the vengeance often wreaked by the Labour Unions on servants of the employer and on traitors to the organization, the same word must be used with a severer moral implication of the shooting down of workmen at the orders of men like Carnegie, not even by the authorized police force or militia of the State, but by privately hired assassinators such as the notorious Pinkerton used to supply.

The labour movement in America is not generally Collectivist. Collectivism is alien to the American temper and ideal, which looks rather to a community of free men controlling, through personal ownership, their own industry. The demand of American labour has been rather for the sharp and efficient punishment of such crimes against property as are involved in conspiracies to create a monopoly in some product and the use of great wealth to "squeeze out" the small competitor. Such demands found emphatic expression in the appearance in the 'nineties of a new party calling itself "Populist" and formed by a combination between the organized workmen and the farmers of the West, who felt themselves more and more throttled by the tentacles of the new commercial monopolies which were becoming known by the name of "Trusts." In the elections of 1892, when Cleveland was returned for a second time after an interval of Republican rule under Harrison, the Populists showed unexpected strength and carried several Western States. In 1896 Democrats and Populists combined to nominate William Jennings Bryan as their candidate, with a programme the main plank of which was the free coinage of silver, which, it was thought, would weaken the hold of the moneyed interests of the East upon the industries of the Continent. The Eastern States, however, voted solid for the gold standard, and were joined, in the main, by those Southern States which had not been "reconstructed" and were consequently not included politically in the "Solid South." The West, too, though mainly Bryanite, was not unanimous, and McKinley, the Republican candidate, was returned. The Democratic defeat, however, gave some indication of the tendencies which were to produce the Democratic victory of 1916, when the West, with the aid of the "Solid South," returned a President whom the East had all but unanimously rejected.

McKinley's first term of office, saw the outbreak and victorious prosecution of a war with Spain, arising partly out of American sympathy with an insurrection which had broken out in Cuba, and partly out of the belief, now pretty conclusively shown to have been unfounded, that the American warship Maine, which was blown up in a Spanish harbour, had been so destroyed at the secret instigation of the Spanish authorities. Its most important result was to leave, at its conclusion, both Cuba and the Philippine Islands at the disposal of the United States. This practically synchronized with the highest point reached in this country, just before the Boer War, by that wave of national feeling called "Imperialism." America, for a time, seemed to catch its infection or share its inspiration, as we may prefer to put it. But the tendency was not a permanent one. The American Constitution is indeed expressly built for expansion, but only where the territory acquired can be thoroughly Americanized and ultimately divided into self-governing States on the American pattern. To hold permanently subject possessions which cannot be so treated is alien to its general spirit and intention. Cuba was soon abandoned, and though the Philippines were retained, the difficulties encountered in their subjection and the moral anomaly involved in being obliged to wage a war of conquest against those whom you have professed to liberate, acted as a distinct check upon the enthusiasm for such experiments.

After the conclusion of the Spanish war, McKinley was elected for a second time; almost immediately afterwards he was murdered by an Anarchist named Czolgosz, sometimes described as a "Pole," but presumably an East European Jew. The effect was to produce a third example of the unwisdom—though in this case the country was distinctly the gainer—of the habit of using the Vice-Presidency merely as an electioneering bait. Theodore Roosevelt had been chosen as candidate for that office solely to catch what we should here call the "khaki" sentiment, he and his "roughriders" having played a distinguished and picturesque part in the Cuban campaign. But it soon appeared that the new President had ideas of his own which were by no means identical with those of the Party Bosses. He sought to re-create the moral prestige of the Republican Party by identifying it with the National idea—with which its traditions as the War Party in the battle for the Union made its identification seem not inappropriate—with a spirited foreign policy and with the aspiration for expansion and world-power. But he also sought to sever its damaging connection with those sordid and unpopular plutocratic combinations which the nation as a whole justly hated. Of great energy and attractive personality, and gifted with a strong sense of the picturesque in politics, President Roosevelt opened a vigorous campaign against those Trusts which had for so long backed and largely controlled his party. The Republican Bosses were angry and dismayed, but they dared not risk an open breach with a popular and powerful President backed by the whole nation irrespective of party. So complete was his victory that not only did he enjoy something like a national triumph when submitting himself for re-election in 1904, but in 1908 was virtually able to nominate his successor.

Mr. Taft, however, though so nominated and professing to carry on the Rooseveltian policy, did not carry it on to the satisfaction of its originator. The ex-President roundly accused his successor of suffering the party to slip back again into the pocket of the Trusts, and in 1912 offered himself once more to the Republican Party as a rival to his successor. The Party

Convention at San Francisco chose Taft by a narrow majority. Something may be allowed for the undoubtedly prevalent sentiment against a breach of the Washingtonian tradition of a two-terms limit; but the main factor was the hostility of the Bosses and the Trusts behind them, and the weapon they used was their control of the Negro "pocket boroughs" of the Southern States, which were represented in the Convention in proportion to their population of those States, though practically no Republican votes were cast there. Colonel Roosevelt challenged the decision of the Convention, and organized an independent party of his own under the title of "Progressive," composed partly of the defeated section of the Republicans and partly of all those who for one reason or another were dissatisfied with existing parties. In the contest which followed he justified his position by polling far more votes than his Republican rival. But the division in the Republican Party permitted the return of the Democratic candidate, Dr. Woodrow Wilson.

The new President was a remarkable man in more ways than one. By birth a Southerner, he had early migrated to New Jersey. He had a distinguished academic career behind him, and had written the best history of his own country at present obtainable. He had also held high office in his State, and his term had been signalized by the vigour with which he had made war on corruption in the public service. During his term of office he was to exhibit another set of qualities, the possession of which had perhaps been less suspected: an instinct for the trend of the national will not unlike that of Jackson, and a far-seeing patience and persistence under misrepresentation and abuse that recalls Lincoln.

For Mr. Wilson had been in office but a little over a year when Prussia, using Austria as an instrument and Serbia as an excuse, forced an aggressive war on the whole of Europe. The sympathies of most Americans were with the Western Allies, especially with France, for which country the United States had always felt a sort of spiritual cousinship. England was, as she had always been, less trusted, but in this instance, especially when Prussia opened the war with a criminal attack upon the little neutral nation of Belgium, it was generally conceded that she was in the right. Dissentients there were, especially among the large German or

German-descended population of the Middle West, and the Prussian Government spent money like water to further a German propaganda in the States. But the mass of American opinion was decidedly favourable to the cause of those who were at war with the German Empire. Yet it was at that time equally decided and much more unanimous against American intervention in the European quarrel.

The real nature of this attitude was not grasped in England, and the resultant misunderstanding led to criticisms and recriminations which everyone now regrets. The fact is that the Americans had very good reason for disliking the idea of being drawn into the awful whirlpool in which Europe seemed to be perishing. It was not cowardice that held her back: her sons had done enough during the four terrible years of civil conflict in which her whole manhood was involved to repel that charge for ever. Rather was it a realistic memory of what such war means that made the new America eager to keep the peace as long as it might. There was observable, it is true, a certain amount of rather silly Pacifist sentiment, especially in those circles which the Russians speak of as "Intelligenzia," and Americans as "high-brow." It went, as it usually goes, though the logical connection is not obvious, with teetotalism and similar fads. All these fads were peculiarly rampant in the United States in the period immediately preceding the war, when half the States went "dry," and some cities passed what seems to us quite lunatic laws—prohibiting cigarette-smoking and creating a special female police force of "flirt-catchers." The whole thing is part, one may suppose, of the deliquescence of the Puritan tradition in morals, and will probably not endure. So far as such doctrinaire Pacifism is concerned, it seems to have dissolved at the first sound of an American shot. But the instinct which made the great body of sensible and patriotic Americans, especially in the West, resolved to keep out of the war, so long as their own interests and honour were not threatened, was of a much more solid and respectable kind. Undoubtedly most Americans thought that the Allies were in the right; but if every nation intervened in every war where it thought one or other side in the right, every war must become universal. The Republic was not pledged, like this country, to enforce respect for Belgian neutrality; she was not, like England, directly threatened by the Prussian menace. Indirectly threatened she was, for a German victory would certainly have been followed by an attempt to realize well-understood German ambitions in South America. But most Americans were against meeting trouble halfway.

Such was the temper of the nation. The President carefully conformed to it, while at the same time guiding and enlightening it. For nearly two years he kept his country out of the war. The task was no easy one. He was assailed at home at once by the German propagandists, who wanted him, in defiance of International Law, to forbid the sale of arms and munitions to the Allies, and by Colonel Roosevelt, who wished America to declare herself definitely on the Allied side. Moreover, Prussia could understand no argument but force, and took every sign of the pacific disposition of the Government at Washington as an indication of cowardice or incapacity to fight. But he was excellently served in Berlin by Mr. Gerard, and he held to his course. The Lusitania was sunk and many American citizens were drowned as a part of the Prussian campaign of indiscriminate murder on the high seas; and the volume of feeling in favour of intervention increased. But the President still resisted the pressure put upon him, as Lincoln had so long resisted the pressure of those who wished him to use his power to declare the slaves free. He succeeded in obtaining from Germany some mitigation of her piratical policy, and with that he was for a time content. He probably knew then, as Mr. Gerard certainly did, that war must come. But he also knew that if he struck too early he would divide the nation. He waited till the current of opinion had time to develop, carefully though unobtrusively directing it in such a fashion as to prepare it for eventualities. So well did he succeed that when in the spring of 1917 Prussia proclaimed a revival of her policy of unmitigated murder directed not only against belligerents but avowedly against neutrals also, he felt the full tide of the general will below him. And when at last he declared war it was with a united America at his back.

Such is, in brief, the diplomatic history of the intervention of the United States in the Great War. Yet there is another angle from which it can be viewed, whereby it seems not only inevitable but strangely symbolic. The same century that saw across the Atlantic the birth of the young Republic, saw in the very centre of Europe the rise of another new Power. Remote as the two were, and unlikely as it must have seemed at the time that they could ever cross each other's paths, they were in a strange fashion at once parallel and antipodean. Neither has grown in the ordinary complex yet unconscious fashion of nations. Both were, in a sense, artificial products. Both were founded on a creed. And the creeds were exactly and mathematically opposed. According to the creed of Thomas Jefferson, all men were endowed by their Creator with equal rights. According to the creed of Frederick Hohenzollern there was no Creator, and no one possessed any rights save the right of the strongest. Through more than a century the history of the two nations is the development of the two ideas. It would have seemed unnatural if the great Atheist State, in its final bid for the imposition of its creed on all nations, had not found Jefferson's Republic among its enemies. That anomaly was not to be. That flag which, decked only with thirteen stars representing the original revolted colonies, had first waved over Washington's raw levies, which, as the cluster grew, had disputed on equal terms with the Cross of St. George its ancient lordship of the sea, which Jackson had kept flying over New Orleans, which Scott and Taylor had carried triumphantly to Monterey, which on a memorable afternoon had been lowered over Sumter, and on a yet more memorable morning raised once again over Richmond, which now bore its full complement of forty-eight stars, symbolizing great and free States stretching from ocean to ocean, appeared for the first time on a European battlefield, and received there as its new baptism of fire a salute from all the arsenals of Hell.

INDEX

A

abandonment, 107, 175
Aberdeen, Lord, 116
abolitionists, 132, 133, 135, 163
act(s), 3, 75, 86, 126, 127, 167, 192, 211, 217, 223, 228
Acts of Congress, 211, 217
Adams, John Quincey, 40, 57, 61, 62, 63, 66, 67, 68, 71, 91, 93, 94, 98, 99, 103, 189
Adams' appointment(s), 7, 40, 46, 107, 113, 184
agitation, 135
Alabama, 160, 161, 170, 189, 211
Alexander I. of Russia, 86
Aliens Law, 62
allies, 35, 82, 234, 235, 236
amendment(s), 54, 65, 69, 121, 159, 166, 168, 211, 214, 215, 216
Amendments to the Constitution, 211
America, ix, xvii, xix, xx, 1, 2, 4, 8, 10, 15, 16, 18, 19, 20, 21, 22, 23, 25, 26, 28, 29, 35, 37, 39, 40, 42, 43, 44, 53, 57, 59, 60, 62, 68, 70, 73, 76, 77, 79, 80, 83, 84, 85, 86, 87, 90, 91, 93, 95, 99, 100, 101, 107, 111, 113, 114, 117, 131, 158, 165, 180, 189, 203, 204, 228, 229, 230, 231, 232, 235, 236
American Ambassador, 87, 189
American colonies, 11, 18
American constitution, 39, 164, 170, 232
American Fathers, 44, 130
American forces, 29
American Navy, 79, 180
American policy, 42, 61
American prosperity, 76
American Socialism, 231
American trade, 76
Anderson, Major, 170, 171
André, Major, 33
antagonism, 3, 55, 56, 109, 135, 137, 138, 181
Antietam, Battle of, 187, 189
Anti-Masonic Party, 111
Anti-Slavery Societies, 132, 225
Anti-War Whigs, 123
Appomattox Court House, 199
Arizona, 121, 124, 141
Arkansas, 85, 169, 173
armament, 34, 151, 177
army of the Potomac, 179, 184
Arnold, Benedict, 33, 34

assassinated, 227
assassinates Lincoln, 206, 231
assassination, 206
Atlanta, Georgia, 8, 32, 82, 91, 105, 160, 161, 196, 197, 215
Attorney-General, 103, 145

B

Baltimore, Lord, 4, 7, 132, 153, 175, 185
Baltimore, Maryland, 4, 6, 7, 8, 10, 11, 39, 41, 49, 55, 132, 153, 169, 174, 185, 186, 187, 193, 201
bank deposits, 104
bank(s), 28, 56, 57, 69, 101, 102, 103, 104, 105, 110, 146
bargain(ing), xvi, 55, 68, 69, 86, 94, 116, 160, 222
Beaumarchais, 31
Beauregard at Bull Run, 178, 179, 180, 182, 184, 211
Beauregard, General, 178, 179, 181
Belgium, 234
Bill for a National Bank, 56, 84
Bill for re-charter, 102
Black Abolitionist, 153, 162
Black, Judge, vii, 137, 153, 162, 164, 170, 201, 222
Blaine, James G., 226, 227, 228
Blair, Francis, 174
Bland, Richard, 17
Boer War, 232
Boone, Daniel, 71
Booth, John Wilkes, 205, 206
border ruffians, 142, 149
Border States support, 49, 153, 155, 188, 197, 202, 207
Boston Tea Party, 19
Boston, Massachusetts, v, 5, 11, 12, 17, 18, 19, 20, 22, 25, 49, 57, 58, 61, 70, 72, 81, 91, 99, 120, 125, 132, 133, 134, 135, 139, 142, 163, 175, 203, 212
Breckinridge, 153, 192
British expedition, 29
British fleet, 25, 79, 80
British forces, 28
British Government, 19, 21, 22, 27, 28, 29, 31, 39, 42, 79, 138, 144, 180
British Minister(s), 17, 20
British possession, 86
British representative, 35
British troops, 26, 27
Brown, John, 6, 143, 151, 163, 166, 172, 206, 217
Bryan, William J., 232
Buchanan, James, 145, 149, 157, 158, 159, 163, 170, 177, 192
Bull Run, 178, 179, 180, 182, 184, 211
Bunker's Hill, Battle of
Burgoyne, General, 28
Burgoyne's surrender
Burke, Edmund, 16
Burnside, General, 190
Burr, Aaron, 65, 66, 67, 70, 72, 73, 74, 75, 109
Butler, Benjamin, 216

C

Cabinet, 52, 56, 57, 86, 96, 99, 102, 104, 107, 159, 205, 207
Calhoun, John Caldwell, 8, 78, 90, 96, 97, 98, 100, 101, 102, 105, 109, 114, 115, 116, 117, 118, 120, 121, 126, 134, 135, 139, 143, 148, 155
California, 87, 115, 121, 123, 124, 141, 144, 153, 159, 162, 228
Canada, 8, 9, 28, 29, 39, 79, 110
candidate for the Presidency, 91
Canning, George, 87
capital of the Confederacy, 28

Index

capitalist, 133, 226, 227
Capitalist party, 133
Carnegie, Andrew, 231
carpet-baggers, 219
Cass, General, 123, 159, 163
Catholic(s), xiv, 4, 7, 39, 40, 138, 144
Catholicism, 5
cavalry leader, 32
Chancellorsville, Battle of, 189
Charles I., 4
Charles II., 6, 7
Charleston, South Carolina, 31, 43, 49, 63, 90, 97, 98, 99, 100, 122, 152, 153, 155, 156, 157, 158, 159, 160, 163, 165, 170, 171, 172, 173, 177, 180, 198, 219, 221
Chatham, William Pitt, Earl of, 28
Chattanooga, Battle of, 195, 196
Cherokee Indians, 105
Chesapeake, 3, 22, 79
Chicago, Illinois, 152, 187
Chickamauga, Battle of, 195
Chinese, 228, 229
Civil Rights Bill, 212
Civil War, vii, 48, 52, 136, 142, 144, 149, 155, 163, 164, 166, 167, 171, 172, 178, 190, 192, 211, 227, 228
Clay, Henry, 72, 77, 79, 83, 84, 85, 90, 93, 94, 95, 98, 99, 100, 101, 102, 103, 105, 112, 113, 118, 123, 124, 125, 129, 136, 139, 140, 159, 174
Clay-Calhoun, 100
Cleveland, Grover, 228
Clinton, Democratic candidate for Vice-Presidency, 57
Coalition against Jackson, 95
Cobbett, William, 38, 59
collectivism, 137, 231
collectivist, 137, 231
colonies, 3, 5, 6, 8, 9, 10, 11, 12, 15, 16, 17, 18, 20, 21, 23, 31, 35, 49, 53, 86, 117, 137, 165, 237

colonists, 6, 7, 8, 10, 11, 12, 15, 16, 17, 18, 19, 20, 23, 27, 30, 31, 41, 115, 138
colonization, 8, 87
Colony of Virginia, 4, 8, 10
Columbia, South Carolina, 31, 43, 49, 63, 90, 97, 98, 99, 100, 122, 155, 156, 157, 158, 159, 160, 163, 165, 170, 171, 172, 173, 177, 180, 198, 221
Columbus, Christopher, 1, 2, 176, 198
commander-in-chief, 26
Compromise of 1850, 129, 139, 141, 147
confederacy, 8, 33, 39, 43, 44, 69, 72, 73, 165, 167, 168, 170, 174, 175, 176, 177, 178, 180, 181, 182, 184, 185, 187, 189, 190, 192, 193, 194, 195, 196, 197, 198, 201, 206, 207, 209, 220
Confederate congress, 178
Confederate Debt, 202, 210
Confederate envoys to Europe, 180
Confederate leaders, 190
Confederate states, 175, 185, 217
Confederate(s), 164, 170, 171, 175, 178, 180, 181, 183, 185, 186, 187, 190, 195, 198, 201, 202, 205, 210, 211, 217
confederation, 35, 153, 168
Congress, 20, 23, 26, 40, 42, 46, 49, 51, 56, 61, 62, 63, 69, 74, 77, 78, 85, 94, 95, 97, 99, 100, 102, 103, 104, 105, 106, 112, 121, 139, 140, 141, 145, 149, 156, 158, 161, 162, 167, 172, 180, 187, 192, 203, 207, 208, 209, 212, 213, 214, 215, 216, 217, 221, 227, 228, 230
Connecticut, 5, 81, 85
conscription, 40, 192
constitution, 16, 43, 44, 48, 50, 51, 54, 56, 62, 65, 66, 67, 69, 70, 90, 93, 95, 97, 103, 107, 125, 133, 135, 138, 141, 143, 145, 146, 149, 153, 156, 157, 164, 166, 167, 168, 169, 173, 201, 202, 211, 214
Continental Congress(es), 20, 21, 25, 35, 42, 43, 47

242 Index

convention, 43, 48, 49, 54, 66, 81, 84, 99, 100, 103, 122, 123, 149, 152, 153, 157, 202, 234
convention at Charleston, 153
Copperhead(s), 190, 191, 197
Cornwallis and Tarleton, 32
Cornwallis, Lord, 31, 34, 35, 183
cotton industry, 98
Cotton States, 10, 84, 97, 159, 160, 164, 169
Cowpens, Battle of, 32
Crawford, William, 90
Creek(s), 80, 82, 86, 187
Crittenden Compromise, 159, 160
Crittenden, Senator, 159, 160
Cuba, 160, 232
Czolgosz, assassinates McKinley, 233

Democratic candidate, 66, 114, 145, 153, 234
Democratic Party, 66, 107, 109, 110, 149, 153, 197
Democratic Societies, 61
Democrats, 53, 57, 59, 105, 112, 117, 118, 119, 123, 137, 139, 153, 197, 207, 222, 232
District of Columbia, 125, 147, 186
Douglas, Stephen, 72, 130, 139, 140, 141, 142, 146, 147, 148, 149, 150, 152, 153, 159, 172, 204
Draft Riots, 192
Dred Scott case, 145
Dred Scott decision, 152
Dutch Colonies, 6

D

Davis, Jefferson, 139, 144, 159, 163, 164, 166, 168, 170, 171, 182, 190, 196, 197, 199, 201, 207, 215
De Grasse, in command of French fleet, 34
Declaration of Colonial Right, 20
Declaration of Independence, 20, 22, 23, 25, 34, 38, 49, 50, 60, 63, 89, 147, 150, 156, 165, 203, 204, 214, 228
Declaration of Neutrality, 59
Deist(s), 40
Delaware, 6, 174
democracy, xi, xx, 1, 12, 17, 25, 30, 38, 42, 47, 57, 58, 59, 60, 62, 65, 75, 83, 90, 91, 94, 106, 107, 109, 113, 116, 118, 130, 137, 138, 165, 204, 227
Democratic, xiii, 17, 38, 41, 42, 43, 46, 52, 53, 57, 60, 62, 66, 67, 89, 91, 93, 98, 101, 107, 109, 110, 113, 114, 117, 118, 123, 140, 142, 145, 149, 153, 159, 169, 192, 197, 204, 222, 227, 229, 232, 234
Democratic banquet, 98

E

Eaton, Major, 96
Eaton, Mrs., 96
elections, 67, 95, 104, 143, 169, 191, 232
Electoral College, 47, 48, 52, 61, 66, 93, 95, 107, 154, 158, 222
Emancipation Proclamation, 188, 196, 201, 222
embargo, 76
Emerson of John Brown, 151
England, ix, xv, xx, 3, 4, 5, 6, 8, 9, 10, 11, 15, 17, 18, 20, 26, 27, 30, 31, 34, 35, 37, 38, 39, 40, 45, 46, 54, 56, 58, 59, 62, 68, 73, 77, 78, 79, 80, 81, 82, 83, 87, 105, 116, 119, 125, 131, 136, 144, 156, 160, 181, 182, 188, 206, 234, 235
English colonies, vii, 1, 2, 3, 7, 8, 9, 15, 30, 41, 91
English colonies in America, 3
era of good feeling, 85, 89
Erie Railway scandal, 226
Erskine, British Minister at Washington, 77

Europe, xv, 2, 3, 5, 8, 9, 10, 29, 38, 57, 59, 75, 77, 82, 86, 107, 110, 111, 130, 142, 174, 180, 228, 234, 235, 237
European battlefield, 237
Everett, nominated as candidate for Presidency, 153

F

Farragut, Admiral, 184
Federal Government, 45, 55, 56, 74, 83, 125, 161, 162, 167, 170, 177, 182, 188, 192, 202, 214
Federal laws, 170
Federalist Party, 63
Federalist(s), 47, 57, 61, 63, 67, 68, 70, 72, 89, 137
Fessenden, Senator, 203
Fifteenth Amendment, 45
filibustering, 160
Filmore, Millard, 124
first Battle of Bull Run, 179
first Continental Congress, 21
flag of the Confederacy, 171
Florida, 3, 8, 74, 80, 82, 85, 97, 160, 163, 165, 221
Floyd, Secretary for War under Buchanan, 159, 177
Force Bill, 99, 100
forces, 9, 20, 34, 89, 99, 158, 173, 176, 178, 181, 195, 198, 201, 210
foreign war, 6, 81
Fort Donelson, 177, 194
Fort Henry, 181
Fort Sumter, 170
Forts Henry and Donelson, 181
forty-seven-forty-or-fight, 116, 118
Fourteenth Amendment, 226
France, xvii, xxi, 8, 9, 22, 30, 31, 34, 35, 39, 43, 54, 58, 59, 60, 62, 68, 75, 77, 105, 177, 182, 234

Franklin, Benjamin, 16, 30, 35, 43, 49, 139, 211
Frederick the Great, 237
Fredericksburg, 184, 190
Free Soil settlement, 142
Free State, 85, 112, 123, 124, 143, 148, 154, 159, 162, 179, 201
Free Trade, 11, 44, 97, 99, 100, 156, 225
Frémont, General, 144, 187, 197
French, xi, 8, 9, 16, 22, 26, 30, 31, 34, 38, 39, 43, 45, 46, 54, 57, 58, 62, 68, 73, 75, 80, 86, 115, 178, 203, 211
French Canadians, 39
French fleet, 22, 34
French Revolution, 57, 75, 86
French war(s), 9, 26
Fugitive Slave Law, 125, 134, 148, 166, 169
fugitive slaves, 125, 136, 151, 186, 213

G

Garfield, President, 227
Garrison, William Lloyd, 132, 133, 135, 140, 143, 147, 160, 163
Gates, General, 29, 33
General Scott, 158, 173
Genet, 59, 60, 62
George III, 15, 18
Georgia, 8, 32, 82, 91, 105, 160, 161, 215
Gerard, James W., 236
German, xvii, 18, 27, 28, 34, 234, 236
German propaganda, 235
Germany, 236
Gerry, a member of the Convention, 43
Gettysburg, 190, 193, 194, 205, 220
Gettysburg, Battle of, 190, 193, 194, 205, 220
Ghent, Peace of, 82
Governor, 12, 16, 34, 156, 169, 174
Governorship of New York, 72

Index

Grant, Ulysses S., 181, 184, 193, 194, 195, 196, 198, 199, 205, 210, 211, 216, 217, 220, 221, 222, 226
Great Britain, 8, 15, 16, 27, 31, 77, 79, 82, 106, 119, 150, 189
Greeley, Horace, 163, 187, 191, 215
Grenville, George, 15, 17
Guiteau, murders President Garfield, 227
Gulf of Mexico, 80
Gulf States, 163

H

Hamilton, Alexander, 43, 51, 52, 53, 55, 56, 57, 58, 59, 60, 61, 62, 66, 67, 69, 70, 72, 73, 84, 85, 89, 101, 137, 165
Hampton Roads, 182, 197
Hanging Rock, 32, 74
Hanging Rock, Battle of, 32, 74
Harper's Ferry, 151, 152, 187, 206
Harrison, General Benjamin, 112, 113, 184, 232
Harrison's Landing, 184
Hartford Convention, 99
Hawkins, Sir John, 11
Hayes, President, fraudulent election of, 222
Henry, Patrick, 8, 17, 51
holt, 163
Holy Alliance, 86, 87
Hooker, General Joseph, 183, 189, 195
hostility, 62, 138, 234
House of Representatives, 47, 48, 66, 93, 105, 121, 146, 213, 222, 227
Howe, Lord, 27, 29
Hyde family, 8

I

immigration, 8, 114, 138, 228, 229, 230
impeachment of Andrew Johnson, 216, 217
Imperialism in U.S., 232

inaugural address, 67, 166, 168
inauguration, 67, 172
independence, 35, 43, 61, 73, 86, 87, 114, 119, 190, 197, 201
Independence, 22, 50
independence of the colonies, 35
Indians, 7, 10, 11, 16, 105
Ingersoll, Robert, 40, 227
Irish, 96, 138, 164, 193, 220

J

Jackson, Andrew, xx, 32, 74, 91
Jackson, Stonewall, 179
Jacksonian Revolution, vii, 89, 95, 137, 191
Jackson's Veto Message, 103
James I., attitude of, towards Catholics, 4, 10
Jefferson, Minister, 21, 22, 150, 203, 237
Jefferson, Thomas, 21, 22, 150, 203, 237
Jewish, 231
Johnson, Andrew, 197, 207, 208, 211, 212, 216, 217, 221
Johnstone, General Joseph E., 178, 183, 196, 197, 199, 201, 205, 210

K

Kansas-Nebraska Bill, 143
Kentucky, 63, 71, 72, 77, 90, 97, 98, 100, 146, 168, 169, 174, 175, 181, 187
Kentucky Resolutions, 63, 97, 98
Know-Nothing movement, 229
Know-Nothing(s), 137, 138, 229
Ku-Klux-Klan, 220, 221, 222

L

labour movement in, 231
Labour Unions, 231

Index

law of Nature, 17
law(s), 4, 8, 13, 16, 17, 20, 23, 24, 33, 38, 39, 42, 45, 49, 57, 58, 60, 63, 74, 80, 89, 105, 136, 145, 159, 162, 167, 169, 180, 186, 198, 223, 228, 235
Lawrence, free soil settlement of, burnt, 142
Lecompton, 149, 152
Lecompton Constitution, 149
Lee, Robert E, 6, 22, 168, 173, 183, 184, 185, 186, 187, 189, 191, 193, 195, 196, 198, 199, 201, 211, 215, 221, 222
Liberator, 132, 147
Lincoln, Abraham, 72, 118, 131, 146, 154, 174, 192, 205, 216
lines, 33, 47, 53, 58, 61, 79, 82, 110, 123, 124, 126, 133, 140, 160, 192
Little Giant, 139, 148, 153, 172
Liverpool, 189
Lone Star State, 115
Long Island, Battle of, 28, 29
Longfellow, 151
Look-Out Mountain, Battle of, 195
Louisiana, 8, 9, 68, 69, 71, 73, 77, 115, 141, 160, 202, 205, 221
Louisiana Purchase, 68, 141
Lovejoy, 135
Lowell, James Russell, 119, 123, 161, 163
Lusitania, 236
Lyon, Captain, 174

M

Macaulay, 117
Madison, James, 43, 51, 76, 77, 79, 83, 90
Maine, 5, 8, 85, 232
Maryland, 4, 6, 7, 8, 10, 11, 39, 41, 49, 55, 132, 169, 174, 185, 186, 187, 193, 201
Maryland! My Maryland!, 185
Mason, 7, 42, 48, 132, 162, 180, 181
Mason and Slidell, Confederate envoys to Europe, 180, 181
Mason-Dixon line, 42, 48, 132, 162
Massachusetts, v, 5, 12, 18, 19, 20, 22, 25, 49, 57, 58, 61, 70, 72, 81, 91, 99, 120, 125, 139, 175, 203, 212
Maximilian, 211
Mayflower, 5
McClellan, General, 168, 169, 179, 182, 183, 184, 187, 189, 194, 197, 207
McDowell, General, 178, 179, 183, 184
McKinley, William, 232, 233
McLane, Jackson's Secretary to the Treasury, 102, 104
Meade, General, defeats Lee at Gettysburg, 191, 193, 194
Merrimac, the, exploits of, 182
message of Dix, 164
Mexican, 114, 119, 121, 123, 146, 194, 211
Mexican territory, 121
Mexican throne, 211
Mexican War, 123, 147, 194
Mexico City, 120
military, xi, xvi, 8, 20, 25, 27, 29, 31, 32, 33, 34, 37, 38, 45, 58, 61, 76, 80, 92, 94, 103, 112, 114, 120, 143, 144, 171, 174, 176, 178, 179, 181, 182, 185, 186, 187, 188, 190, 192, 193, 197, 198, 215, 216
Missionary Ridge, 195
Missouri Compromise(s), 85, 90, 115, 124, 125, 129, 141, 142, 143, 145, 159
Missouri Whisky Ring, 226
Missouri Whisky scandal, 226
monitor, 182
Monroe Doctrine, 87, 117, 211
Monterey, defeat of Mexicans at, 120, 122, 123, 139, 237
Morgan, murder of, 111
moribund, 42
murder, 38, 73, 132, 143, 151, 198, 206, 207, 209, 231, 236
murder of Lincoln, 206, 209

N

Napoleon, 27, 38, 68, 75, 79, 82, 139, 206, 211
Napoleon I, 211
Napoleon III, 211
Napoleonic Wars, 77, 139
Nashville, Tennessee, 72, 74, 81, 91, 92, 96, 110, 141, 144, 164, 169, 173, 175, 181, 197
National Bank, 56, 84
National Debt, 55
National Republicans, 83
naval, 79, 103, 181
Navigation Laws, 10, 16, 17
navy, 116, 211
Negro, 11, 26, 41, 48, 49, 50, 84, 101, 105, 131, 134, 136, 140, 144, 145, 150, 151, 164, 180, 187, 197, 202, 203, 204, 207, 209, 210, 213, 214, 216, 217, 218, 219, 220, 221, 222, 226, 228, 230, 234
Negro Governments, 222
Negro rule, 217, 221, 222
Negro Slavery, 41, 50, 84, 105, 134
Negro Suffrage, 203, 216, 218
Negroes, xx, 5, 11, 41, 150, 151, 186, 187, 188, 193, 196, 198, 203, 214, 215, 218, 219, 220, 229
neutrality, 59, 75, 82, 175, 180, 189, 235
New England, 4, 6, 7, 8, 11, 39, 43, 58, 61, 72, 79, 80, 81, 91, 93, 115, 119, 120, 138, 143, 151, 153, 206
New Hampshire, 5, 81
New Jersey, 6, 7, 234
New Mexico, 121, 124, 141, 161
New Orleans, 80, 82, 91, 164, 184, 215, 216, 237
new Tariff, 100
New World, 3, 7, 79, 137, 180
New York, 6, 7, 11, 27, 28, 29, 53, 57, 66, 72, 91, 102, 109, 139, 144, 163, 171, 192, 230
New York City, 57, 192
New York Tribune, 163
North Carolina, 164, 169, 173
North, Lord, 19, 29, 31
Northern Abolitionism, 132
Northern Colonists, 11, 30
Northern Democrats, 188
Northern States, 12, 125, 132, 136, 145, 160, 191
Nullification, 63, 98, 99, 100, 122, 156
Nullifiers, 70, 98, 99, 100, 101, 163

O

of Georgia, 10, 91, 105, 168, 196
Ohio, 72, 79, 84, 112, 159
Old Hickory, xxi, 92, 112
Oregon, 115, 116, 118, 140, 228

P

Palmerston on Jackson, 106
Palmetto flag, 157, 219
Parliament, 15, 16, 18, 19, 40, 46
Party System, xv, 118
patriotism, xvi, 39, 53, 66, 80, 101, 124, 137, 147, 172, 208
peace, 4, 9, 10, 30, 35, 39, 42, 48, 53, 68, 71, 75, 77, 78, 81, 82, 85, 106, 120, 121, 124, 130, 131, 190, 191, 196, 216, 217, 235
Penn, William, 6, 7
Pennsylvania, 7, 8, 10, 11, 16, 28, 39, 60, 156, 191, 193, 212, 213
Pensacola, 82
Perry, Commander, 79
Personal Liberty Laws, 136, 162
Philadelphia, 7, 28, 43

Index 247

Philippine Islands, 232
Phillips, Wendell, 163
Pickett's Brigade, 193
Pierce, Franklin, 139, 211
Pinckney, of South Carolina, a member of the Convention, 43
Pinkerton, private assassinators hired by, 231
policy, 4, 6, 12, 18, 28, 54, 55, 56, 58, 60, 62, 70, 76, 77, 78, 81, 83, 87, 95, 97, 99, 102, 104, 105, 113, 115, 118, 122, 124, 131, 137, 142, 143, 146, 147, 157, 159, 161, 162, 163, 166, 168, 169, 188, 196, 201, 203, 205, 208, 209, 210, 212, 213, 214, 217, 219, 221, 222, 225, 233, 236
political creed, 17, 58, 70, 103, 155
Polk, chosen as Democratic candidate for Presidency, 117, 118, 123
Pope, General, 184, 187
Popular Sovereignty, 142, 146, 149, 152
Populist(s) Party, 231
Prayer of Twenty Millions, 188
presidency, 43, 45, 46, 47, 51, 52, 62, 75, 77, 90, 93, 105, 106, 109, 114, 117, 126, 169, 192, 217, 222, 226
president, xix, 8, 43, 45, 46, 47, 51, 52, 54, 61, 67, 68, 71, 72, 73, 74, 75, 76, 77, 79, 80, 91, 93, 94, 95, 96, 98, 99, 100, 101, 102, 103, 104, 105, 106, 107, 110, 111, 112, 113, 118, 119, 121, 124, 126, 149, 154, 156, 157, 158, 159, 162, 163, 164, 165, 166, 168, 169, 171, 172, 173, 175, 179, 185, 187, 188, 191, 192, 195, 197, 201, 202, 205, 206, 207, 208, 209, 210, 212, 213, 214, 215, 216, 217, 221, 226, 228, 230, 232, 233, 234, 236
President Monroe, 77, 83, 85, 86, 87, 90, 91, 97, 99, 117, 211
President of the United States, xix, 45, 61, 71, 73, 154
President Wilson's veto, 230
Presidential candidate, 79

proclamation, 12, 20, 74, 87, 180, 186, 187, 188, 189, 217
Progressive Party, 130, 234
prosperity, 10, 11, 76, 79, 134
Protectionist policy, 225
Protestants, 4, 5
Prussia, 9, 80, 234, 236
Puritan(s), xv, 4, 5, 7, 8, 11, 39, 61, 91, 134, 138, 143, 235
Puritanism, 6, 213

Q

Quebec, 9, 79
Quincey, Josiah, 70

R

racial riot, 215
Radical Republicans, 197
Radical Republicans Chase favoured by, 152
Radicals, 207, 212, 215, 216
Raleigh, Sir Walter, 3, 4, 5, 10
Randolph, John, 59
Randolph, Peyton, 20, 21
Reconstruction, ix, xx, 201, 202, 203, 205, 206, 208, 212, 213, 214, 215, 222
Reconstruction Bill, 215
Reconstruction policy, 205
religious equality, 5, 38
Renaissance, 2, 3
Republican candidate, 152, 222, 227, 232
Republican Party, 146, 152, 161, 197, 203, 206, 217, 221, 225, 226, 227, 233
Republican(s), 32, 40, 57, 67, 75, 94, 144, 145, 146, 148, 149, 151, 152, 153, 154, 156, 157, 158, 159, 161, 162, 163, 166, 172, 173, 192, 197, 203, 206, 207, 209, 215, 216, 217, 221, 222, 225, 226, 227, 232, 233

Revolution of 1689, 4, 54
Rhode Island, 5, 81
Richmond, Virginia, 3, 4, 7, 10, 17, 34, 37, 38, 39, 41, 49, 55, 91, 112, 131, 151, 155, 164, 165, 169, 172, 174, 178, 179, 180, 182, 183, 184, 185, 187, 189, 193, 195, 199, 237
Rochambeau, co-operates with Washington against Cornwallis, 34, 183
Rockingham Whigs, 17
Roosevelt, Theodore, 233, 234, 236
Rosecrans, General, 195

S

San Francisco, 234
Saratoga, Burgoyne, 28, 29, 31, 33, 35
satires, 123
scallywags, 219
Scotch-Irish, 8
Scott, Dred, 120, 145, 146, 152, 153, 160, 237
Secession, vii, 74, 81, 114, 122, 155, 156, 157, 159, 160, 161, 163, 166, 167, 168, 169, 170, 171, 172, 173, 174, 179, 202, 208, 209, 211, 215, 219
Secessionism, 164
Secessionists, 44, 70, 157, 164, 165, 167, 169, 177
second Battle of Bull Run, 184
second Continental Congress, 20, 22
Secretary for War, 74, 97, 159, 177
Secretary of State, 60, 68, 91, 94, 113, 114, 116, 159, 170, 171, 211
Secretary to the Treasury, 52, 105, 145
Sedition Law, 62, 63
Seminole Indians, Jackson pursues, 86
Senate, 46, 47, 84, 95, 98, 102, 105, 113, 121, 126, 139, 150, 156, 159, 162, 215
Seven Years' War, 9, 15

Seward, William, Senator, 139, 144, 152, 171, 181, 205, 211
Shannon, duel with the Chesapeake, 79
Shay's insurrection, 60
Shenandoah Valley, 178, 184, 198
Sherman, General William T., 198, 199
Sherman's March, 198
Shiloh, attacks at, 177, 181, 194
slave insurrection, 130, 151, 210
slave population, 131, 201
Slave State(s), 7, 49, 50, 84, 114, 120, 122, 125, 131, 132, 142, 161, 166, 169, 174, 180, 188, 191
Slave Trade, 49, 125, 134, 144
slave-owning, 41, 91, 123, 149, 207
slavery, vii, xiv, 3, 11, 41, 48, 49, 50, 84, 101, 110, 114, 116, 120, 121, 122, 123, 124, 126, 129, 130, 131, 132, 133, 134, 135, 138, 139, 140, 141, 143, 145, 146, 147, 148, 152, 159, 160, 161, 163, 164, 166, 168, 169, 172, 173, 179, 187, 188, 191, 196, 197, 201, 202, 210, 213, 217, 218, 223, 225
slave-traders, 223
Slidell (see Mason and Slidell), 180
socialism, xiii, xiv, 231
South America, 87, 236
South Carolina, 31, 32, 34, 43, 49, 63, 90, 97, 98, 99, 100, 122, 155, 156, 157, 158, 159, 160, 163, 165, 170, 171, 172, 173, 177, 180, 198, 221
Southern Abolitionism, 133
Southern Confederacy, 44, 101, 144, 157, 174, 182, 188
Southern opposition, 141
Southern slave-owners, 133
South-West, 80, 84, 114
Spain, 1, 3, 8, 9, 31, 34, 68, 73, 82, 85, 86, 114, 156
Spanish colonies, 3
Spoils System, 68, 95, 107
Spottsylvania, Battle of, 195, 211

spy, 33
Squatter Sovereignty, 142
Stamp Act, 15, 18, 51
Stanton, appointed Secretary for War, 192, 217
Stars and Bars, 171
Stars and Stripes, 51, 157, 165, 171, 172, 176
State debts, 55, 56
State Department, 104
State Rights, 43, 45, 47, 69, 91, 100, 176, 222
State Sovereignty, 44, 45, 70, 81, 90, 98, 110, 155, 157, 166, 170, 173, 175
Stephens, Alexander H., 160, 168, 210
Stevens, Thaddeus, 212, 213, 214, 216, 221
Stowe, Mrs. Beecher, 131, 133
Sumner, Charles, xxi, 139, 150, 162, 203, 205, 209, 211, 212, 213, 214, 215, 216, 217, 221, 223, 228
supremacy, 24, 34, 87, 223
Supreme Court, 57, 97, 103, 145, 146, 152
Suratt, Mrs., 205
surrender of Johnstone, 205

T

Taft, President, 233
Talleyrand, 62, 69, 212
Tammany Hall, 57
Taney, Roger, 40, 103, 104, 105, 145, 148, 163
Tariff of Abominations, 97
Tarleton, leader of South Carolina, 32, 34
taxation of the colonies, 16
taxed tea, 18
Taylor, Zachary, 120, 122, 123, 124, 237
Tea Tax, 18
Tennessee, 72, 74, 81, 91, 92, 96, 110, 141, 144, 164, 169, 173, 175, 181, 197

territories, 7, 10, 69, 71, 141, 142, 143, 145, 146, 148, 159, 161, 228
Texas, 114, 115, 116, 117, 119, 120, 160, 169
the Federalist, 43, 44, 45, 51, 54, 57, 58, 61, 63, 66, 69, 70, 71, 73, 75, 76, 137
the Wilderness, 189, 195, 220
Thirteenth Amendment, 201, 202
Tippercanoe, nickname of Harrison, 112, 113, 123
Tories, 31, 34
Townshend, Charles, 18
treason, 20, 33, 74, 75, 80, 100, 207, 229
Trent, 180
Trusts, 232, 233
Tyler, 112, 113, 117, 207

U

Uncle Tom's Cabin, 135
union, xv, 42, 43, 44, 48, 51, 53, 54, 55, 56, 67, 70, 72, 74, 78, 80, 81, 83, 85, 98, 99, 100, 102, 115, 117, 120, 121, 122, 123, 124, 125, 129, 133, 135, 137, 140, 148, 153, 155, 156, 157, 158, 160, 161, 162, 163, 164, 165, 166, 167, 170, 172, 173, 174, 175, 176, 178, 180, 181, 182, 184, 185, 186, 187, 188, 189, 190, 191, 193, 194, 196, 199, 201, 202, 208, 210, 221, 226, 231, 233
Union forces, 182
Union troops, 184, 185, 193
United States, ix, xxi, 1, 2, 7, 15, 23, 44, 56, 57, 59, 60, 62, 68, 73, 75, 76, 80, 86, 87, 101, 104, 106, 115, 116, 117, 119, 120, 121, 122, 133, 137, 141, 145, 156, 157, 167, 168, 170, 173, 180, 182, 189, 203, 207, 214, 215, 228, 232, 234, 235, 236
United States Bank, 56, 101, 104
United States Constitution, 15, 43, 44, 45, 48, 50, 51, 54, 56, 62, 65, 66, 67, 69, 70,

90, 93, 95, 97, 103, 125, 133, 135, 138, 141, 143, 145, 146, 149, 153, 156, 157, 164, 166, 167, 168, 169, 173, 201, 202, 211, 214
United States Navy, 182

V

Vallandingham, a typical, 191, 192
Van Buren, 96, 102, 106, 109, 110, 112
Vermont, 5, 81
veto, 103, 127, 215, 216, 217
Vice-Presidency, 57, 66, 112, 113, 197, 233
Vice-President, 47, 67, 72, 77, 96, 98, 113, 124, 160, 168, 207
Vice-President of the Confederacy, 160
Vicksburg, capture of, 193, 194, 195
Vikings, 2
Virginia, 3, 4, 7, 10, 17, 34, 37, 38, 39, 41, 49, 55, 91, 112, 131, 151, 155, 164, 165, 169, 172, 174, 178, 179, 180, 184, 185, 187, 189, 193, 195
Virginian dynasty, 89, 90
Virginian legislature, 131
Virginian Unionist, 195

W

war hawks, 78
war of 1812, 83, 86, 97
War of Independence, 41, 55, 80
war with Mexico, 74
War Party, 77, 233
war with England, 116, 118, 140, 211
war with Great Britain, 101
war with Spain, 74, 232
Washington, Booker, 210, 218
Washington, city of, 125
Washington, George, vii, 8, 10, 26, 27, 28, 29, 32, 33, 34, 35, 37, 42, 43, 51, 52, 54, 55, 57, 59, 60, 61, 67, 68, 71, 77, 78, 80, 83, 85, 87, 90, 91, 93, 96, 98, 101, 106, 110, 115, 140, 156, 157, 160, 169, 170, 174, 178, 181, 182, 183, 184, 185, 195, 196, 205, 219, 236, 237
Webster, Daniel, 78, 99, 101, 102, 105, 113, 125, 126, 139
Wellington, proposal to send to America, 82
Whig leaders, 113
Whig Party, 109, 113, 119, 138, 145, 153, 225
Whigs, Rockingham, repeal Stamp Act, xxi, 56, 104, 105, 107, 109, 112, 118, 120, 122, 123, 137
White House, 67, 95
Whitman, Walt, 171
wilderness, 116
Wilkes, Captain, 180, 181
Williamsburg, Hooker defeated at, 183
Wilmot Proviso, 121, 147
Wilson, Woodrow, 234
Wolfe, James, 9

X

X.Y.Z. Letters, 62

Y

Yorktown Peninsula, 34, 183